RECREATIONAL TOURISM

RECREATIONAL TOURISM

Vikash Choudhary

CENTRUM PRESS
NEW DELHI-110002 (INDIA)

CENTRUM PRESS
H.O.: 4360/4, Ansari Road, Daryaganj,
New Delhi-110002 (India)
Tel: 23278000, 23261597, 23255577, 23286875
B.O.: No. 1015, Ist Main Road, BSK IIIrd Stage,
IIIrd Phase, IIIrd Block, Bangalore-560085 (INDIA)
Tel: 080-41723429
Email: centrumpress@gmail.com
Visit us at: www.centrumpress.com

Recreational Tourism

First Edition, 2010

PRINTED IN INDIA

Printed at Mehra Offset Press, Delhi

Contents

Preface

There has been relatively little research done in recreation and tourism climatology, and much of it appears to be motivated by the potential usefulness of climate information for planning in tourism and recreation. The research often addresses the theme of recreation climate as an adjunct to a variety of decision making processes ranging from those related to such things as the development and location appropriate recreational facilities, or determining the length of the recreation season during which a facility will operate, to those as specific as planning future activities involving personal decisions of when and where to go for a holiday. There is also interest in the indirect effects of climate.

For example, Perry (1997) suggests that people leave swimming pools and golf courses on wet days and converge on nearby towns in search of amusement indoors. Therefore, depending on the weather sensitivity of the recreational activity, climatic information can help in the planning, scheduling and promoting of alternative indoor entertainment facilities. Perry (1997) also describes the use of climate information in publicity campaigns to condition tourists' expectations of climate at certain locations. It is clear that if climatic information is to be useful in decision making, it needs to be presented in a form appropriate to the problem. De Freitas (1990) shows that standard weather data or even secondary climatic variables are not always reliable indicators of the significance of atmospheric conditions. Recreationists respond to the integrated effects of the atmospheric environment rather than to climatic averages.

The characteristics of weather and climate are not necessarily determinants of tourism but constitute an important factor in both financial terms for tourism operators and the personal experiences of tourists. Various places in the world have a "tourism potential" and weather and climate set limits. For example, tourism administrators do not promote places with a little potential or appeal as this would not be profitable. On the other hand, the tourist who chooses to visit such places would suffer inconvenience (e.g. transport costs) or discomfort (e.g. heat or cold stress). Financial loses can also result from weather variations and changes. Rainy summers or less snowy winters can have significant impacts on tourism.

Weather and climate can affect decisions about holiday destination or the kind of activities engaged in. Weather can play a significant role in the three phases of a trip: before, during and after. Meteorological conditions also affect on-site behaviour of tourists and recreationists.

A multi-disciplinary and inter-disciplinary approach has been followed to compile this book giving priority to the interests of its readers and professional users.

—*Vikash Choudhary*

1

Introduction

Recreation or fun is the expenditure of time in a manner designed for therapeutic refreshment of one's body or mind. While leisure is more likely a form of entertainment or sleep, recreation is active for the participant but in a refreshing and diverting manner. As people in the world's wealthier regions lead increasingly sedentary lifestyles, the need for recreation has increased.

The rise of so called active vacations Recreation and nature tourism are increasingly important activities with many implications both economic and environmental. As society changes so the demands and trends for recreation and nature tourism change and develop. This poses many challenges for planners and managers of recreational areas and providers of services. This review article focuses on the situation in Europe but does not ignore some major trends and issues arising elsewhere, while much of the research can be traced back to ideas and methods developed elsewhere, such as the U.S.A.

To set the scene the main social and environmental trends are presented that show how the changing nature of society feeds through in expectations and demands for recreation and nature tourism. Demographic changes, consumer behaviour and the increasingly mobile and connected lifestyles of European citizens have produced trends for outdoor recreation preferences and for broadening travel horizons. Knowing about these trends enables planners and entrepreneurs to change their recreation or tourism offer to meet these demands.

However, these demands have to be seen in the context of changing pressures and sensitivities of the environments, frequently natural, in which recreation and nature tourism activities are located. Climate change is a prime example of these pressures. Many countries have developed sophisticated survey and other monitoring tools and instruments to identify demand, to monitor levels and types of activity, changing preferences and pressures on the environment. While recreation is often led by demand from people who wish to participate in certain activities there are also increasingly well recognised benefits to health and wellbeing from closer contact with nature.

Policy makers in the health sphere are taking a keen interest in this and in the means for encouraging sedentary populations to engage with physical activity in natural environments. The evidence base for this is improving and is reviewed in this paper. Management of environments and visitors produces many conflicts which must be resolved. Recent surveys of forest recreation have enabled a European-wide pattern to be identified which will help planners and managers identify issues to be considered.

The paper draws on work being undertaken as part of two EU funded Cost Actions: "Cost E33: Forest Recreation and Nature Tourism" and "Cost E39: Forests, Trees and Human Health and Wellbeing". These allow experts from around Europe to network and to pool research and practice.

Drivers and Trends in the Demand for Outdoor Recreation and Nature Tourism in Europe

Recently a number of attempts have been made to try to anticipate the trends in outdoor recreation demand likely to result from changes already underway in society. One example has been carried out in England by the Henley Centre/Headlight Vision who produced a report for the Countryside Agency which attempted to evaluate trends likely to affect outdoor recreation over the next 15 to 20 years. This report identified a large number of drivers that may affect recreation. The initial list can be grouped into a number of major themes that are likely to affect different countries and regions in different ways and to different degrees. These are presented below. Some are also supported by other evidence while others emerged from stakeholder workshops and are yet to be realised. Some of these are mainly social and demographic issues while others are environmental.

Social and Demographic Drivers and Trends

Demographic changes. These changes include the ageing society, where people are living longer, a trend for people to have children later, lower birth rates leading to families with fewer children, a wider range of household types, increases in ethnic diversity as a result of migration, a flow of young people to cities from the countryside, rural depopulation, reducing populations in some countries and increasing populations in others. These changes result in different patterns in the use of leisure and recreation time, for example older retired people may have many years of time for participating in recreation although as they grow older their physical abilities reduce. Another example is the decrease in traditional households, so that family outings to recreation sites are less the norm. As people have children at later ages they are able to spend more time travelling or take more holidays.

It is difficult to underestimate the impact of this driver over time. Many statistics demonstrate the major effect of demographic changes, such as population reduction in rural areas in many parts of Europe. In the U.S.A., however, population growth through immigration is a significant factor.

The affluent society. As developed countries become more prosperous and people have higher average incomes they are able to spend more of their income on leisure and recreation activities. This is also linked to the convenience culture, to the rise of the empowered consumer who wants more choice and to changing work patterns enabling people to use leisure time more flexibly. As economies mature and people already possess most of the tangible consumer products that they want they start to desire intangible products such as experiences, often gained through leisure and recreation, and especially through travel to far off places and in the pursuit of extreme adrenaline sports and experiences.

The evidence of this can be seen in some of the statistics related to nature tourism in developing countries. In 2005, there were more than 800 million international tourist arrivals globally, an increase of 5.5% on 2004. It is estimated that the market for nature tourism is increasing at six times the rate of tourism overall. Some of the factors that have contributed to this growth trend in nature tourism are that people are looking for new experiences, adding diversity to their experiences, combining business travel with holidays and looking to "get back to nature".

In Europe, pressure on leisure time is leading people to go on more, but shorter, trips (ETC, 2006). In addition, increased incomes and the growth of single-person households among the youth market (16–35 age group) which accounts for over 20% of global tourism, are expected to result in more active holidays, particularly adventure nature tourism (ETC, 2006).

The information society. This, with the all-pervasive influence of the internet, and of the increasingly common use of mobile phones means that people are able to obtain information and to communicate with each other very quickly and at any time of day or night. As a result people make plans about their leisure and recreation time very quickly, at the last minute and they also change them easily. They also make decisions on the basis of information available from recreation and tourism providers on the internet, buy travel tickets, hotels and equipment over the internet and write feedback about their experience on it.

Health and wellbeing. Society is increasingly concerned about the physical and mental health of its citizens, with many conditions such as obesity and stress seen as reaching epidemic proportions. Part of the concept of wellbeing is also associated with social inclusion, where people from disadvantaged communities are able to take part fully in society. Disability, age, poverty and poor living environments are often associated with each other and with poor health and wellbeing. This has led to a desire to make the outdoors, especially more natural areas accessible and used by as many people as possible. There is also what can be termed a re-tuning to nature, where people feel a desire to become reconnected to the natural world from which they feel disconnected by modern lifestyles. The increasing evidence for this is reviewed in a later section of this paper.

There has been recent work at trying to develop indices of life satisfaction that take into account the role of human, social, built and natural capital at a country level. This suggests that social inclusion, as part of social capital, and natural areas as part of natural capital, are both part of the equation of life satisfaction.

Environmental and community awareness. According to the Henley Centre/Headlight Vision report people have a generally greater awareness of the environment and its problems, such as global warming, pollution and deforestation. Membership of environmental organisations is increasing and governments are taking environmental issues seriously at a national and international level. Single issue politics concerning different environmental aspects are also on the rise. Many people with such interests also want to engage in nature or ecotourism but they also wish to take part in activities that may have a benefit for their local environment or for that of another country. There is also a rise in communal yearning, where people want to feel part of a community and to contribute to it during their leisure time by participating in community activities. This increasing awareness of the environment and community can also help the managers of protected areas implement measures that may restrict recreational access, because people understand the need for this action.

Environmental Drivers and Trends

Landscape change: This factor is associated with the environment within which people live, work and spend their leisure and recreation time. As a result of increasing urbanisation, rural depopulation, pressures on the environment, climate change and changes in the economics of food and timber production, brought about by policy changes and global trade, the landscape is changing in different ways in different countries. In western Europe, for example, urban growth is generated by economic development, transport infrastructure and by demographic changes. This may be controlled to greater or lesser degrees by planning policies and instruments. There is also a trend for the identification of the countryside as people move away from the towns and cities to rural landscapes where the quality of life and community is seen to be better. In rural and peripheral regions landscapes are becoming abandoned as farming is uneconomic and people migrate to the towns. This can have positive effects on the environment, as pollution reduces and natural habitats increase, leading to attractive places for recreation. However, this can also reduce the quality of the landscape, the infrastructure for recreation and tourism may be at risk and the people who remain may not be well equipped with the entrepreneurial skills needed to take advantage of the potential for recreation and nature tourism

Climate change: With the increasing concern over climate change and the negative impact that emissions from vehicles have on the environment, visitor transport issues should be viewed as part of an integral network and alternatives created to the car or aeroplane. Climate change is one of the biggest long-term threats facing not only the tourist industry but also the planet and the impacts are beginning to be felt around the world. Potentially, climate change could lead to the loss of many destinations whose appeal depends on the natural environment (ETC, 2006). For example, climate change poses a serious threat to the future health of coral reefs through the increased frequency and intensity of mass bleaching events. The research conducted by not only identified the main resistance and resilience factors of coral reefs to bleaching but also management tools and strategies that can and need to be implemented to enhance reef resilience. Areas where nature tourism is dependent on high quality reef ecosystems will need to take this advice on board to minimize the impacts of climate change.

If terrestrial species are unable to move or adapt to new climatic conditions, local extinctions may occur. Vulnerable or already stressed ecosystems will be the first to be affected by climate change. Scientists have been monitoring changes in phenology for many years. Phenology is the simplest process in which to track changes in the ecology of species in response to climate change. Menzel and Fabian (1999) reported that in Europe, over 30 years, spring events, such as leaf unfolding, had advanced by 6 days and autumn events, such as leaf colouring, were delayed by 4.8 days. Responses by individual species to climate change may disrupt interactions with others. Crick *et al.* (1997) analysed data from the British Trust for Ornithology's nest record scheme collated between 1971 and 1996. Of the 65 species studied, 20 had significant trends towards earlier egg laying with an average of 8.8 days.

Bird watching (avitourism) was the fastest growing nature-based tourism in the United States in 2002. Any wildlife features that people want to enjoy will be affected by changes in the timings of these events. The threat of climate change has also seen an increase in the number of people visiting Alaska or Antarctica. With melting ice caps, people are obviously determined to visit these areas before they disappear.

The intensity and frequency of weather events are also increasing. In recent years, the severity of hurricanes hitting the Caribbean, Central and North America has increased These events will result in loss of land and infrastructure, negatively impacting species living in the area but may also deter tourists from visiting. Simpson *et al.* (2007) have conducted extensive research in Tobago on the impact of climate change on tourism in the area. The three main observed effects were found to be:

1. Changes in weather patterns; rainfall patterns causing seasonality blurring and; increase in intensity of extreme events such as storm surges and hurricanes.
2. Coastal erosion of beaches and cliffs.
3. Coral bleaching.

To reduce the impact of climate change on nature tourism it is necessary not only to adapt but to mitigate causal effects. Simpson *et al.* (2007) discuss research, planning, management and action that is required to reduce, and mitigate, the potential impact that climate change will have on nature tourism in Tobago. Many of the suggestions require action before the planning or construction stage where this is still possible.

A crucial interdependence exists between the climate, the environment, tourism and communities. Sustainable, responsible tourism policies should be implemented and integrated into local, regional and national government strategies. Government policy plays a very important role in the development of tourism industries that are financially and ecologically sustainable. Many natural zones cross administrative and political boundaries and this must be taken into account when developing ecotourism. Without having all nations that border an area involved, conflicts will be unavoidable.

Once the drivers and trends are understood, it is necessary for policy makers, planners and managers to have some knowledge and understanding of the likely changes in behaviour and demand that may affect specific areas. This is the field of visitor monitoring which, while established first in the U.S.A. has become an important tool in Europe. The next section reviews some of the systems used to assess and monitor changes in recreation behaviour and for assessing changes in visitor demand.

Monitoring Changes in Recreation Behaviour and Assessing Changes in Demand

The need for national level information about recreation demand was already recognised forty years ago in the United States. The first National Recreation Survey (NRS) was conducted in 1960. The continuity of a core set of participation and demographic questions used in surveys since then has ensured that trend construction and comparisons of recreation at the level of the U.S. population over the years have been possible.

Similar efforts have been taking place in other countries such as Canada, Denmark, Norway, Finland and Sweden but the contents and extent of the nationwide recreation surveys varies considerably. Without such surveys it is very difficult to calculate the level of resources needed to supply recreation, or to determine the way that trends resulting from the factors described above manifest themselves in demand. The surveys enable providers of outdoor recreation to change their strategies to meet the challenges of these changing demands.

The latest National Survey of Recreation and Environment (NSRE) 2006, recently completed in the United States, includes information collection about recreation participation and recreation trips, covering 50 different outdoor activities. In Scandinavia, Denmark has conducted a series of recreation surveys which offer the possibility to compare forest recreation participation over time: Danish surveys cover the overall levels of visitation to forests, and include a remarkable set of data about forest and landscape preferences. The survey in 1993/94 reached a response rate of over 80%, from samples of almost 3,000 persons.

In Finland, only one nationwide recreation survey has been conducted but there are plans to repeat the study in 2008–2010. The Finnish survey data included about 10,000 respondents. The main issues measured were participation in outdoor activities, recreation trips close-to-home and trips which also included an overnight stay. However, while there are many differences in concepts, terms and units of measurements, some international comparisons are possible. In Table 1, participation rates of some of the most typical recreation activities in six countries have been collected to express the diversity, similarity and differences of recreation behaviour among different nations. The idea of harmonizing approaches for recreation information monitoring, so that international comparisons can be made and so that Europe-level analysis is possible, has been discussed in the research community, particularly in the Cost Action E33. It will be seen if more comparable data is available in future.

Table 1: Participation rates in some recreation activities in six European countries, Canada and the United States in the 1990s and 2000s.

Recreation activity	***Participation rate in %***						
	Denmark	***Finland***	***Holland***	***Italy***	***Norway***	***Canada***	***USA***
	a)	***b)***	***c)***	***d)***	***e)***	***f)***	***g)***
Walking	63	68	74	40	84		67
Hiking		19		38	82		24
Bicycling		55	68	6	47		29
Jogging, running	14	16	16	4			26
Camping		18		2		19	14
Picnicking	10	28		45		26	49
Hunting	1	8		4	9	5	7
Picking berries and other 'forest fruits'	2	57			35	11	
Picking wild mushrooms	3	41		21	13		
Cross-country horseback riding	1	2	6	3	4	2	5
Studying and enjoying nature	56	51		21		31	
Cross-country skiing		40		2	50	4	3

(a) A mail questionnaire regarding forest recreation on a sample of 2,826 of the Danish adult population in 1993–94, conducted by the Danish Forest & Landscape Research Institute.

(b) A telephone survey, sample of 12,709 among the whole population conducted by Statistics Finland and Finnish Forest Research Institute in 1998–2000.

(c) A diary survey by Statistics Netherlands (CBS) in 1995–96.

(d) A mail questionnaire on sample of 3,000 of the whole Italian population in 1995; recreation activities in forest.

(e) The Nature Survey, sample of 86,951 Canadians by Statistics Canada in 1997.

(h) NSRE telephone survey of sample of 12,000 people in 1994/95.

On-site Inventories: Monitoring Visitor Flows

On-site recreation inventories, i.e. visitation monitoring systems, are an important part of the whole management policy of recreation and protected areas in many countries.

The recreation monitoring system most often applied is a science-based system for data collection, data management and reporting, which supplies updated visitor information on a continuous basis for policy makers and managers. Monitoring systems differ between countries, but often standardization of methods and harmonization of information content has taken place within one country or at least within one public land agency.

The most common visitation information measured includes number of visits, duration of visit and distribution of visitors over the recreation area. Information gathered from visitors usually consists of socioeconomic factors such as sex, age, income and municipality/region/country of residence, length and means of travel and amount of money spent. Visitor behaviour patterns describe the level and type of participation in recreation activities, the length of stay in the area and the make up of the group who made the visit. Visitor satisfaction, motives and the expectations of visit and experiences are also studied in most cases. As a result of Nordic-Baltic project on visitor monitoring a new manual is going to be published in 2007. The coming manual offer recommendations to choose variable, measures and sample methods for visitor monitoring.

The United States Forest Service has implemented a sophisticated on-site visitor monitoring system called the National Visitor Use Monitoring System (NVUM). With this system, one fourth of the 160 national forests in the country are sampled each year through a system of site-day sampling. Activities, duration of visit, satisfaction, trip spending profiles and sites visited are collected and GIS referenced to provide location-specific, regional, and national estimates to guide policy, management, maintenance, budgeting and customer responsiveness.

Table 2: Number of visits in Finland's national parks over the years 1996–2005. Source: Metsähallitus (2006), Finland.

Year	*Number of visits*
1996	714,000
1997	749,000
1998	771,000
1999	787,000
2000	833,000
2001	852,000
2002	1,012,000
2003	1,123,000
2004	1,285,000
2005	1,410,000

In Denmark, automatic monitoring of the car-based forest visitation at four selected forest areas was established in the mid 70's and has been going on ever since. In addition, on-site inventories have been carried out in more than 300 forest areas in 1976–77 and again in 1996–97 in more than 500 Danish forest and nature areas.

In the United Kingdom, visitor counting and surveys are also widely applied and used in planning and management processes. Finland has standardized visitor study procedures in order to obtain comparable visitor information from all state owned recreation and protected areas. The national recreation management policy uses visitor surveys in order to develop customer-driven management in recreation areas. In many other European countries, even though a majority (85%) has conducted some studies about recreational visits to specific recreational sites, systematic and standardized visitor information collection systems are still in a developmental stage.

An example of trends based on systematic visitor counting in national parks comes from Finland. The Metsähallitus (Forest and Park Service), which manages the majority of state owned forest lands in Finland, has monitored recreational use in national parks and state owned hiking areas for over ten years (Table 2).

It shows how the basic trend is for an increased level of visitation. The pattern varies across each park and this enables the identification of places where visitor levels start to place pressure on natural resources, for example, or those locations that are particularly sensitive to recreation activities.

Trends in Recreation Participation

The science based information of existing trends in recreation behaviour is best documented in the United States, where monitoring of participation in outdoor activities has continued since early 1960's. According to Cordell *et al.* (1999); Cordell (2004, 2005) and the Interagency National Survey Consortium (NSRE, 2003), participation in all outdoor activities has been increasing when measured in terms of the total numbers of participating people (Table 3). This increase in total participation rates is partly due to the increasing population. However, the numbers of visits and visiting people matters when looking at the pressures of recreational use on natural resources, which tend to be finite.

Table 3: Measured changes in 1982–2002 and forecasting rate of change in outdoor recreation participation 2010–2050 in the United States.

Participants, millions	*Measured*			*Index of forecast c)*				
	1982 a)	*1994 b)*	*2002 c)*	*2010*	*2020*	*2030*	*2040*	*2050*
Cross-country skiing	5.3	6.5	8.1	1.15	1.23	1.49	1.67	1.91
Downhill skiing	10.6	16.8	18.1	1.09	1.16	1.36	1.54	1.82
Snowmobiling	5.3	7.1	11.7	1.00	1.05	1.08	1.13	1.22
Hunting	24.7	18.6	23.7	0.97	0.98	0.98	0.98	0.99
Hiking	24.7	47.8	69.7	1.04	1.11	1.19	1.24	1.31
Back packing	8.8	15.2	22.2	0.93	0.99	0.91	0.91	0.94
Camping primitive	17.7	28.0	33.9	0.92	0.98	0.87	0.84	0.84
Walking	93.6	133.7	175.4	1.07	1.15	1.22	1.27	1.33
Fishing	60.1	57.8	72.2	1.05	1.12	1.17	1.21	1.27
Sailing	10.6	9.6	11.1	1.06	1.13	1.24	1.33	1.48
Motor boating	33.6	47.0	51.8	1.06	1.13	1.21	1.29	1.40
Horseback riding	15.9	14.3	20.5	1.07	1.18	1.28	1.39	1.54

Sources: a) Cordell et al. (1997), b) NSRE (2003), c) Cordell (2004).

In the United States, most rapidly increasing numbers of participants are in walking, sightseeing, swimming, picnicking and boating. In general, traditional outdoor activities such hiking and camping are still growing at a moderate rate, while consumptive activities such as hunting are declining. New types of activities such as viewing fish and wildlife and motorized outdoor activities such as snowmobiling or jet skiing are activities that are increasing most in popularity. Table 4 shows these trends.

Table 4: Expected changes in popularity of outdoor activities in future (Cordell, 2004, 2005).

Fastest growing activities	*Slowest growing activities*
Kayaking	Motor-boating
Snowboarding	Primitive camping
Jet skiing	Sailing
View or photograph fish	Visit historic sites
Snow-mobiling	Downhill skiing
Ice Fishing	Snorkelling/scuba
Sledding	Visit beach/waterside
View wildlife	Anadromous fishing
Back packing	Caving
Day hiking	Small game hunting
Bicycling	Migratory bird hunting
Horseback riding	Picnicking
Canoeing	Warm-water fishing
	Saltwater fishing
	Swimming

As in the United States, the traditional consumptive activities of hunting and picking wild berries and mushrooms seem to be in decline in popularity in Scandinavia. Instead, snowmobiling is increasing in popularity. In most European countries there is no long term monitoring or statistics of outdoor recreation, so that it is less easy to spot these trends, but it is very likely that many of the trends that are now seen in the United States, likely to develop in Europe.

This section has shown that the assessment of behaviour and demand is essential for creating a picture of emerging patterns and trends so that policies can be developed and planning take place with the best information possible. However, it is obvious that these systems are mainly available and implemented in developed countries with often mature economies and where legislation and other instruments are available to manage supply and demand. They are less likely to be available in developing countries.

Trends in the Development of Nature Tourism

Nature tourism is a rapidly expanding activity throughout the world which encompasses many different activities but essentially includes those which involve participants engaging with nature. The industry segment takes place in predominantly natural settings with the added emphasis of fostering understanding and conservation of the natural environment.

Nature tourism can take many forms, ranging from the passive (enjoying a view, painting) to the active (white-water rafting, mountain biking) and from the consumptive (fishing, hunting) to the non-consumptive (walking, bird-watching). Ecotourism, a term that has been increasing in popularity in recent years, is one niche market within the larger nature tourism market. The International Ecotourism Society defines ecotourism as "responsible travel to natural areas that conserves the environment and improves the wellbeing of local people" (TIES, 1991).

Stueve *et al.* (2002) estimated that natural areas, and their closely associated local cultures, and the various related tourist, recreational and leisure activities, contribute around half the total economic activity attributable to the travel and tourism sector. This equates to approximately US$ 340 billion in 2005. Tourism is the principle 'export' (foreign exchange earner) for 83% of developing countries. Nature-based tourism diffuses economic benefits to rural or peripheral regions because the main natural and heritage attractions are often away from urban or industrial areas.

Potential Benefits of Nature Tourism to Communities

Many private, public and community landholders are turning to nature tourism as a profitable adjunct or replacement for farming, forestry or fisheries. In the past, the main function of forests in Europe was that of wood production. Today, in many European countries that are largely forested nature tourism is increasingly seen as an important chance to diversify the means of livelihood in rural areas. With the decline in the importance of this as a management goal in many regions, nature tourism is often looked upon as a means for rural development.

The possibilities and interest of developing nature tourism vary between European countries. In Finland, almost 80% of the population live in urban environments and, in 2004, 40% of the adult population took nature trips equating to an average of nine trips per person per year.

Currently, nature tourism businesses are often relatively small scale and mostly part-time enterprises combined with agriculture and forests. In some area such as in Lapland, Finland nature tourism is already the most important sector contributing the regional economy. Furthermore, new forests are also being established with public recreation very much in mind, often close to large centres of urban population.

Tourism based on natural environments is an increasing international industry with major economic, social and environmental consequences at both local and global scales.

Many of the conflicts emerging as a result of nature tourism differ between developing and more developed countries. People in developing countries who live in areas that are often most attractive to nature or eco-tourists often rely on products, services, or land from natural areas, to meet their livelihood needs. In these situations, demand on resources can conflict with conservation or tourism requirements. Incursions into protected areas, whether for wildlife poaching or subsistence hunting, are commonplace.

Moreover, tourism may create a dependency on a volatile, seasonal industry and it may conflict with other livelihood activities such as fishing or agriculture. In largely forested countries in northern Europe tourism industry competes with commercial forestry and timber production. Salafsky and Wollenberg (2000) developed a conceptual framework for defining the linkage between livelihood activities and conservation. They found that if there is a direct linkage, so that livelihoods are dependent on biodiversity, or where the local community benefits economically, they are more likely to taken action to counter threats to resources.

There are a number of common strategies required to develop successful nature tourism operations irrespective of region or country. The European Commission produced a comprehensive report that detailed and developed fifteen principles for the management of rural tourism that can be adapted and applied to nature tourism.

The document also contains information on the components of good practice for rural tourism. Three of the areas for which guidance was provided concerned working together to a strategy, delivering a quality (rural) tourism experience and strengthening quality management and monitoring processes

The Increasing Evidence Base for Health Benefits of Outdoor Recreation and Access to Nature

As identified in the section on the drivers of future outdoor recreation, health and wellbeing is an increasing area of research. The body of literature in Europe supporting positive links between active and passive use of natural environments and human health is increasing but still relatively fragmented.

Evidence suggests that forests and other nature areas help in people's recovery from stress and attentional fatigue. Outdoor recreation is well on the way to becoming an important element of a healthy living and a remedy against the deficiencies of a modern life separated from nature. People with special needs such as the elderly or those with physical or mental disability often gain therapeutic benefits from activities conducted in natural environments. Mental wellbeing is supported also through the role that play takes in helping to establish personal and community identity for children and young people.

By offering an attractive environment for recreational activities, forests may seduce people with a sedentary life style to become more active during their leisure time. Activities such as recreational walking and cycling already have a positive effect on health. It has been shown that more green space within the living environment leads to people visiting natural environments more often. However, a higher number of visits to green areas does not automatically mean that these people are more physically active.

For example, people living in a less green environment may still walk often, but do so more frequently in a built-up area as opposed to a green space. Urban forests and parks near to where people live are especially important for elderly and young people who are restricted in their capacity to travel. The most active users of neighbourhood forests are probably children.

There are also programmes that try to stimulate people to become physically active within the local natural environment, for example in the United Kingdom. When they do go for a walk, a lack of nearby nature-based opportunities tends to increase the number of people using a car and subsequently leads to driving longer distances to visit an attractive natural area. The key factor for active use is easy access to the areas, preferably within walking distance from home. In a survey study in Salo, Finland half of the respondents noted that the main reason for not using urban recreation areas was the distance to get there.

The most sought after experiences are mainly enjoying the natural scenery, peace and quiet. These qualities are sought, if possible, near home, but increasingly they can be found only in rural and peripheral urban areas. Finnish nature tourists, for example, look for quiet and peaceful surroundings as well as the possibility to move independently in a natural environment.

In addition, hiking trails and constructed facilities for the outdoors were emphasized, while guided activities and excursions were seen as less important. The Finns seem to retain a relatively close association with nature and to retain the skills needed to manage independently in natural places. However, the urbanization process also taking place in Finland may increase the demand of guided activities in the future.

Tourists mainly evaluate the environment in terms of landscape, where attractive scenery becomes one of the most important reasons for the choice of destination. In Finland, almost 80% of people live in cities or population centres, but almost half of Finns (48%) are interested in taking a nature trip within a year and 26% within the next few year. Most people (28%) were interested in taking a trip to a national park, hiking, fishing or hunting area owned by the state. Private cottages were also a relatively popular travel destination (16%). Tourists were willing to travel an average of 380 km from their home municipality to a nature area.

Today, the majority of national parks are located in Lapland, some 800–1000 kilometres from the capital, Helsinki Metropolitan area. Therefore, the demand for shorter travel distance puts more pressure for developing nature tourism services in commercial forests located in South-Finland, mainly in private ownership.

If open to the public, recreational use of forests tends to be rather intensive in highly populated countries such as the Netherlands. Forests, however, have a relatively large "social capacity" per hectare, because of the screening effect of trees there can be many people present without the area feeling crowded.

The perception of crowdedness obviously also depends on visitor expectations. However, people's recreational motives vary and different user interests often lead to conflicts. For example, those who want to go for a walk in a quiet and natural environment may feel disturbed by others, who pursue hobbies such as horseback riding and mountain biking. In the future, motorized use of natural areas is likely to be in increasing conflict with activities linked with experiencing peace and quietness and solitude.

Psychological wellbeing does not necessarily have to be derived through physical activity. An important positive health effect of viewing and experiencing nature is its stress reducing effect. Research aiming to replicate original studies in the United States has led to similar results in Sweden. Just visually experiencing a natural setting can be shown to reduce stress.

Stress relief, as measured through muscle tension, blood pressure and electrical brain activity, can be demonstrated within some minutes of exposure to a green environment. Moreover, viewing or visiting natural environments (compared to built urban environments without natural elements) after stressful or mentally fatiguing situations, produces greater physiological changes toward relaxation and faster recovery of attention-demanding cognitive performances.

There are only a few epidemiological studies on the relationship between nature and health. A study in Sweden by Grahn and Stigsdotter (2003) demonstrated that the more often one visits green areas the less often one reports sickness from stress. An epidemiological study performed in the Netherlands by showed that residents of neighbourhoods with abundant green space tend, on average, to enjoy better general health. This positive link was found to be most apparent among the elderly, housewives, and people from lower socioeconomic groups.

Moreover, a recent study in Finland conducted in two largest cities showed that perceived stress symptoms and self-reported health was influenced by the total amount of time spent in natural areas. Similar results have been found in the U.K. The results suggest that exposure to nature areas increases positive emotions while negative emotions decrease only when exposure to natural areas is relatively high. Weekly contact with nature within work or study was found to increase positive emotions and decrease negative emotions.

It is unclear to what extent the mechanism behind this restorative effect is evolutionary in character and/or cognitively mediated. Studies related to restorative environments show that people use favourite places often located in natural environments to regulate their self-experience and feelings.

Moreover, these places are usually aesthetically appreciated and provide an opportunity for self-expression. Restorative outcomes, i.e. relaxation, decrease in negative feelings, forgetting worries, and recovering attention focus have characterised visits to natural favourite places. A high aesthetic quality may not be required for a stress reducing effect, but might be helpful to attract people to the recreation area. One precondition, however, is quite generally thought to be important for restorative effects: safety.

The (assumed) presence of potentially dangerous other people will diminish positive health effects. As mentioned before, common motives for visiting forests and natural environments are experiencing solitude, peace and quietness. These qualities may also be conducive to the stress-reducing effect. However, crime statistics, for example in the United Kingdom, show that physical attacks are rare in woods, and that such concerns are often based on perceptions rather than reality. One of the key factors for security is visibility, which requires active management of the understorey, and giving the impression that the area is controlled.

Another possible mechanism relating nature to health is that of social interaction and cohesion. While European research in this topic is still scarce, several studies conducted in Chicago suggest that green space, especially trees, may help to facilitate (positive) social interaction with neighbourhood members.

This is suggested to reduce feelings of social isolation, which is a risk factor related to depression. Although it is still unclear what are the most relevant mechanisms behind the health effects, recent Dutch research has shown that the relationship between the amount of green space in the living environment and self-reported health is positive, even after controlling for relevant socio-demographic and socioeconomic characteristics. Moreover forests contribute to a better quality of living environment in the cities, for example by improving air quality and consequently the health of urban residents. The leaves of trees can take up many pollutants, e.g. ozone, nitric acid vapour, nitrogen dioxide, ammonia, sulphur dioxide and particles (aerosols and dust). Some of these pollutants can cause serious health problems. Trees also provide valuable shading from the sun. An individual tree can provide Sun Protection Factor (SPF) of 6 to 10, which means a level of exposure to ultraviolet radiation of one sixth to one-tenth of full sun

Conflicts Arising from Outdoor Recreation and Nature Tourism and Sustainable Management of Resources and Environments

The previous section examined the general issues of nature tourism and some of the conflicts that arise, mainly between over development and damage to the resources from too many visitors. This section considers the conflicts involved in the management of natural areas, especially forests, across different parts of the world. Here there are not only conflicts between recreational or tourism visitors and the natural resource but also among and between recreational activities. This presents many challenges to managers.

However, not all conflicts occur everywhere and there are distinct regional patterns that emerge from an analysis of different countries. The first part looks at the situation in Europe which is best known to the authors from work on Cost Action E33. This is followed by summaries of the situation from other regions.

Europe

The following review is based on the analysis of a survey which was undertaken for the Cost Action E33 programme mentioned above. It was the first attempt to produce a picture of the situation across the whole of Europe and it reflects the situation of the present time. Survey questions were designed to reflect expert knowledge, in relation to forest functions, forest management, and forest based recreation management.

One survey form was sent to a representative of each country, who was asked to complete the survey in collaboration with other national experts knowledgeable in the respective fields. This type of questioning prevented one single expert from responding solely on the basis of personal observations and opinions.

The results include the answers from forest practitioners and researchers working within the respective regional or national forestry administrations of each country. The survey was addressed to the national representative member of the Cost Action programme, who was invited to be responsible for the questionnaires in his or her country based mainly on personal invitations leading to a high response rate (over 80%).

In the following, some results of this survey concerning conflicts in recreation management are presented. The first approach showed a rather diverse picture which showed some basic trends. However, a more differentiated analysis and discussion with the experts was able to identify significant regional variations.

The most important types of conflicts across Europe. It can be seen that in countries which are characterized only by a small amount of forest and those with an intensive and very productive forestry (such as Finland and Norway) most of the conflicts occur between "recreation and forest use", mainly timber harvest activities where health and safety considerations as well as difficulties in using harvested areas for recreation were cited as reasons.

In densely populated countries the conflicts between different user groups tended to dominate (for example Belgium, Denmark and

Germany). This is because there are often many user groups competing for space. In the Mediterranean countries and France hunting is considered as the most severe problem causing conflicts with recreation. However, analysis of the pattern of conflicts arising from outdoor recreation and nature tourism and the sustainable management of resources and environments revealed significant regional differences. Overall, five regional groups of countries emerged which are characterised by similar foci, conflicts and management tasks:

- The Atlantic region.
- The Central European region.
- The Mediterranean region.
- The Nordic region.
- The Continental region.

Below, the main concerns and challenges for each region are described. The relative priority of these topics is influenced significantly by the overall amount of forest, the population density, the legal situation, and, especially, access.

The *Atlantic Region* is characterised by a very low proportion of forest cover per country, usually in the region of 5–11%. In Iceland, Ireland, Denmark, the U.K. and the Benelux countries, the provision of recreation opportunities is of utmost importance as forests represent one of the main types of accessible land use for recreational purposes. The high population density and relatively low proportion of forest (< 11%) leads to an emphasis on recreation as a major policy objective for forest management and a subject of a focus both in research and practice.

The main challenges for management are the aesthetic enhancement of plantation forests for the purpose of recreation and the development of urban forestry (among others, Heytze and Herbert, 1990; McCormack and O'Leary, 1995; Bell, 1997). Compared to other regions, the main conflicts are crowding and the recreational demands of different ethnic groups. In the Benelux countries and in the U.K. the combination of intensive recreation and nature conservation also poses a special challenge. Additional challenges for management are on the one hand the supply of recreation opportunities and conflict resolution between different user groups, crowding, and rubbish dumping. On the other hand the increasing demand for an open access to forests is of increasing relevance for recreation and tourism. Surveys and monitoring of visitor numbers, changing demands and efforts to ensure that there are accessible forest areas close to where people live are an integral aspect of forest management.

In the *Nordic Region* challenges are completely different. These countries contain an extremely high proportion of forest (up to 69%). In Sweden, Norway, and Finland, multi-functional forestry must include the traditional "every man's rights" which include berry picking, mushroom collecting, and free access for all recreation and sports activities, which are considered of utmost importance by the entire population. The main conflicts are between forestry and recreation. Large clearcuts and road contruction are mentioned as major problems by many researchers and managers from these countries. Compared with these issues, the severity and frequency of other conflicts is considered to be rather low.

Forest managers have to deal with an increasing number of conflicts with the use of snow mobiles in winter, unauthorised motorized camping and erosion caused by mountain biking. The management concepts differ across the various Nordic countries. While management in Finland is mainly based on a standardized method for visitor surveys there is no tradition in Norway for systematic collection of data and users of nature, except for national surveys organized by Statistics Norway.

By contrast monitoring in Norway is primarily biological monitoring. Management has to deal with the precondition of free access. Therefore restrictive management actions such as limiting the number of visitors able to visit an area, or the use of entrance fees to ration visitor numbers are unlikely to be feasible, while softer actions such as visitor information, signposting and guided tours are more acceptable. In the Nordic region increasing ecotourism is a new challenge for forest management.

In the countries of *Central Europe*, such as Germany, Switzerland, and Austria, as well as large areas of France, typically about one third of the area is under forest cover and all countries provide free access to the forest. Conflicts arise mainly between different user groups and between recreation demands and nature conservation priorities. Conflicts exist in areas with greater restrictions from nature conservation and they predominantly involve outdoor sports. These conflicts also occur in forests close to urban areas. In the mountain areas, off-piste skiing, back country skiing and snow shoeing as well as mountain biking lead to conflicts.

The planning of new recreational infrastructure has a long tradition in Central Europe. Visitor management is a constant challenge for managers, especially in and close to densely populated areas. Management and monitoring of recreation mainly occurs as an integrated task of forest inventory or management planning. Only in special cases is there independent planning for recreation and nature tourism. New forms of conflict resolution have been developed using contracts and voluntary agreements with sport associations, especially concerning rock climbing and cross-county skiing.

The *Continental Region* face a different set of challenges, partly as a result of the legacy of the Soviet or communist era, restitution of forest lands to their former owners and rural depopulation. Recreation has always been an important management concern, but frequently appropriate infrastructure, or controlled access may be absent. Many prerequisites for more intensive tourism use are also missing. The restructuring of agriculture, and the widespread conversion of arable land to shrubs and eventually to forests is leading to significant changes in the rural landscape. The main conflict area is between recreation and nature conservation.

Most of the protected areas have been established in Eastern Europe during the last 20 or 30 years, many of them in traditional recreational locations, for example in Latvia and along the Baltic coast line and in mountainous areas. The mountainous areas of the Czech Republic, Slovakia and southern Poland are facing increasing problems, especially with ski touring, cross country skiing, snow shoeing and snow mobiles as well as climbing and mountain biking.

The planning, management and monitoring systems are similar to those used in the Central region. They are mainly connected with forest inventory and management or with the management plans for protected areas. Around bigger cities and urban areas, the recreational planning as well as the management of the recreational infrastructure is more intensive. The most popular management actions used in these countries are restrictive ones, particularly rules and regulations, but also prohibitions, although their acceptance by the public appears to be rather low. Experts in the region also mentioned the education of future management personnel as a challenge, especially with regard to training in the areas of recreation and or eco-tourism. New challenges derive from the forest ownership transformation process in these countries.

The *Mediterranean Region* also contains about one third of its area as forest, but here it is different type of forest, often being sparse in terms of tree cover and composed of trees suited to the climate but which are also flammable. Timber production is not important so one of the main additional uses in forests is tourism, which requires landscapes of high aesthetic quality, and also leads to further demands such as fire management, the provision of recreational infrastructure, and the restoration of previously intensively used areas.

Rubbish dumping by private individuals was mentioned by the experts as a "tradition" in almost all Mediterranean countries causing a lot of problems for forest management. Some areas are currently subject to intensive reforestation, or at least to the stabilization of marginal forests in semi-arid areas. All these activities also need to consider demands for nature conservation.

In most of the mediterranean countries there is no independent planning or monitoring of recreation and nature tourism in forests. In Greece and Italy, for example, recreational planning is mainly done in special cases, especially around larger cities to provide recreational opportunities. In Cyprus a close cooperation between the Cyprus Tourism Organization, the Forestry department and other stakeholders has fostered strategic planning and monitoring of forests, rural tourism and nature tourism projects. Future challenges were mainly seen in an increasing need for environmental education, new demands like "nature tourism" and the necessity for visitor monitoring.

North America

In the U.S.A., with a tradition of strong private property rights and no public access to private land, the main resources for outdoor recreation have, for a long time, been the public lands managed by the National Park Service, the U.S. Forest Service, the Bureau of Land Management (BLM) and the network of state parks managed by each state. Significant infrastructure development was put in place several decades ago and the period of the 1980s saw reductions in federal funding to these agencies.

In the U.S.A., the population is set to increase as a result of immigration and the ethnic mix of the population is also expected to change so that patterns of leisure and recreation are likely to be different. Health concerns such as the "epidemic of obesity" and the need to increase the physical activity levels of the American population are also at the forefront of policies connected with outdoor recreation. Meanwhile, the pressures placed on well-loved and accessible national parks such as Yosemite lead to severe conflicts of visitor numbers, activities and the protection and management of natural resources.

There have traditionally been differences between the different management agencies, the National Park Service being concerned with scenery, nature and recreation management and therefore a more focused remit than the Forest Service or BLM which each have goals to develop and use a wide range of natural resources.

This, such as timber cutting in old-growth forests of the Pacific Northwest has led to conflicts over resource use and nature conservation, scenic preservation and recreation. Tools to manage visitors and visitor pressure have featured in the management systems of the agencies for some time and these continue to be developed and applied.

One of the strong points of these approaches such as the Recreation Opportunity Spectrum is to connect the nature of the visitor experience with the type of landscape setting within which this experience takes place. Another tool, Limits of Acceptable Change is used to manage the changes to the ecology that occur as a result of high levels of visitor use. In addition, given the popularity of motorised vehicles in the U.S.A., conflicts between these and the natural resources are a constant theme requiring management action and monitoring.

The U.S. Forest Service has a research programme that undertakes research in to provide information about recreation use of forests, supply and demand of recreation opportunities, and impacts of resource management activities and landscape change on recreation activities (USDA, 2006).

A broad range of topics are studied including:

- Relationships between ecological conditions and recreation activities: impacts of fire on recreation activities.
- Cultural differences in outdoor recreation use: minority ethnic group participation in outdoor recreation; access to leisure and urban open space opportunities.
- Psychological and social dimensions of the recreation experience: human values and perceptions associated with recreation activities; sense of place and recreation management; experiential aspects of wilderness; impacts of criminal activity in forests on recreation; use of recreation fees; recreation visitor conflicts.
- Recreation assessment and trends: visitor service quality assessment; national recreation assessment and trend analysis (NSRE); national visitor use monitoring (NVUM); scenic quality assessment.

Many of these activities are reflected in the aspects described in earlier sections and demonstrate that many of the concerns are common to a wide range of areas around the world.

Principles of Sustainable Nature Tourism

Given the kinds of possible conflicts described above it is important to be able to develop sustainable methods for managing recreation and tourism. Metsähallitus, the state Forest and Park Service in Finland, is responsible for managing most of the country's protected areas as well as supplying partly the country's forest industry. The organisation has developed nine principles which summarise the key elements of managing sustainable nature tourism in protected areas:

1. Natural values should be preserved and all activities should promote nature conservation. Features are small groups; erosion and impacts monitored; nature is the prime reason for the visit; marked trails; tourism into area with suitable features; nature education and awareness are central.
2. The environment must be subjected to as little pressure as possible. Every effort is taken to avoid damage and disturbance; no trace of visitors should be left behind; emissions minimised and renewable energy sources preferred.

3. Local traditions, cultures and communities must be respected. Visitors are encouraged to learn about the communities and cultures in the area; local communities are considered in the provision of information and activities; guides familiar with local conditions.
4. Visitors should increase their understanding and appreciation of nature and cultures. Information should be available prior to the visit; information available on arrival, guides well trained; information and interpretation easily accessible and attractive; visitors are able to contribute to the management of the area.
5. Improved recreational facilities must be provided for visitors. Needs of visitors considered; facilities to suit demand and conditions; visitors to enjoy peace and quiet as well as guided activities; facilities and services developed in cooperation with local businesses.
6. Visitors should be encouraged to enjoy both mental and physical recreation. Facilities provided for range of visitors i.e. hikers and bikers as well as casual recreational walkers; easy and demanding routes available; opportunities for a variety of activities in natural surroundings.
7. Local economies and employment must be promoted. Local businesses to be used wherever possible; employment given to local people wherever possible.
8. Publicity materials should be produced responsibly and carefully. Information must be reliable and up-to-date; publicity is conducted openly and interactively and does not work against nature conservation.
9. Activities must be planned and organised cooperatively. Visitor's opinions are important; training organised with local businesses; all stakeholders involved in planning.

In developing a nature tourism operation, it is essential to clearly identify the destination and to have a unique selling point. The natural assets of a destination play an increasingly important part in presenting and marketing a tourism experience. If an area is listed as a World Heritage Site, for example, this indicates globally outstanding natural and/or cultural significance. This can potentially cause conflicts where an increased number of visitors cause intense pressure on the infrastructure and support services within the area. Eagles *et al.* (2000) estimated that in 1996, there were more than 2.6 billion visitor days of recreation activity in the parks and protected areas of Canada and the U.S.A. This level of activity is likely to have major economic, social and environmental impacts.

It is essential to develop partnerships between tourism, environmental and community interests. These partnerships all need to have a shared understanding of the processes and benefits but also of the commitments entailed. A large number of Codes of Conduct for tourism have been developed by a range of organizations regarding environmental, sociocultural and political features and behaviour.

Many of these are pertinent to nature tourism: the World Tourism Organisation of the UN *Global Code of Ethics for Tourism* (World Tourism Organization, 2001); the United Nations Environment Programme *Principles on the Implementation of Sustainable Tourism* (UNEP, 2000); the World Wildlife Fund (WWF) *Ten Principles for Mediterranean Tourism*; the Pacific Asia Travel Association (PATA) *Code for Environmentally Responsible Tourism*; the WWF *Guidelines for Community-Based Ecotourism Development* (WWF, 2001), and the *Environmental Guidelines* of the World Travel and Tourism Council (WTTC, 1998).

These codes are designed to ensure that all the actors involved understand what is trying to be achieved but also that everyone is working towards the same process and goal. Within the codes, issues such as waste disposal, disturbance to wildlife and habitats, respecting cultures, supporting education and complying with the country's safety standards, are covered.

To be successful and to retain the support of the local community, any nature tourism operations have to provide economic benefits. It is important that these benefits are shared with the community and not all taken out of the area.

Parks often supply the most important part of the nature tourism experience, but typically capture little of the value of the stream of economic benefits. Nature tourism depends on a high quality environment to attract visitors. As a result, the negative effects of tourism need to be minimised. This will also help to reduce conflict with local communities. Moreover, nature tourism should contribute actively to the conservation of natural and cultural heritage.

If the area is allowed to degrade, either through lack of management or through over-exploitation, then the area will lose its attractiveness to visitors. The direct impacts of tourists, such as trampling and litter, have been fairly extensively studied. However, impacts which are more diffuse, indirect and intermittent which are difficult and expensive to measure such as waterborne pathogens or interference with plant pollination ecology are less well-understood. To reduce conflicts and tensions between local populations and tourists, it is imperative that these effects are also considered and researched.

To be sustainable, it is important that any nature tourism development encourages community involvement and participation. Local and indigenous communities should be included in planning, development and operation. Local people should be involved from the outset, at the planning stage right through to gaining the economic benefits of the operation as a result of employment generated by the project or by being key stakeholders.

However, one of the problems of local community participation is that it can be difficult for it to be equal. Some people choose not to participate or it may not be possible for some to participate so that they benefit economically. One of the key problems is that tourism may not actually link well enough to local communities dependent on natural resources and traditional rural livelihoods.

Ghimire and Pimbert (1997) have presented a six-part typology of participation ranging from passive participation where people are told what will happen with no input to decisions to interactive participation where people are involved in joint analysis where new local groups are formed or strengthened and they take control over local decisions and practices (this parcipation ladder is quite frequent in participatory planning research).

All stakeholders should be encouraged to engage in the planning process and in liaison between tourism enterprises, government bodies and environmental planners. Participatory management is a key tool in ensuring participation in planning, decision-making and management. One important task is to develop tools and approaches to improve integrating local knowledge into decision making and planning processes. In developing countries especially, it is important to encourage management styles based upon local rules and collective action. This should ensure long-term preservation of national resources as well as a sustained supply of resources required by nature tourists.

Management of Nature Tourism

A number of indicators have been developed to enable tourism stakeholders and nature tourism operators to assess the sustainability of their activities. These cover issues such as the wellbeing of host communities, tourist satisfaction and management of scarce resources. For example, the World Tourism Organisation produced a book entitled *Indicators of Sustainable Development for Tourism Destinations* in 2004, the Department for Culture, Media and Sport (DCMS) produced *National Sustainable Tourism Indicators* in 2001 (DCMS, 2001) and the Association of Caribbean States (ACS) have developed a set of indicators that are quantifiable and applicable through a Tourism Sustainability Index in order to create a Sustainable Tourism Zone for the Caribbean.

When developing new areas for Nature Tourism, it is important to consider the carrying capacity of the area, not only in terms of the local community but also for the visitors. Natural areas are often diverse landscapes with a number of features attractive to different groups of people for different reasons.

However, diversity often leads to conflict, where visitors who are seeking different experiences find themselves in the same setting. In the future conflicts will increase between clients seeking for peace and quietness in the wilderness and clients interested in motorised outdoor activities.

Eagles (2001) suggests that the negative impact of tourism on park resources is less influenced by absolute numbers of visitors, and more influenced by weak tourism policy, management and staffing often caused by very low levels of finance.

Managers of protected areas worldwide face the challenge of conserving natural and cultural heritage for future generations, ensuring that conservation values are not degraded by the current generation's use and appreciation of these areas. There is a danger that, by identifying and promoting prominent natural areas for tourism, the numbers visiting and their associated impacts can actually degrade what most people value in the area. Visitor use can negatively affect the environment as well as the quality of visitor experiences.

In order to improve any services offered, ensure all stakeholders are satisfied and the integrity of the environment is maintained, it is essential that \strategies and impacts are monitored, evaluated and reviewed. It is also important to undertake market research on the visitors to assess their satisfaction with the area and facilities. This will enable the development of pragmatic and effective recommendations for addressing any existing and future problems.

Conclusions and Research Needs for the Future

This review paper has presented a wide range of issues that are of concern to policy makers, planners and researchers at the present time. Given the fast changing social, economic and demographic conditions as well as the increasing pressures on the environment and the uncertainties around climate change, the subject of outdoor recreation and nature tourism is one that needs to be kept continually under review.

It is clear that a societies develop, economies mature and people around the world become more affluent, live longer and have more spare time recreation and tourism become increasingly important activities. The statistics for the growth of outdoor recreation and nature tourism reinforce this importance.

The review also demonstrates that many of the drivers of changing levels and types of demand are not completely predictable and that considerable uncertainties exist in terms of which drivers will continue to have an effect and which may weaken over time. The nature of the impact of new technology is also uncertain but it is likely to be large in scale. In the light of the analysis of trends identified above, what are the research needs for the future? Each section of the paper has examined different facets of outdoor recreation and nature tourism and as a result is able to generate a number of research needs.

The Drivers of Recreation

As a result of the discussion of the drivers of recreation there are needs for research to strengthen the base assumptions and to validate the trends as they emerge over the next years. For this a series of baseline studies from a range of countries followed up by longitudinal surveys conducted every 5–10 years would help policy makers and planners in the development of their policies and plans.

The discussion on demand monitoring, which is an essential aspect of this kind of study also throws up several important lines of research:

- Systematic monitoring of the recreation behaviour of the population – national level recreation surveys – sampling individuals or households.
- Systematic recreation monitoring on-site, site specific visitor assessment and visitor surveys.
- Harmonization of key variables for international comparisons.
- Harmonization of methods for national statistics over time, trend construction, forecast modelling to allow international comparison, especially at the pan-European level.
- Development of methodology to suit the changing society: the use of internet survey, GPS-tracking etc.
- Pressure on natural resources and conflict management because of new activities and technologies such as motorised recreation in Europe.
- Recreation opportunities and environmental changes such as climate change, rural landscapes disturbed by afforestation or uncontrolled housing development, poor quality of water resources.
- The increasing number of people enjoying nature tourism trips shows no signs of abating and, if predictions are to be believed, numbers will only continue to rise. As a result, policy makers, planners and managers are going to have to deal with increasing demand so that instruments to evaluate and plan for this are needed.

Health and Wellbeing

This short review of the potential effects of nature on health and wellbeing shows that the evidence base is increasing but is not strong enough to have a major impact on policy. Gaps in research were identified in a research mapping study carried out for the U.K. department of Communities and Local Government which showed that this area has as yet a patchy research record throughout the developed world. Some priorities for research were suggested, in relation to a number of themes such as:

Economic Values

- Funding mechanisms for green space.
- The value of economic regeneration.
- Quantification in monetary terms of health benefits (of exercise etc.) e.g. savings to the health budget.
- Costs of crime and vandalism.
- The value of local employment provided by green space.

Health

- Benefits in relation to key target groups, especially children, older people and disabled people.
- Longitudinal studies to test and validate health benefits over time.
- Barriers to the use of green space for health and wellbeing.
- The effects of risk aversion on levels of use of green space for health and wellbeing.

Social and Community

- The availability of nearby green space for children's play.
- Intergenerational studies into play and the use of green space, as affected by, constrained or encouraged by parents or grandparents.
- The effects of fear and feeling unsafe as barriers to using spaces of different types by different social groups.
- The difference between actual and perceived levels of crime in different spaces.
- The social setting of crime.
- Planting for safety.
- The use of lighting to increase levels of use and to reduce fear.

Physical Aspects

- Accessibility to green spaces "from the front door" in order to reduce the need to use transport.

Management and Maintenance

- Maintenance of informal green spaces used a lot for play.
- What skills are needed by staff to prepare for current and future demands of management and maintenance.
- Methods of communication and information provision to the wide range of user groups in different spaces as a means of helping to raise awareness, build confidence and manage risk and fear.

Conflicts Between Recreation and Nature Tourism on Sustainable use of Resources and Environments

In the area of conflicts between visitors and the environment the following needs have been identified:

- To ensure that visitors have as minimal impact as possible it will be necessary to continue gathering information on the intensity of recreational use that is made on areas and also to assess the way they behave during their visits. By having a greater understanding of the benefits gained by individuals of access to natural areas, it will allow planners and managers to focus their activities and operations more effectively.
- Climate change is perhaps the biggest threat to nature tourism. However, it is an issue that is beyond the control of recreation and nature tourism planners. Those involved will need to conduct research into the impacts climate change could have on the environment and businesses in a range of habitats and regions. It is also important to understand how to adapt to the changing conditions. Ideally, recreation and nature tourism operators should also implement mitigation plans so that impact is reduced initially.
- Nature tourism's continued expansion offers opportunities to generate increased income and employment, both nationally and in remote rural areas, and to provide increased incentives for biodiversity conservation in state protected areas and on private lands. However, these must be balanced with the risks of continued environmental degradation and greater pressure on protected areas, many of which lack the resources for effective management and are unprepared for significant growth in visitor numbers.

- The development and application of visitor management systems to different regions and for different circumstances will help to provide planners and managers with more sophisticated and sensitive tools than they have at present.
- Techniques need to be further developed to enable existing areas to deal with increased pressures. This may include setting limits on visitor numbers or activities to ensure the environment remains undamaged.
- Research into the use of technological advancements, so that the development of additional tourism areas will have less of an impact on the environment and to ensure the sustainability of the venture in the long-term.
- For some of the conflicts identified, general research is required. However, for certain issues, research and information needs to be more specific to the region, area or people. For example, reducing conflicts between local people and nature tourists will be region and resource specific. It is possible to identify common themes, such as participation, but as each community is unique, applying general guidelines will also be problematic.

The research in the field described here is increasing all the time and new findings about all the subjects discussed here constantly emerge. It is the intention to keep this review itself under review and to revisit it when significant new material affects the conclusions and predictions.

2

Sustainable Tourism

Tourism is one of the most important and expanding sectors of the world economy. It is also a major source of foreign exchange earnings for many developing countries. Tourism, because it has become such a large industry, has many impacts which can be felt and seen worldwide and that effect all forms of life. The effects of these impacts can be advantageous but they can also cause many disadvantages and bring many problems with them. If tourism is managed properly (sustainable tourism), however, it can increase the benefits for or positive impacts on the social and natural environment of an area and reduce the negative effects significantly.

In this topic participants will be introduced to the topic of tourism. We will look at what tourism is exactly and briefly explore its most important features. This section aims to develop a "common information background" among the seminar participants.

The Development of Tourism

Travel Before the 20th Century

Travel before 1850 was uncomfortable, dangerous, exhausting and longer. People travelled because they had to. Earlier forms of travel included trade, pilgrimages, education, conquests etc. During the renaissance reasons for travel were for pleasure, education and knowledge. Popular journeys around this time: the "Grand Tour", trips to the antiques in Greece and Italy. Later: London, Paris and Vienna.

During the industrialization there was a significant increase in tourism due to improvements in mail system, road networks and forms of transport (railway/steamboats) and an increase in income. First package tour was organized and offered around this time (1841) by Thomas Cook (Leicester to Loughborough by train with afternoon tea).

The tourism industry developed quickly from the middle of the 20th century. More time and more money to travel, dramatically improved communications and transport network (passenger flights). The urge to discover new places became greater. The 1960s saw the beginning of mass tourism because of an increased number of services and products in tourism due to cheaper flights and package holidays.

The number of people travelling has increased three fold since the 1980s from 236 million international travellers in 1986 to 760 million in 2004. The negative impacts of tourism are generally connected to the huge increase in people travelling over the last half a century. We are more aware of tourisms impacts since the number of people travelling increased.

What is Tourism?

Definitions

WTO definition of tourism: "Tourism comprises the activities of persons travelling to and staying in places outside their usual environment for not more than one consecutive year for leisure, business and other purposes not related to the exercise of an activity remunerated from within the place visited. Tourism is different from travel. In order for tourism to happen, there must be a displacement: an individual has to travel, using any type of means of transportation (he might even travel on foot: nowadays, it is often the case for poorer societies, and happens even in more developed ones, and concerns pilgrims, hikers). But all travel is not tourism".

There are many other definitions of tourism. Tourism of less than 24 hours with no overnight stay (day tourism) is generally not included in tourism statistics.

Useful Tourism Terminology

Length of Tourism

Day Trippers: Tourists who do not spend the night in collective or private accommodation when visiting a destination, tourists spending less than 24 hours spent at a destination.

Short Break: 2-4 days with 1-3 overnight stays.

***Overnight Visitor*:** Someone who stays for one night only in collective or private accommodation at a destination.

Territorial Definitions

***Inbound Tourism*:** Nonresident tourists travelling into and within a given country.

***Outbound Tourism*:** Residents of a given country travelling into and within another country.

***Domestic Tourism*:** Involves residents of the given country travelling only within that country.

***International Tourism*:** Tourists travelling into a given country from another country or travelling out of a given country into another country (combination in inbound and outbound tourism).

Data and Measurements Relevant to Tourism

Country of origin – travel intensity, travel frequency, total number of journeys taken, average length of journey, destination, choice of transport, organization.

Border crossings – arrivals, departures, others, nationality, motive, length of stay, time of year, expenditure.

Destination – arrivals, nights spent, entrance into leisure facilities etc.

Tourism as an industry sector, its specifics in comparison with other branches Tourism is in comparison with other industries dependent on national, regional and local resources of a country. It is an industry, which is bound to territory. Other industries generally depend on natural resources and/or services. Furthermore tourism depends on traditions, culture, etc. These features are incorporated into tourism businesses becoming part of the tourism industry. This in turn creates a cross-sectoral, dynamic approach to tourism with a corresponding management schema. Tourism is a service industry which means that it depends strongly on human resources at all levels (regional, national, international) and from many different service sectors, e.g. accommodation, gastronomy, travel agencies, travel writers & publishers etc. Each of these sectors is really an industry of its own. Human resources include all the people who work in the tourism industry at all levels, from the cleaners who tidy the hotel rooms to the individuals who manage tourism resorts. This dependence on human resources means that the quality of tourism fluctuates constantly. The people employed in the tourism industry are often those employed for a shorter amount of time than in those in other industries. Skills learnt involving tourism often do not stay in one place for very long because of this high roll over rate. Combining these resources to produce well managed tourism that works well is often difficult. This also leads to the fluctuation in quality mentioned above. Other industries are generally dependent on human resources on one or two different levels (regional/national, national/international), their resources are all involved in the same type of industry, e.g. car production, computer technology etc. and the turn over rate of the human resources is more stable than in tourism.

Tourism also undergoes continuously high fluctuations in terms of its products. This is also a big difference in comparison with other industries. The tourism product market changes constantly trying to keep up with tourism trends. Each year new more specialised products are introduced to the market. Different products become in and other products out. Each year many tourism companies fail to keep up with this change and go out of business. Other businesses generally produce one type of product and diversify within that product, e.g. Nike produces trainers but hundreds of different types of trainers.

Categories and Types of Tourism

There are many different ways to categorise tourism. These include:

* length of journey (day trip, short-term tourism, relaxation tourism...).
* reason for travel (business, health, relaxation...).
* holiday organization (individual, complete package holiday...).
* activities/interests.
* distance to the destination (local, national, international tourism) etc.
* There are many different types of tourism. Some of these types can been.

seen below:

* recreational holiday.
* relaxation and recuperation holiday.

* bathing/beach/sun holiday.
* sports tourism.
* educational tourism.
* study/sightseeing tourism.
* adventure tourism.
* pleasure tourism.
* visiting relatives or friends.
* health/wellness tourism.

These categories overlap making precise classification difficult: The most significant categories are recreational and bathing/beach holidays followed by study, cultural and long distant adventure travel. Many holidays combine the above mentioned categories. Types of tourism particularly relevant for the Biosphere Reserves: summer tourism in the mountains (hiking, walking, biking, learning about the natural and cultural heritage, relaxing etc.), winter tourism in the mountains (down hill skiing, cross-country skiing, extreme skiing, snowboarding, tobogganing etc.), educational tourism, study/sightseeing tourism rural tourism, cultural tourism, fitness/wellness, spa-tourism, congress/seminar, scientific tourism, cycle/hiking tourism, ecotourism, water tourism and other forms of nature based tourism.

Types of Tourism vs. Motive for Travel

A motive is the reason why tourists (want to) travel somewhere.

There are many different motives e.g. relaxation, peace and quiet, enjoyment, to learn something new etc.

Motives play an important role in tourism especially in tourism marketing.

They will be looked at in more detail in the marketing part of this seminar.

The Tourism Chain

Tourism consists of a highly complex system of activities and services with numerous interconnections to other sectors on different spatial levels, these activities and series form a phenomenon more commonly known as the tourism chain. The tourism chain can be separated into different phases, which echo the stages of travel. These are: the journey preparation, journey to and from the chosen destination and the tasks when the tourist has returned home which conclude the holiday. Each of these phases encompasses different activities or services. The complexity of the chain also means that a large number of players are involved in the various tourism activities.

If tourism is to be effectively developed and managed, it presupposes a fundamental understanding of the complexity and characteristics of the global tourism system.

The strategy of drawing certain benefits from tourism-mainly of an economic nature implies taking advantage of free-market mechanisms for ecological and social purposes, and this means, in turn, accepting the logic of a system mainly driven by private enterprise, in which competitiveness and operational profitability are both the core purpose and at the same time the prerequisite for its very ability to function. Protected area administration, government institutions, NGOs and rural target groups that want to actively participate in tourism, therefore, will have to begin thinking, at least partially, in these terms.

The Tourism Chain

* Stage.
* Client's activity.
* Means Provider.
* Generating interest Marketing, information, advert.
* Travel agencies, destination managements.
* Product check-out and reservation.
* Marketing, advert, information and communication channels.
* Travel agencies, destination managements, providers of various services.

Preparation

Preparation of equipment and gear Purchase, repairs, rental. E.g. salesmen of equipment for sport, hiking and travelling, bookshops, photo-shops, equipment rentals and repairs, etc.

Journey

Transport from home to a tourist destination Car, bus, train, ship, plane, bicycle, on foot. Transport companies, car and bike rentals, traffic infrastructure operators.

Accommodation

* Hotels, guest houses, hostels, camps and other facilities.
* Operators of facilities. Taking meals Restaurants, own preparation, etc. Operators of facilities, shopkeepers.
* Free-time activities Hiking, sport, relaxing, etc.
* Guides, instructors, sellers of equipment, operators of playgrounds and other centres, etc.
* Learning activities Visiting museums and castles, sightseeing in towns and their vicinities, and the like.
* Visiting protected territories and the like. Managers of facilities and territories, tour-guides, bookshops, etc. Cultural activities.
* Concerts, festivals, custom presentations and the like.
* Managers of facilities, music bands and theatre troupes, and the like..
* Working activities Meetings, seminars, exhibitions, fairs, conferences, presentations, excursions, etc.
* Providers of facilities, interpreters. Shopping and local service.
* Purchase of souvenirs and local products. Purchase of other necessities.
* Banks, money exchange, car repairs, health care and the like.
* Transportation services. Craftsmen, producers and sellers of souvenirs and local products.

Shops in the locality. Bank and exchange service providers, car repair owners, health care facilities, and the like. Transportation companies, taxi, car and bike rentals.

Stay

Other activities:

* Spa service, educational activities and the like.
* Operators of facilities, providers of services, and others.

Journey Back Home

* Transport from tourist destination home.
* Car, bus, train, ship, plane, bicycle, on foot.
* Transport companies, car and bike rentals, traffic infrastructure operators Equipment-maintenance and repair works.

* Washing, cleaning, etc. Repairing items, and the like. Laundries, car/bike repairs, craftsmen and the like.

Activities After Returning Home

* Recording and sharing of memories.
* Making photographs, writing articles or web-pages, participating in discussion and other meetings, etc.
* Photo-labs, providers of information and communication technologies, operators of facilities.

Current trends and statistics in tourism

* Exact quantification of world tourism masses is difficult. According to the World Travel and Tourism Council, "tourism and its related economic activities generate 11% of Global Domestic Product, employ 200 million people tourism supports 215 million jobs indirectly], and transport nearly 700 million international travellers per year". This number was 760 000 in 2004.
* It represents 10.4% of the worlds total GDP ($4218 billion US) and 12 % of trade exports.
* Tourism is also one of the top 5 exports in 83% of countries worldwide and is the main source of foreign income for 38%.
* Domestic tourism is expected to grow strongly. Domestic tourism is estimated to be about 10 times higher than international tourism globally.
* Europe; the Americas, East Asia and the Pacific count for 80% of total tourism arrivals.
* Europe accounts for nearly 2/3rds of global tourism. Its share decreased recently.
* Every second European travels somewhere on holiday at least once a year. Only 9% of Europeans usually travel outside of Europe.

Future Predictions

Number of international tourism arrivals is expected to double by 2020, the tourism receipts will have reached $2 trillion and every one in 4 arrivals will be long haul.

* Trends.

* Behavioural.
* Increased awareness for the environment.
* Increased travel experience.
* Higher consciousness of quality and value for money.
* More selected choice of destination.
* Tourists have become more physically and intellectually active.
* Tourists look for new destinations and new tourism products.
* Tourists want to visit places, which are environmentally friendly and socially just.
* Older people and handicapped people are travelling more.
* Increase in use of technology-internet (especially within the tourism sector).
* More tourism destinations are adopting the planned and managed approach to developing tourism and wish to develop good quality sustainable tourism.
* More frequent but shorter holidays taken throughout the year.

In Activities

More and more tourists wish to participate in recreation, sports and adventure and to learn about culture history and the natural areas of the places visited.

Forms of adventure tourism are expanding rapidly as are other specialised forms of tourism including cultural, nature, 'roots' (tourism visiting their ancestral home areas), health and religious tourism. Culture and ecotourism are being increasingly developed as a way to protect the natural beauty and cultural heritage of an area. Increase in health and spar tourism.

Impacts of Tourism on the Natural and Cultural Environment

Tourism can be a lucrative source of revenue for a destination, but it can also have major negative impacts on it. These impacts are not only physical, but also cultural. The impacts vary according to the number and the nature of tourists as well as the characteristics of the site at which tourism activities take place. Individual tourists may have relatively small impacts, but every time large numbers of tourists gather at a destination and the resources are overused, tourism causes a variety of severe impacts. These negative impacts can only be managed effectively if they have been identified, measured and evaluated. Only then can a tailored management of impacts be established. The goal of this topic is to familiarise the participants with the negative and positive impacts of tourism on the environment.

Dimension of Impacts

The impacts of tourism on the environment can be classified in different ways:

* negative-positive.
* ecological-economic-social.
* direct-indirect.
* financial-non-financial.
* local-regional-global.
* short term-long term.

Negative Impacts

Negative ecological impacts: The negative impacts of tourism on the natural environment can be put into three categories: Consumption of natural resources like water, energy, soil, landscape and others Pollution of air, water, littering and solid waste Disturbance and destruction of natural habitats All these impacts occur either through tourism development, such as the construction of hotels or development of the infrastructure, as well as through tourism activities themselves.

Environmental impacts on ecosystems: Whenever the negative impacts on the natural environment are dealt with, it should be considered that these impacts rarely effect only one entity, but that the ecological impacts of tourism usually effect ecosystems as a whole.

Environmental impacts on cultivated land: The impacts on the natural environment do not only effect pristine nature areas, but also cultivated land, which is an important part of the natural and cultural heritage of a region and ecologically valuable because it's the habitat of many species.

Environmental impacts on the global level: Environmental impacts of tourism occur at the local, regional and global level. Climate change and the depletion of the ozone layer are two mayor effects of the increasing global traffic and industrial development, in which tourism plays an important role. Environmental impacts that primarily have effects on the local and regional level also effect the environment globally in the long run. Basically, loss of biological diversity is a major consequence of these impacts.

Tourism itself is affected by the consequences of environmental impacts on a global level: natural disasters are normally followed by a decline of tourism. Climate change causes weather uncertainties which can affect the attraction of tourism destinations (skiing resorts, beach holidays).

Negative sociocultural impacts: All viable societies create traditions, accept elements from outside, invent rituals and, by reinvesting themselves, are undergoing a constant process of cultural change. Tourism aid change and development and thus have major effects on the cultural development of a society. The reaction of societies towards tourism is diverse: some reject changes, others involucrate them into their traditions and some will abandon their cultural roots altogether. However, the inevitably spreading international culture is becoming universal, due to influences such as television and multinational cooperations. Tourism also spreads this uniform culture even bringing it to remote and isolated places and, very often, to sensitive, vulnerable cultures. While cultural change is an unavoidable, natural part of human culture, the sudden and forced changes that tourism often brings can cause the complete breakdown of a society and may consequentially cause the loss of entire cultural tradition. Cultures that are economically vulnerable and politically subordinated are those most at risk from cultural changes, which are unwanted by most of the societal members. Sociocultural impacts of tourism are often hard to identify or to measure and a subject of personal value judgements. Generally spoken, tourism brings about changes in value systems and behaviour of the people and cause changes in the structure of communities, family relationships, collective traditional life styles, ceremonies and morality. The ambiguity of sociocultural impacts is due to the fact that tourism may have impacts that are beneficial for one group of a society, but which are negative for another.

Negative Socioeconomic Impacts: The tourism industry generates substantial economic benefits to both host countries and tourists' home countries. Economic improvement is the primary motivation to promote a region as a tourism destination, because tourism can cause massive economic development. But it also has hidden costs with unfavourable economic effects. Rich countries usually profit more from tourism than poorer countries. Least developed countries are at least able to realize the benefits of tourism. Large-scale transfer of tourism revenues out of the host country and the exclusion of local businesses and products reduce the revenues of tourism which could otherwise benefit the local population.

Positive Impacts

Positive Socioeconomic Impacts

The main positive socioeconomic impact of tourism is that it generates income for the host economy as well as foreign exchange earnings. Furthermore, tourism stimulates investment in the regions economy and infrastructure, which leads to the generation of employment and, again, to an increase in income for the local population. Employment may be created directly in the tourism industry through hotels, restaurants, nightclubs, taxis, souvenir sales and other tourism related services, or indirectly through the supply of goods and services needed by tourism-related business. Tourism development often implicates infrastructure improvements such as better water and sewage systems, roads, electricity, telephone and public transport networks, thus improving the quality of life for residents. By stimulating economic development tourism contributes directly to government revenues by the taxes on the implementation of income from tourism and indirectly through contributions that originate from taxes and duties levied on goods and services supplied to tourists.

Positive Impacts on the Natural Environment

Tourism income not only improves the economic situation of a destination, but can foster environmental protection. Direct financial contribution to conservation is generated through entrance fees for protected areas, grants with which tour operators and other tourism providers support conservation measures, taxes which the government partly uses for financing environmental protection. Tourists appreciate a healthy and beautiful natural environment and reject destinations where the pollution and destruction of the natural environment takes place. Tourism can therefore raise the awareness of the local population concerning environmental problems and enhance the motivation for conservation activities or promote the improvement of conservation management. Another positive impact of tourism on the natural environment of a destination is that it provides an alternative to unsustainable economic activities, e.g. deforestation of the rainforest, intensified agricultural practices and highly polluting industries.

Positive Sociocultural Impacts

Tourism as a force for peace: One motive for travelling is the desire to interact with people and to get to know foreign cultures. Cultural exchange supports understanding between peoples and cultures, can lead to the reduction of prejudices and thus contribute to the decrease of tension between societies.

Revaluation of Local Culture and Tradition: The experience of locals with tourists that appreciate local cultures, show interest and valuation of traditions and cultures goods and enjoy being with locals can increase the sense of regional identity and pride. The tourists' demand for the original and authentic elements of the destination's culture can cause a renaissance of indigenous cultures, cultural arts and crafts and the rejuvenation of events and festivals that are getting forgotten due to modern development and adaptation to western lifestyles. Tourism supports new or revitalised tradition by creating a demand for them. The cultural and historical traditions whose revitalization is encouraged by tourism often contribute to the environmental conservation and the sustainable management of natural resources.

Strengthening of Local Communities: The economic revenues of tourism can facilitate the reduction of emigration through the creation of jobs and improving the local population's income. Tourism, when managed sustainably, can bring the idea of new strategies and concepts of community administration and regional planning to a region. The participative approach of sustainable tourism can encourage the civic involvement and increase the pride of the local population. Tourism can also increase the chances of education and job training because it demands qualified staff for tourism businesses.

Conclusions

Tourism is not a "white industry": It has many negative impacts on the natural and cultural environment of the host regions and on a global level. The positive impacts of tourism can contribute to a sustainable regional development which benefits local people, fosters environmental conservation and improves the quality of life of local communities. The goal of sustainable tourism development is to minimize the negative impacts and to realize as much positive impacts as possible.

Natural and Cultural Heritage

The goal of this topic is to emphasise the fact that natural and cultural heritage is the main motivation for a visitor to come to a region. By defining natural and cultural heritage and landscape the participants should be able to identify the specific characteristics of their region which are the fundamentals for tourism. Sustainable tourism is always based in the region's own attractions-not in something brought in from abroad (e.g. a fully air conditioned tropical greenhouse-landscape in a northern region or an indoor ski park in a region where there is never enough natural snow for skiing).

What is Natural and Cultural Heritage?

The heritage of a region consists of its physical natural and cultural environment, its natural phenomena and its cultural traditions and immaterial cultural goods. Heritage is always affiliated with a region and/or a society (or part of society) and it is based on the region's history.

It has its origin in the past, it has been passed over from one generation to the next and maintained until the present. While cultural heritage is directly related to the region's and society's history, natural heritage also has its roots in the past as it forms the natural environment for former vegetation and wildlife and for mankind, undergoing constant development and changing through geological and hydrological processes, evolution and human influence.

Why is it Important for Tourism?

The natural and cultural heritage of a region is the main motivation for a tourist to visit the region. It is either the main reason for a trip, e.g. cultural or nature tourism, or it provides a complementary offer for other types of tourism, e.g. congress tourism, recreation and sports tourism. The outstanding natural and cultural features of a region are those which make a place "special"-and worth a visit.

Natural Heritage

Natural heritage consists not only of flora and fauna, but also of every other part of the natural environment, e.g. the inorganic nature such as rocks, geologic formations, rivers, lakes, mountains as well as the relation between these natural components as ecosystems. The main components of the natural heritage are vegetation and wildlife, geology, hydrology and natural phenomena or events such as the climate, volcanic or astrological incidents, the course of the year, evolution and the changes in the ecosystems. They are of differing importance for tourism. This difference is shown in the table on page 3. Besides their importance as tourism attractions each component of the natural heritage may be the topic of educational and scientific interest.

Cultural Heritage

Any existing cultural phenomena, from the material, e.g. stone-made cathedrals, the arts and handicrafts, to the immaterial goods of a society such as music, dances, legends and rites, and the interaction between these features form the cultural heritage of a region and/or society. Cultural heritage is, as the word "heritage" demonstrates, based in the past, it forms a part of tradition. But that doesn't mean that contemporary culture like music, theatre, literature or fine arts and the like don't belong to cultural heritage. The most important characteristic of cultural heritage is that it is somehow related to a region and its people and that it represents the specific environment from which it originates. Sometimes it's difficult to decide whether a cultural phenomena is endemic, adopted or imported and therefore belongs or not to the cultural heritage.

Landscape

Landscape describes a regions shape and characteristics. Its primarily a part of the natural heritage as it is largely formed by geological, hydrological and botanical features, but it is strongly influenced by mankind and the societies economic activities. It can therefore be seen as an interface between natural and cultural heritage. The landscape is an essential contributing factor to the visitor's impressions of and feelings about a region. Perceiving and admiring the landscape is an indispensable part of the travel experience. Landscape is usually not seen as a specific subject of interest-normally single features such as rock formations, geological phenomena or vegetation, e.g. forests or meadows, are what attracts the visitor. It is, however, experiencing these features in the context of the whole landscape of the area which makes visiting them extra special. Many tourist activities are based on the experience of landscape, like all kind of nature tourism, and nature oriented physical activities as hiking, biking, swimming, etc.

Why Should Heritage be Protected?

The natural and cultural heritage is often vulnerable to the impacts of modern development, consumer lifestyles and globalization. In addition, the use of heritage in tourism may directly threaten its integrity. The local people and visitor's lack of environmental awareness, cultural insensitivity, improper management and insufficient legal framework and law enforcement can lead to deterioration of physical and immaterial natural and cultural goods. To provide the basis for tourism development not only in the present, but also for future generations, natural and cultural heritage must be protected.

How Can Heritage be Protected?

There are several approaches to protecting of heritage which are not necessarily related to tourism, e.g. environmental conservation laws, programmes and education, monument protection and cultural revitalization programmes. Legislation, direct protection via barriers, guarding and the exclusion of harmful activities and visitor management are the main measures which should be taken to protect the heritage from the negative impacts of tourism. Educational activities to increase environmental awareness and peoples appreciation of the natural and cultural heritage should be considered especially when developing tourism in sensitive natural and cultural sites. Considering protection and making use of tourism development as a means of conservation is a basic principle of sustainable tourism development.

Uniqueness Versus Unique Experience

From the point of view of the visitor's experience, unique natural "wonders" like the Grand Canyon, the Great Barrier Reef or the wildlife of Kruger National Park may be, at first sight, main attractions that most other regions can't compete with. But this doesn't necessarily mean that a region without such big attractions cannot be a place for an outstanding natural experience. The key to this experience is interpretation.

Explaining and informing about natural features like plants, animals, rivers or rocks and their role within complex ecosystems will change the visitor's perspective from just a fleeting experience to an insight into the wonders of the natural world. The same is true for cultural heritage-everybody wants to see the Eiffel tower or St. Peter's, and compared to them, the little village church may be of less importance. But what makes a visit special is the insight and understanding of a region's history, culture and the people as a whole-murals can tell exciting stories, dances can demonstrate great spirit and rites and habits can be inspiring-thus forming a vivid and unique experience.

Principles of Sustainable Tourism

What is Sustainable Tourism?

There is no widely accepted definition for sustainable tourism. Perhaps one of the better known definitions however is that of the World Tourism Organization: "Sustainable tourism development meets the needs of present tourists and host regions while protecting and enhancing opportunity for the future, It is envisaged as leading to management of all resources in such a way that economic, social, and aesthetic needs can be fulfilled while maintaining cultural integrity, essential ecological processes, biological diversity, and life support system." Sustainable tourism development should be ecologically sustainable (long term), economically viable, as well as ethically and socially equitable. Sustainable tourism should integrate the natural, cultural and human environment; it must respect the fragile environmental balance that characterises many tourism destinations, particularly in environmentally sensitive areas. It has a long term perspective. The principles of sustainable tourism find their roots in the phenomena sustainable development.

What is Sustainable Development?

There are many different definitions for sustainable development. The most well known one is from the Brundtland report: "Sustainable development is development that meets the needs of the present without compromising the ability of future generations to meet their own needs."

A more detailed definition is: "Sustainable development focuses on improving the quality of life for all of the Earth's citizens without increasing the use of natural resources beyond the capacity of the environment to supply them indefinitely. It requires an understanding that inaction has consequences and that we must find innovative ways to change institutional structures and influence individual behaviour. It is about taking action, changing policy and practice at all levels, from the individual to the international."

Sustainable Development is built upon 3 dimensions (ecological, social-cultural, economic) which are closely related; interact with each other, and need to be considered and addressed in an integrative manner.

Why are Sustainable Development and Sustainable Tourism so Important?

Sustainable development is important because the way that society has been developing cannot continue if we want to ensure that resources are available for future generations. The resources we are using within our society are limited and they are depleting at a rapid rate. Sustainable development is seen as a solution to this problem.

The importance of sustainable tourism is derived from the importance of sustainable development. Tourism is one of the worlds biggest industries. Since the 1980s the number of international travellers has increased almost three fold, from approximately 240 million in 1980 to roughly 700 million. This figure is expected to double again by 2020. The limits of the natural, social and cultural resource base, which constitute the fundamentals of tourism, will be unable to cope with the continuing tourism growth unless we do something about it. The central challenge for the tourism industry, its businesses and destinations, is: how can the tourism activity, and the growth expected over the next two decades, be managed in such a way as to ensure that it respects the limits of its resource base, and of those resources' capacity to regenerate, whilst being commercially successful? Sustainable tourism attempts to solve this problem.

Another factor is that although tourism brings many benefits to a country e.g. important contribution to gross national product, it can lead to investment in infrastructure with benefits that spread beyond tourism, and can provide a rationale for promoting environmental protection etc., if it is managed incorrectly it can result in negative environmental impacts on land and resources, including impacts on vegetation, wildlife and ecosystems, impacts arising from waste management, travel and transport; and in socioeconomic and cultural impacts affecting local communities, social relations and cultural values. Sustainable tourism tries to produce tourism which is mainly advantageous rather than disadvantageous for a destination and its inhabitants.

The History of Sustainable Development

As a concept sustainable development finds its roots in landscape, agricultural and town planning thousands of years ago. The term "sustainable development" as we know it and understand it today, however, was first used at the end of the 60s beginning of the 70s and is an articulation of previous ideas about sustainable development in the context of a global industrial and information society.

Historical Development Before the 1980s

It is estimated that through excess consumption the capacity of the earth's resources started to be exceeded around the middle of the 18th century. This was caused by the industrial revolution and the consequent increase in the need for energy as well as better living standards, causing an increase in population which in turn resulted in an increased need for food products and new more modern methods implemented in agriculture. During and after the industrialisation the concept behind SD gained increased recognition and importance in many countries. People became concerned about the effects of industrialisation on the environment and realised «that if it were not controlled, the process [the industrialisation] could destroy the physical environment and lead to a very poor quality of life for the population».

Model settlements were established and many organizations concerning the protection of the natural environment were founded. Governments and local councils also began to look towards longer-term development and tried to protect the development of towns and cities. The second world war was another mile stone in sustainable development. Plans for rebuilding Europe recognised the necessity for Europe's sustainable development. In the 1960s and 1970s people increasingly began to recognise that the way the world was developing was the cause of many environmental and social problems and that development had to become more sustainable to protect resources for future generations. The fuel crisis, extreme pollution, rapid growth in poverty in the third world, diseases etc. strengthened this increased consciousness development is inevitable but that it does not have to occur in a way, which will lead to the depletion of resources and the eventual destruction of the fundamentals of our planet.

Sustainable Development Since the 1980s

There has been a rapid increase in interest in the topic since the 1980s. A few of the most important events which have occurred involving sustainable development are mentioned below.

The «World Conservation Strategy» (1980 International Union for the Conservation of Nature and Natural Resources (IUCN))-one of the first reports to talk honestly about sustainable development. The Brundtland Report «Our Common Future (1987 World Commission on Environment and Development)-perhaps one of the most well known reports about sustainable development and a mile stone in the history of the phenomenon. The Earth Summit in Rio de Janeiro in 1992, however, was probably the most important event in the development of SD. It was a major conference, organised by the UN, held in Rio de Janeiro, and attended by 108 heads of State or Government. Leaders at the Earth Summit built upon the framework of Brundtland Report to create agreements and conventions on critical environmental issues such as climate change, decertification and deforestation

The outcomes were:

- Agenda 21-a comprehensive programme of action for global action in all areas of sustainable development.
- The Rio Declaration on Environment and Development-a series of principles defining the rights and responsibilities of States.
- The Statement of Forest Principles-a set of principles to underlie the sustainable management of forests worldwide.
- The United Nations Framework Convention on Climate Change and The Convention on Biological Diversity.

Throughout the rest of the 1990s, regional and sectoral sustainability plans were developed. A wide variety of groups, ranging from businesses to municipal governments to international organizations such as the World Bank, adopted the concept and have interpreted it in their own way. Progress on implementing sustainable development plans, however, has been slow. Lots of documents and conferences, but little implementation/action.

Various bad occurrences related to tourism as well as the sudden increase in mass tourism in the 1960s triggered a lot of tourism critique and led consequently to the introduction of the phenomenon sustainable tourism or, as it was more commonly known at that time, «green» (gentle) tourism into the debate. It is also a phenomena that has developed out of the growth of sustainable development. International action in this area, however, did not really take off until the early 1990s. After initial scepticism, however, tourism has been officially recognised as an important issue in international environmental politics, both in relation to the Convention on Biological Diversity and to Agenda 21.

Some Important International Conferences and Reports

The establishment of the *"International Guidelines for Biological Diversity and Tourism Development"*. These fulfil the concept of sustainable tourism and should be considered by all relevant bodies as the tool for future planning and management of tourism. The Quebec Declaration, within the framework of the International Year of Ecotourism 2002, was implemented by the Commission on Sustainable Development (CSD), as a contribution to bring the different views of NGOs and the tourism industry into line in accordance with sustainable tourism. The Commission for Sustainable Development adopted Decision 7/3 on tourism and sustainable development at its 7th session in New York in 1999.

This decision includes the adoption of an international work programme on sustainable tourism development and an invitation to the CBD to *"further consider, in the context of the process of the exchange of experience, existing knowledge and best practice on sustainable tourism development with a view to contributing to international guidelines for activities related to sustainable tourism development..."*.

Today sustainable tourism is a term, which is widely used. Many governments and actors within the tourism industry have already developed or have started to develop sustainable tourism policies.

There are a wide range of organizations that deal with and campaign for sustainable tourism. There has been a large increase in public awareness about the subject.

The Principles of Sustainable Development

Overlying Principles

1. *Integration of environmental and economic decisions* – consideration of environmental impacts from economic decisions and vice versa)
2. *Stewardship* – protection of the social and physical environment and maintain a viable economy for the present and future generations.
3. *Shared responsibility*-acknowledgement that sustaining the environment and economy is our responsibility.
4. *Global responsibility*-think globally, act locally.

Social Principles

5. *Cultural identity*-Value increase and protection of cultural diversity and identity, including local specialities, and local community support.
6. *Protection of health and comfort by:* Ensuring secure, healthy and good standards of living for all community inhabitants Implementing prevention and quality in health care.Ensuring access to water, food, accommodation and heating for acceptable prices. Providing access to knowledge and skills required to enable individuals to be self-sufficient and therefore be a useful part of society. Supporting participation of all community groups and other stakeholders/ interest groups in decision making and considering the impacts these decisions may have on society.
7. *Public participation* – the participation of all stakeholders effected by development in the decision making process is necessary.
8. *Understanding and respect*-Consideration must be given to the aspirations, needs and views of various communities and individuals effected by development.
9. *Access to information* – promotion of the opportunity for equal and timely access to information
10. *Integrated decision making and planning*-encouragement and support of decision making and planning processes that are open, cross-sectoral and that incorporate time horizons relevant to long-term implications.

Environmental Principles

1. *Use of natural resources*-effective and efficient use of natural resources. Use of resources should not exceed their rate of growth.
2. *Waste minimisation* – reduction, recycling and reuse, or proper disposal of materials. Waste production should not lie above the absorption capacity of the earth.
3. *Conservation*-maintenance and conservation of the essential ecological processes, biological diversity, life-support systems and aesthetic value of our environment. Increase peoples awareness about the importance of biodiversity and its value.
4. *Prevention*-anticipation, prevention or mitigation of significant adverse environmental and economic impacts of policy, programmes and decisions.
5. *Enhancement* – enhancement of the long term productive capability, quality and capacity of our natural ecosystems.
6. *Rehabilitation and reclamation* – restoration of damaged or degraded environments.
7. *Scientific and technological innovation*-research, development, test and implementation of technologies essential to develop environmental quality.

Economical Principles

1. *Basic material and immaterial needs* – should be fulfilled and guaranteed.
2. *Minimum standard of living*-must be guaranteed.
3. Profitable/ viable business.
4. Economic utility and stability
5. *Economic growth*-qualitative not quantitative

The Principles of Sustainable Tourism Management

The challenges of key importance for the development and implementation of sustainable tourism exist worldwide. The specific nature and intensity of these challenges, however, vary from place to place. Moreover, particular geographical areas, such as the Mediterranean and the Alps have their own specific problems and challenges.

The following principles should underlie any approach to sustainable tourism (this saves confusion with the variation in different definitions) and they relate to how sustainable tourism might be achieved and what its implications could be. Sustainable tourism management is an approach which:

> *Minimizes the negative environmental, social and cultural impacts of tourism Generates economic profit from tourism for local people and improves their quality of life, their working environment and their access to technology and information.*

Allows local people and other stakeholders to participate in decision making processes involving tourism development which could effect them.

Informs all stakeholders of tourism development which could effect them. Contributes to natural and cultural preservation and conservation and promotes the importance of and protects biodiversity.

Provides tourists with more meaningful tourism experiences, e.g. meeting, cooperating, communicating and working with local inhabitants etc. bringing the tourist closer to the culture of the destination. Enables visitors to observe and understand environmental and cultural relationships and contexts. Is sensitive to local people, as well as other stakeholders, their needs, rights and aspirations.

Sees policy, planning and management as extremely important to combat the problems caused by non sustainable tourism. Emphasises that there are limits to tourism development can be very frustrating because there are limits to how much can be achieved in the short and medium term. It is a slow process of development.

Generally involves frequent conflicts between stakeholders over resources, implementation etc. Compromises may be necessary. ETE has developed a set of principles for sustainable tourism development in Banska Stiavnica in Slovakia. These principles are a good example of sustainable tourism principles in a destination.

3

Types of Sustainable Tourism vs. Conventional Tourism Types

Sustainable tourism is an overhearing concept. All forms of tourism can be sustainable – even mass tourism-when it's managed properly! But certain types of tourism tend to be viewed as being more inherently sustainable as others, namely ecotourism, pro-poor tourism, community-based tourism, fair-trade tourism, cultural tourism and rural tourism. The relationship between forms of tourism considered sustainable and those considered unsustainable can be seen in the diagram below.

Non-sustainable Growth of Tourism

Sustainable Tourism Development

Unplanned activities e.g. building a guest house ad hoc, without knowing if it is beneficial; building a slope for downhill skiing – could not be successful, but ecological damage remains; duplicate activities in a region, useless competition and resource squandering.

Development concepts and plans responsible business plans; of tourism development in a region Makes possible a responsible and coordinated use (therefore in decreased amounts) of accessible resources. Central planning and decision-making decisions about regional projects are made in Bratislava; when making plans, regions are not considered, and the like. Decisions made at local level, involving local people and businessmen subsidiary; true public participation in zoning plan preparation; (entrepreneurs and citizens decide what they want and what they don't want in tourism, of course assisted by experts) Unlimited development when planning and implementing tourism-related activities, the tourism interests are considered only, nothing else; Regulated development in time and space restrictions are respected, e.g. acceptable number of visitors in village, nesting time of birds, carrying capacity of a territory, etc.

Intensive use of landscape and resources things get concentrated on a few places; effort is made to get the most out of a client; negative impacts of intensive development are ignored. Extensive use of landscape and resources effort is made to disperse visitors in the territory; to get out of the client only what is necessary; efforts to regulate impacts are respected.

Understanding tourism as a universal remedy for social and economic problems in a region unprofessional approach that ignores the basic economic and logical aspects of development; cannot depend on one sector – high risk, low capability to withstand threats; low rate of using the potential of landscape and community. Understanding tourism as one of the tools for solving social and economic problems in a region it is necessary to have a wider portfolio of branches, so if one fails or faces problems, the others can keep the economy going; better use of the potential of the landscape and community Focus on economic goals only orientation on financial profit. Harmonisation of economic, social and environmental goals benefits include not only financial profit, but also e.g. good feelings, education, cultural exchange, pleasant atmosphere, clear conscience, pretty and diverse landscape, and the like. Universal support of tourism activities without differentiation no priorities are determined, resources are just scattered with no true result required; difficult-to-measure results, though usually there is no interest to measure them.

Differentiated and targeted support of tourism activities defining priorities–what is important for the region, what has to go first and what can wait; well measurable results, effort to transfer experience in to next phases. Implementation of individual projects in the region individual interests are promoted, interests and needs of others are not respected; however, this could be "only" a consequence of bad coordination. Coordination of projects in the region effort is made to increase synergy in the region. Construction and development for the purpose of satisfying unlimited demands-"the more visitors the better" method absence of professional analysis (or they are not respected) –

they define what is best for the region and where is the focus meaningful. If having a lot of visitors, low income is sufficient and so the quality can be worse; effort to get quick money, not reflecting consequences.

Determining the limits of a territory—"the most proper visitor" method analysis and surveys are prepared and respected; rather to have fewer but better paying visitors – this, however, requires higher standards and quality (long-term process). New constructions (lodging, recreation centres, various parks, etc.) easier way, but causes more damage to the environment (occupying new areas, influencing biodiversity, etc.); quicker money, easier preparation.

Use of existing objects usually complicated and more expensive; however, the strengths of the region are promoted and used. Copying not local and not typical models and construction technologies in architecture uniformity; global materials, technologies and companies it is an easier way but decreases the quality of experience.

Implementing architectural elements and construction technologies typical for the region difficult way, but increases the quality of experience however, biases exist and results are expectable in midterm horizon. Use of cars intricate problem, difficult to solve; the entire society is based on cars; have a strong negative impact on the environment – exhausts, spatially demanding, safety problems, degradation of tourism, etc. Promoting public and non-engine ways of transportation difficult goal because public transport (PT) is usually less comfortable and low quality; PT – significantly less pollution, considering the number of transported people; non-engine transportation – positive impacts on health, no pollution, more intensive experiences. Seasonal character of demand and/or offer being satisfied with the peak time periods when enough money is made for the year but it is accompanied by a number of social (seasonal employment, crowded centres) and environmental impacts. Permanent demand and/or offer easier on the social and economic environment. Stereotypic and universal products for everyone degrading the visitor to a „piece"; decreasing the quality of experience, stronger feelings of dissatisfaction, and the like; the visitor is then less sensitive to the landscape and community.

Tailor-made products for small groups atmosphere of friendship and pleasant experiences; good feeling from visiting the region; visitor supports the community and landscape protection. The visitor's passive acceptance of the environment lying on the beach, going up and down on skis, etc. the visitor is then less sensitive to the landscape and community.

Interactive relation between the visitor and the environment visitor learns more and then understands the need to protect the community and landscape and is supportive of this protection. Favouring cheap but unqualified labour force attempts to have increased profit, even for the price of long-term losses; frequently, this is also a consequence of a bad external situation. Efforts to employ highly qualified people thinking in long-terms; investing in local people, who live in the place and presumably will stay there for longer.

Use of labour force from outside of the region exploitation of employees and violation of human rights; low quality of work; Use of local labour force this is a responsible approach to the region where profit is acquired; this way, usually, the visitor's experience is better, out flow of financial profit from the region too.

Ecotourism and Sustainable Tourism

There tends to be a lot of confusion in definition between the two terms. In some countries the term ecotourism is used instead of sustainable tourism. Ecotourism, however, should be considered as a concept separate to sustainable tourism. It is, as mentioned above, a type of tourism or tourism sector, which is considered to be inherently more sustainable than other forms. Definition of ecotourism: "responsible travel to natural areas that conserves the environment and improves the wellbeing of local people."

Sustainable Tourism in Protected Areas

Protected areas (PAs) are important destinations for a growing tourism segment (nature or ecotourism) which uses intact and diverse nature, landscapes and biodiversity as major attractions. This represents both a potential threat to, and an opportunity for conservation goals. On the one hand, negative environmental and other impacts have to be minimised; on the other hand, nature tourism can provide significant benefits, both for conservation agencies and for local people living in and around PAs. One of the most important challenges that many PA agencies and conservation NGOs face today is satisfying these requirements in a sustainable way.

Tourism in protected areas should be based on the special character of the protected area and includes:

Tourism based on appreciating nature, such as studying, photographing or painting nature or landscapes and activities such as mountain walking, climbing, caving, diving, cross-country skiing, cycling or canoeing, where they are enjoyed primarily to discover nature, rather than as a sport. Cultural and educational tourism aimed at increasing people's understanding of the protected area and its surroundings, for example, school visits, nature camps, visiting natural and cultural sites, learning local crafts. Quiet, small-scale or small group activities which maintain the area's peace and quiet and wild qualities.

Strategic Planning for Regional Tourism Development

Why Strategic Planning?

There are four main reasons why strategic planning is useful for tourism development. These are mentioned in this section.

A region could have great potential for tourism development. It is, however, necessary to consider this potential carefully in order to ascertain how this potential can be used in a way, which will make tourism development good for the region. A good strategy can help to do just that! It helps the people managing such development to create sound conditions for tourism development in the region, it also enables individual stakeholders to recognise their position in the development process and it sets out guidelines for the implementation of tourism activities in a profitable way.

Tourism development in a destination is a long-term, systematic process. In contrast the projects of individual stakeholders are almost always of a short-term, rarely midterm, character. It is, therefore, necessary to create a framework, into which the individual projects will fit, thus supporting the long-term character of tourism development. Strategic planning provides this framework.

The tourism products of a region are influenced by a number of different factors and consist of a variety of major or minor products and services, which are provided by various stakeholders. If a region intends to create conditions for tourism development there and to sell tourism product harmonising and coordinating these products is necessary. Strategic planning can assist and organise this process. Having a good strategy is also helpful when applying for financial support from banks, funds, etc.

Basic Requirements

If a tourism development strategy (or any local/regional strategy) is to be successful and effective, it must be created through a process of cooperation between all stakeholders and adopted by them in a form which is convenient. The final document should be an outcome of intensive discussions and negotiations amongst stakeholders. General agreement must be achieved in visions and goals, as well as in actual measures towards meeting them.

When creating a tourism development strategy it must be clear in advance that the stakeholders actually want it and that they will respect it and therefore stay true to it's contents. It can only be viable as a document when it is supported and required or at least confirmed by the people, who will use it, i.e. by the stakeholders. In addition, it should not be initiated when the main aim behind it is to make money from various sources. Even if a strategy is officially adopted, e.g. by local parliament or a tourism association, it remains an informal and voluntary tool. A strategy should achieve its goals through the voluntary commitment of all the stakeholders. A strategy is flexible and open. Neither the process of preparing a strategy nor the final document should be fully defined in advance. Only the basic framework is predetermined.

The strategy and action plans which are derived from it, should be realistic and achievable and should not focus on activities and goals which maybe tremendous but which are unrealistic. A well designed sequence of small, realistic steps can lead to the completion of larger goals, which may have previously seemed improbable.

Tourism development strategies should determine and coordinate the steps to be taken for each industry sector in a region, not just one (e.g. public administration or hotel service).

Essential Parts of a Strategy

A strategy usually consists of five basic parts:

1. Diagnosis of the present state and a problem analysis.
2. Defining the vision and goals of tourism development.
3. Identification of strategies.

4. Programmes and projects put into action.
5. Monitoring and feedback.

Diagnosis of the Present State and Problem Analysis

The diagnosis of the present state of an area, is a description of the existing situation in the field of tourism. It clearly defines a common basis for determining goals, programmes and for joint decision-making and can include:

Analysis of the present situation in the region: natural features (landscape, interesting fauna and flora, rich biodiversity, geological formations, water, protected areas, etc.); cultural features (historical monuments, typical architecture, traditions, customs, music, gastronomy, events, etc.); tourism infrastructure (lodging, eating, attractions, services, etc.); other basic data (distances from cities, airports, bus/train stations; means of transportation to and within the region, density of shopping network, health care, banks, police, various services, etc.,); marketing data (existing market segments; visitors' interests, needs and motivations; modes of marketing; modes and channels of promotion, etc.); legislative environment (national and regional tourism concepts and plans, small business legislation, zoning plans, nature conservation and historical monuments protection, etc.).

Analysis of the external environment: identifies relevant threats and opportunities that need to be faced or used in the tourism development (e.g. trends, political situation, expected legislation, demographic development, etc.). The present situation can be defined and the problems analysed through a number of steps, which include: an inventory of the above mentioned elements; SWOT analysis; benchmarking – the comparison of selected regional parameters with those from another region, which is considered to be at a further point of development; creating scenarios – estimation of possible scenarios for various versions of development. Usually the best and worst scenario are thought out and then compared. The result of this process is the initial identification of aspects which are especially important for tourism development.

Defining the Vision and Goals of Tourism Development

A vision is developed with the aim to answer the following questions: "Where are we going?" and "What do we want to achieve?". The vision justifies the tourism development and defines the development goals, from the perspective of regional and social development. The vision and goals need to be defined through a creative process, where bold, even utopian ideas should explored.

Identification of Strategies

After defining the vision and goals, the basic and strategically important areas of long-term tourism development should be defined. The main direction of the goal-achieving process also needs to be determined. Factors which need to be specified are: what needs to be developed, what given features of the region will be used, what procedures will be pursued, and who will be the main actors.

Depending on the perspective, a number of strategies can be identified. These can be divided into two basic groups:

(a) Sectoral strategies, e.g.: *diversification strategy* – if it is apparent that the existing products/market segments are not sufficient this strategy looks at what new products will be introduced into the market and what market segments addressed; *human resources development strategy* – identification of professions that need to be developed and determining the focus and extent of this development; *marketing strategy* – detailed identification of market segments (target groups) and the selection of a way of marketing, which will attract these segments to the region;

(b) Cross-sectional strategies (all sectors are regarded), e.g.: *win-win strategy* – conflicts that have hindered tourism development need to be solved. This helps to satisfy any doubts that stakeholders or the local population may have about the development and also means that the conflicts no longer block further development; *sustainable development strategy* – defines the principles of a sustainable tourism development.

Operation Programmes and Projects

The strategies identified above should then, in so called *operation programmes* or *action plans*, be converted into the steps that are required for achieving the development goals. *Operation programmes* define, among others, (a) the measures which lead to the goals being met, (b) the organisation and finances required, (c) the time schedule, etc.

The operation programmes are usually sectoral, i.e. deal with measures and actions to be taken within one sector. In the case of tourism development in a region, they can include: creation/improvement of conditions for business in tourism; protection of nature, landscape and the environment; development of human resources in tourism; building infrastructure for tourism; transportation; ensuring clean and safe public areas; marketing and promotion, etc.

Operation programmes, or the measures defined within them, form the basis for decisions about individual projects. Projects are comprehensive groups of short-term activities with real goals. A project should deal with real problems and it's activities and outcomes should be described thoroughly in the operation programme. A number of projects can be included in one operation programme; they can be implemented parallel to or after one another. All projects have a manager and follow a clear project cycle (preparation – implementation – evaluation– feedback).

It is appropriate to create projects and ideas that are related not only to project activities but also to the manner of project management, financing, communication, etc. The following components need to be clearly defined when carrying out projects (in the operation programme or project supply): project justification (i.e. what measures of the operation programme are implemented and what goals of the strategy are intended to be achieved by the given project); project description (localisation, goals and description of activities); description of project outcomes; principles of project financing (indicative budget, financial management, follow-up costs and the way of handling them etc.); people/institutions responsible for project implementation; description of the project management; plan of activities and project milestones.

Operation programmes should be consistent, mutually interlinked and the following aspects should apply to them: they should consist of short-term but complex measures focused on tourism development in the region; these measures should be prioritised, i.e. it should be determined what is more important and what less; programmes focused on operation and maintenance should be perceived as being supportive of development and innovation but not as an individual goal of the strategy; operation programmes should follow an integrated approach, i.e. effort should be made to link those measures from various sectoral operation programmes, which are (a) common/shared, (b) have the same manager, or (c) are possible to finance from the same resource; similarly, individual projects, will be integrated into a "central project". If the individual projects share some of the project activities; these can be interlinked and will also influence one another; projects should have a multiplicative effect, i.e. several new activities should arise from one project. They should, however, not be dependent on the original project; programmes and projects should be innovative, i.e. they should look for and encourage new views and solutions. An innovative element is usually tested on one project and if it is successful, it is included in other projects as well.

Innovations can be implemented in products, methods and approaches. Creativity is an essential part of innovations; particular measures and projects should be as concrete as possible. They should provide deadlines and define the people/institutions responsible for carrying out the measures etc.

Adaptive Management and Monitoring

Tourism development strategies, like any other strategy or development plan, are accompanied by a certain amount of risk and uncertainty. This can be increased when innovations and creative thinking are implemented into the strategy and also in the strategy's preparation process. This is, however, perfectly natural. Nothing can be planned perfectly in advance. When implementing a strategy, unexpected development should be taken into account and if necessary, changes to the strategy and its operation programmes should be made. Quick reactions to inappropriate or unexpected development is the basis of adaptive management.

To achieve this, it is important to take into account the fact that the feedback mechanism is an important part of the process, e.g. feedback from the strategy and its stages, operation programmes and their stages, and the fact that all projects should be evaluated. In addition, the acquired knowledge has to be included in the updated version of the strategy/operation plan, used in the next stage or project. When monitoring the implementation of a strategy, it is necessary to determine what should be monitored, how aspects of the projects should be measured, what the results of the measurement will be used for, who is responsible for what, etc.

Regarding feedback: in the process of a strategy preparation, it is important to remember that updates will be elaborated (e.g. in regular intervals or after achieving a goal). It is; therefore, important to develop a mechanism of evaluation and to incorporate the results of this evaluation in the actualised version of a strategy.

Basic Principles of Developing and Implementing a Strategy

The process of strategy preparation is as equally as important as the strategy itself. During the strategy's preparation, it is already decided whether the given strategy will be a formal, unused document or whether it is will be an actual framework for tourism development in the region. The following two areas need to be considered:

Ownership of Strategy

A tourism development strategy can be only be successful if it is widely accepted by the public in a given region. It should be understood and accepted not only by the authors but also by stakeholders (e.g. entrepreneurs, local parliaments, state institutions in the region, etc.) and primarily by the local population. The reason or group of people behind the strategy preparation process is important in determining the future use of the strategy. This reason or group of people can be one of the following:

(a) Bottom-up – the demand for the strategy development, its principles and content (to some extent) comes from the local population or from a group of public professionals, who do not have the right to make decisions (usually businessmen in tourism). This approach is ideal because it creates "ownership feelings" towards the strategy among quite a large number of people. These people then not only accept and implement the measures defined in the strategy more willingly, but also demand that the local authorities do the same. At the same time, this approach is the most difficult, because it requires extensive communication with the public interesting.

(b) Top-down – the demand for a strategy comes from local authorities (self-administration or state). The local people are then convinced (or forced) to accept the strategy and the measures derived from it. Although this is the approach, which is used most frequently, it is actually the one, which is the most

ineffective because people tend not to trust the authorities and their decisions. When deciding on, whether or not they should accept a strategy, people often look at who is behind the strategy (Popular or unpopular politician? Did I vote for him or not? What political party is he/she a member of?, etc.) before making their decision, rather than at its content. In addition, the wishes and interests of the public are not incorporated into the process or they are taken into consideration but in a formal and ineffective way, which does not have any significant influence on the final strategy.

(c) Middle-out – the demand for a strategy comes from local experts, research institutions or organisations on the middle management level (ones that do not have the rights to make decision but which have the executive capacity and expert knowledge to carry out the strategy). This approach depends strongly on the capability of local experts to take the public interest into consideration and their ability to assert themselves among the local people and on decision-making levels. This approach can be either successful or unsuccessful, depending on the way it is executed.

(d) A combination of the above mentioned approaches – this is the least systematic approach but the one which still occurs quite often. It should, however, be avoided because it creates an intricate set of unclear relations. It is unclear who is responsible for what, who is the author and "owner" of which part of the strategy etc. In addition, those who are to accept and implement the strategy may not know what their tasks are.

Participants in the Strategy Development Process

A successful strategy incorporates the entire community, e.g. the local people, relevant social groups, decision making structures, professional and executive institutions it its preparation and should not be the result of the work of just a small group of people (or even by just a few authors). Generally at least one representative for each interest group should be involved in the process. The best possible results from this approach the following issues should be dealt with:

Who will be responsible for the preparation, implementation and evaluation of the strategy? This is something which needs to be clear to everybody involved and accepted by a large (as large as possible) number of stakeholders.

Who will participate (what people and what institutions) in the strategy preparation? Here, two viewpoints need to be distinguished: the involvement of various types of "action-takers", e.g. leaders, innovators and creative people, "hard-workers", pedants, "decision-makers", etc. so that the result is as harmonic as possible; involvement of representatives for all stakeholders groups and groups of local people (parliament members, entrepreneurs, officers, etc.) in the preparation process as well as the final stages of the strategy implementation. The adoption of the strategy by the public will be less problematic with this approach. At what stages, to what extent and in what activities should the particular stakeholders, or local people, participate?

How (in what form) should the individual stakeholders be involved in the strategy preparation and adoption?

How can a consensus, compromise and generally accepted decisions be achieved? How will the suggestions, ideas, interests and needs of stakeholder be collected?

Though the participation of the local population and the stakeholders is an inevitable prerequisite of a good strategy, equally important is the effective participation of experts – both local experts and those from outside of the region. Tourism, like other industry branches, has its rules, verified procedures and methods. It is essential that the strategy is a methodically correct document – otherwise it will not meet the expected goals. This is why experts should be invited to take part in the procedure and assigned responsibilities. Strategic planning cannot be done without them.

Creating a Vision

What is a Vision?

A vision describes a state in the future, towards which development should be directed. A vision does not provide detailed goals, it is not a state that is truly intended to be achieved but is more the direction that people intend to follow, a description of an ideal state that people dream of. Creating a vision means asking "Where do we want to go?".

Developing a vision is a creative process, which allows daring and utopian ideas. Visions can sometimes be quiet easy to achieve and sometimes it might be impossible. Whether the vision is achievable must be clear to the managers, stakeholders and the local inhabitants of the planning process.

What is Visioning?

Visioning (vision building) is a managed process used by a group of people (community, group of businessmen, local government, company, etc.) to create and build a the vision itself. It is used for participative approaches in a long-term policy agenda setting, using the imagination of the stakeholders as a source of ideas. It allows the participation of a wide public in the development of long-ranged regional plans. It is a democratic way to obtain disparate opinions from every stakeholder and to look for common ground among participants for exploring and advocating strategies for the future.

Visioning determines the direction people want to go in with development activities. It also defines goals, whilst respecting the opinions, needs and wishes of all the participants of the visioning process. This is a strong prerequisite if the goals of the development are to be defined properly and also for designing a good strategy to achieve those goals. Visioning brings the different tourism scenarios, issues, problems, different points of view and competing demands to the forefront. The collected scenarios serve as a basis for generating the end vision. The end vision is based on the opinions, ideas and the diverse perspectives of many people and can therefore be considered a democratically-derived consensus.

Vision building connects stakeholders, refines the environment where the development will take place, creates necessary networks and makes discussions possible. In addition, a vision leads towards the adoption of common goals, programmes and projects.

How to Create a Vision?

Creating a vision with a range of stakeholders or the general public is done through surveys, meetings and voting. There are, however, many different approaches to the process of visioning and towards the adoption of a common vision. Some of these are mentioned below: The creation of a vision in a single or in several stakeholder meetings, informing the public about it afterwards and then discussing the results with stakeholders and the general public which should finally lead to the adoption of one of the visions.

The conduction of a public survey to find out the publics issues with, concerns about and ideas for tourism development and biodiversity conservation. From the results different options for the vision should be developed and discussed. The stakeholders and general public should then vote for one of the options. The conduction of a public survey to find out the issues with, concerns about and ideas for tourism development and biodiversity conservation. Discuss the results in stakeholder meeting(s) and create a vision based on the discussions.

Surveys and discussion not only lead to the adoption of a common vision, but should also identify priorities and major concerns, which need to be integrated into the tourism management plan. They can also provide ideas for goals, which will be derived from the vision and for their implementation. These ideas can then be used in the next steps of the planning process.

It is important to recognize that visioning will require time, staff and will need to be well prepared (for further information on methods of visioning see the literature list at the end of the guide).

Methods

There is a number of methods that can be used to create a generally acceptable vision, most of them being based on, what is called, guided imagination. When implementing this approach, the participants should firstly imagine the ideal state of the place where the tourism is to be develop, secondly, they should try to describe it and write some notes on their ideas and finally they should create a vision. The method of guided imagination for visioning is described in detail in the interactive part for this topic.

Tourism Associations

Tourism Associations as Leader of Marketing

In the tourism sector, the effort of only one producer or hotel manager is usually not sufficient to promote the sustainable tourism products of a region. Cooperation, coordination and joint action are, therefore, important issues for tourism promotion and marketing in a region. Mutual organization, e.g. a tourism association, is generally considered appropriate for the marketing of one or several tourism products or of a tourism region as a whole. A tourism association can be established by local or regional administration or by a cooperation of tourism providers, e.g. hotels, restaurants, guides, tour operators, agencies etc.

The association can focus on the promotion of the whole region as a tourism destination, thus fostering the long term success of many providers instead of concentrating on the individual short term revenues of only one.

In countries where the tourism service is highly developed, e.g. in Austria or Switzerland, tourism associations have been effectively functioning for more than 100 years. They were established by local stakeholders and their aim is to develop tourism in their region. Membership in these associations is frequently obligatory for tourism businesses. In Tirol, Austria for example it is a legal requirement.

The goal of this seminar is to examine various forms of tourism organisations and to explain particularly the role and advantages of tourism associations.

Functioning of an Association

Essential features of tourism associations an open structure with content and responsibilities, which are clearly defined; efficiency and expertise; acceptability by decision-making bodies and sufficient competence; enough personal, financial and methodical resources; management and coordination skills.

Membership

Possible members of an tourism association are:

Individual tourism providers and providers of additional services. Communal government: Its membership has a specific character but it is very important if an association wants to be successful because it improves the coordination of activities and contributes to the image building of the destination. Communal governments often support associations financially but their votes, however, do not have extra weighting in decision-making processes. Non-governmental organizations, citizens' initiatives, local museums, galleries, civic associations and cultural institutions.

Financing

There are different ways to finance the association: Each member of the association pays a membership fee that is either a lump sum or is calculated according to selected criteria. Enrolment fees are single payments paid when a member registers. The generation of individual income for the association, e.g. income from TIC (tourist information centre) operation, from providing information about accommodation, selling souvenirs, organising events, etc. External sources such as visitors' taxes and fees are also a source of income for associations. This is typical for Austria, Germany and Switzerland. State and EU funds can provide support for non-profit organizations, structural funds, etc. Gifts from large businesses and corporations, from dedicated individuals, etc. Sponsorship from other businesses.

Internal Structure

The associations usually have a different legal structure. Most of them are civic associations or associations of legal entities. Their structure usually includes the following:

General assembly of members – elects members of the association's bodies, votes on principal decisions and plans; Board of trustees – is in charge of supervision and control of the association's financial management; Executive body – takes care of the day to day functioning of the association and organises its programme; Board of directors – makes decisions on and manages the work of the executive body.

Preparation committee – has a specific task, which is to specify the image of the association-to-be, prepare data and a proposal of initial documents and open a public discussion about the association, its function and goals. In addition, it should define the associations tasks (issues that the association will focus on) and place them in a realistic time frame and also prepare the founding meeting of the association.

Goals and Tasks of an Association

Tourism Product Development and Coordination of Regional Tourism Development

Tourism associations help to develop the region's tourism products through a continual process that involves as many stakeholders as possible. As a result the services are continually being improved and extended and the ability of the region to compete with other tourist destinations is maintained. In principle, the development of tourism products is the task of a tour operator. If, however, the association helps the individual tourism providers with this work, individual tourism providers can then focus on other things. To foster tourism development, tourism associations can organise events that are attractive for visitors, i.e. cultural, social or sport events, which are part of a region's tourism product. Tourism associations also have an important role in marketing tourism destinations as well as activities that are focused on improving the product and services provided, such as training those working in the tourism sector.

Visions and Concepts of Regional Development

All stakeholders should get engaged in influencing or even creating a tourism development policy (as well as regional development in general). This is not the exclusive task of local governments or local state administration authorities. Members of tourism associations should be actively involved in defining the development objectives of a town or region, while the association itself can be used as a platform for communication. In addition, the association can manage this communication and take part in the preparation and implementation of particular strategic steps of regional development – it links people and interests of tourism stakeholders. An association, which functions well and which is representative also has the power to influence communication with the state administration authorities as well as with the local government. It is therefore able to bring its own particular interests (e.g. adjusting the open-hours in museums or in the process of developing a zoning plan) to the forefront and to promote them. The association puts effort into promoting tourism in the town/region and works towards helping stakeholders make their voices heard at decision-making levels.

Acquiring Public Support

Successful tourism development is only possible if the local public has a positive attitude towards tourism. The association should therefore communicate its work, objectives and plans to local citizens (top-down). At the same time, it creates a platform for a bottom-up communication approach at regional or national levels where the interests of the association's members are promoted. Communication between the association and citizens can be carried out in a number of forms. These can include media activities, various events, publications, training courses (study trips, seminars), round table, discussions, exhibitions, etc.

Operational Function

The association carries out practical activities that benefit a great variety of tourism stakeholders. These are often non-profit activities.

Business Advisory Service

Tourism associations provide or help to search for experts and consultants in various fields.

Marketing

Tourism associations carry out surveys and analyse the level of visitor satisfaction, produce and distribute promotional materials, prepare workshops and presentations for potential partners, invite journalists to the region, who can write about the given destination and its attractions.

Tourism associations coordinate the cooperation of tourism stakeholders and public administration, e.g. the public administration makes sure that the infrastructure for the development of the region is sufficient, while the association is responsible for promoting the destination and its product among the competing tourist sites.

Moderation of Conflicts

The association can also serve as an independent non-biased institution, which deals with visitor complaints or problems or handles conflicts between two stakeholders.

Typical Problems for Tourism Associations in Central and Eastern Europe

Even today there are not many tourism associations in central and eastern Europe that function well. The main reasons for this include:

Psychological barriers: in the past, especially in states in Eastern Europe, the organization of public life was enforced by state authorities and because of this people usually distrust collective institutions.

Lack of appropriate legislation: There are no rules and regulations that would (a) guarantee financial resources to associations and (b) assign them certain rights in tourism development in the region.

Lack of Financial Resources

Absence of a clear and concrete programme: Many tourism destinations have not prepared good regional development plans. These plans would indicate the need of tourism development plans and „justify" the foundation and existence of a tourism association.

Lack of professional staff: The activity of an association must be managed by experienced professionals. Associations, however, usually do not have the money to pay such professionals for their work.

Unreasonable expectations: Inadequate expectations of the way associations' work are induced and cultivated among its members. This often occurs when the association is founded. Lack of motivation: Individual tourism providers have no motivation to become members of a tourism association, they are not able to see the potential of such an association.

Certification in Tourism

What is Certification?

Certification is the implementation and fulfilment of certain criteria or requirements given by the particular certification scheme within a facility, service, product or other entity. The facility etc. receives a certificate or a logo when the schemes requirements or criteria have been fulfilled.

The logo may then be displayed by the facility and serves as confirmation to clients that the facility etc. meets the requirements and respects the goals of the certification scheme whose logo it displays. This logo is generally used for marketing reasons. It shows that the facility or product has fulfilled certain criteria and this can be used to attract more customers. It is a voluntary procedure that, through assessment, monitoring as well as written assurance, shows that a business, product, service, facility etc. meets specific criteria and therefore a particular standard.

Certification programmes in sustainable tourism are also often known as ecolabels. Certification is important because it introduces standards into tourism. This is useful for facilities etc. and for customers. Labels are clear benchmarks for products etc. that are of acceptable standards or that are particularly sustainable. Unfortunately not many people are aware of certification schemes and what they entail or mean.

Reasons for Certification in Sustainable Tourism

Certification can be a good tool for the individual/ company implementing the scheme because it can be used to reach the goals that they are trying to realize. If a tour operator is trying to become more sustainable then a certification scheme can give them the incentive and direction to become more sustainable. It provides smaller steps, which they can apply so that they eventually get to their larger goal.

As mentioned above certification is a good marketing tool for a facility/product or business. Certificates tend to be focused on and therefore attract specific target groups e.g. environmentally friendly/ sustainable tourists, people who by organic produce etc. If a facility is certified for something, e.g. a hotel wants to be certified as being environmentally friendly, the certificate/logo not only informs the target group automatically that the hotel has certain environmental standards but it also increases the attractiveness of the hotel for the target group.

Certification is also useful for customers who use the labels for product/facility orientation. A facility or other entity, which is certified generally shows some kind of good quality and gains the facility credibility in the eyes of the customer.

A certification scheme also shows that the individual, company or facility which is certified, obviously believes in/respects/supports the topic/issue of certification and that their interest is not just in better marketing.

The Basic Characteristics of Certification Schemes

* They are voluntary.
* They exceed the standards which are required by law.
* They usually cost money.
* They allow the facility etc. to use a logo, which makes the facility stand out from its competition.
* They award a logo/ brand to the entity.

This logo is however only allowed to be displayed when the entity obtains the certification, in other words, if they fulfil the criteria set by the scheme. These criteria reflect the goals of and issues behind the scheme.The rules of the certification scheme are generally clearly stated. They define the criteria, mode of application of the certificate, the way it will be evaluated and how the certificate will be presented, how monitoring and control of the scheme takes place as well as the time limit for its application and regional specificities.

Certification schemes include a formalised evaluation process. This process includes self evaluation, external verification, spot checks, evaluation through customers and checks at regular intervals.

The certification scheme should be well marketed. This is necessary if the scheme is to be successful. Without good marketing the certification scheme itself and the benefits it should bring to the facilities implementing the scheme will most likely fail.

Orientation of Certification Schemes

Process-orientated

Goal: continuous improvement, without fixed figures. Certification schemes which focus on process are especially created for facilities or products which are interested for example in becoming more sustainable but want to achieve this by continuously striving to reduce the impacts they have on the environment without actually trying to reach a certain target. For example a hotel may get a certificate of this type may meet the goals defined by the certification scheme (these are usually more general than the criteria) but not individual criteria. An example of a goal might be for example under the heading rubbish: attempting to increase the amount of recycling and reuse of resources in a firm. Whereas criteria for rubbish could be: to use recycled toilet paper. Almost any facility can achieve this type of certification, which reduces the marketing value of the certification.

Performance-orientated

Goal: Achievement of clearly defined criteria. These types of certification scheme certify facilities etc. which do want to reach a certain target through the fulfilment of criteria. In sustainable tourism certification schemes based on fulfilment this means that just meeting the goals of the scheme is not enough. The individual criteria must be met if certification is to be obtained. This means that the facility has to make a lot more effort where its levels of sustainability are concerned. It has to take all the criteria into account and change its approach accordingly.

This certification is more difficult to obtain but has therefore a stronger marketing effect. On the other hand the fact that it is so difficult to obtain means that fewer facilities want to make the effort to become certified.

Types of Certification

Affiliation with a trademark (franchising) the facility fulfils the criteria/goals of a certification scheme, which means that they can benefit from a given affiliation. These benefits may include being able to use the companies logo, marketing strategy, products etc. Increase in comfort specific target groups criteria that need to be met involve improving the quality and comfort of a facility for particular target groups so that it is more attractive for them. Quality the facility attempts to increase the quality of their service for clients or to fulfil set international standards. This is generally involves improvements in the area of management but also other areas.

EMAS, ISO-Standardization Systems

Sustainability the facility attempts to reduce their impacts on the natural and cultural environment.

Regional identity the facility attempts to fulfil criteria which state to what point the facility fits into a certain region. The facility should generally sell regional products, cook regional specialities, promote regional tradition and culture etc. These certificates can also be applied to and are often orientated towards a number of different entities. These may include improving the (environmental) management of a facility, improving the sustainability and quality of (tourism) products e.g. beaches, bathing areas (blue flag), accommodation, tour operators etc., certifying food which has been produced organically etc. Certification schemes may actually strive to improve more than just one of the above mentioned areas and also more than one of the above mentioned entities.

The Development Process

Initial steps:

* Declarations, codes of conduct, contest/awards.

Implementation:

- Public seed funds.
- consultations and networking.
- advising and training measures.

- "soft" criteria and self evaluation.
- marketing.
- stricter criteria and control measures.
- financial sustainability.

Introduction to Marketing in Tourism

Why Marketing in Sustainable Tourism?

The lack of marketing expertise and knowledge of the tourism's industry distribution channels is the main reason why entrepreneurs in sustainable tourism fail. They often assume that because they have an authentic and exciting tourism product, tourists will be interested, failing to understand the nature of the tourism industry as a marketplace. Many donors and policy makers also underestimate the challenge and the costs of distributing the tourism product and do not recognize marketing as a key to economic success, which, in the case of sustainable tourism development, is a part of the sustainability of tourism development.

The aim of this seminar is therefore to clarify and emphasise the fact that marketing is an essential part of sustainable tourism development and that its basic principles should be understood if economic failure, disappointment and discouragement of the ones engaged in sustainable development is to be avoided.

What is Marketing?

Once sustainable tourism development begins, stakeholders of the region design tourism products, create management plans to monitor and prevent unwanted negative impacts and take measures to make the best use of tourism benefits. At this point, just "waiting for the visitor" won't do. Tourists will only purchase the product if they find out information about the product, the product meets their needs and interests, they are able to buy it.

Marketing involves these issues: To have a product which is of interest for a potential visitor, to find out about the customer who might buy it, to make sure that the potential customer is informed about the product, to bring the product to the market, so that the customer is able to buy it, and to keep in contact with the customer and the public to ensure further purchase of the product. Market analysis, product development, distribution and advertising, or more general, promotion are all parts of marketing.

The Key Stages of Marketing

There are many different ways to structure marketing. The stages of marketing management may be different according to the product, the markets and goals of a business. The stages of marketing presented here simply give an overview of the different issues and strategies which should be considered in tourism marketing. For this purpose, marketing here is divided into four stages: analysis, goals and strategies, marketing mix and implementation and control.

Analysis

The first step of marketing is to gain profound knowledge about the potential or given tourism products which one has to sell, about the environment in which the business is developed and about the market, that is, potential customers and existing or future competitors.

According to product development there are two approaches: either to develop the tourism product first and then determine the appropriate market segments where the product may be purchased, or to have a look at the potential customers first: to find out what their interest and needs are, what their budget for a holiday is, what their expectations about quality are, etc., and then develop a product which meets these interests and needs.

Sustainable tourism product development tends to follow the first approach, because it is based on the use of the given environment (natural and cultural resources) and aims not to change the region's lifestyle, characteristics and original features but to provide tourism which the tourist will enjoy. But ignoring the point of view of the visitor may lead to unsatisfying outcomes. The key to a successful tourism product development is a combination of the two approaches, balancing what it is possible to offer with the wishes and needs of the tourists.

Goals and Strategies

This stage is about the creation and operationalisation of an overall marketing strategy. The segmenting strategy aims to select market segments: to which type of tourist should the products be offered? make decisions about targeting: will the product be offered to one or more market segments, to local, regional, national or international markets? Will there be new products introduced or will a diversification of products take place? Is the aim to penetrate the existing market or to develop a new market? The competition strategy decides whether the differences between the own product and other products (here: other providers or other regions) should be pointed out, or whether a 'Me-too-Strategy' should be followed, which means taking advantage of an already existing strong market leader, or whether a Cooperation Strategy should be established with other competitors. This option of particular interest for tourism associations and non-commercial stakeholders in the tourism sector. The customer strategy concentrates on the identification of the right target groups for the product and involves finding out about new, additional target groups, e.g. special interest groups.

The outcomes of this strategy may lead to a change in the developed tourism product or to a diversification of products to meet the needs and wishes of the identified potential customers.

The positioning strategy decides on the main focus of the marketing: quality or price. Combination of strategies Normally, the strategies presented don't exclude one another. A mix of the different strategies will generally take place. There may be different strategies for different business segments.

Marketing Mix or Tactical Marketing: Promotion and Distribution

To implement the marketing strategies, the optimal combination of marketing methods must be selected according to the developed goals and considering the given environment. There are different instruments, often summarized as the four P's: product (or services), price, place (distribution policy) and promotion (communication policy).

Product policy: The product policy concentrates on the adequate product design for the selected market segment. It may consist of combining various product elements (tourism product chain) to achieve the right tourism package or of the design of a single product. The distinction between competing products is part of the product policy. It decides whether to continue with what is already on offer or to change the products on offer (elimination, variation or innovation). In the tourism sector, product policy often concentrates on the improvement of services (e.g. for hotels), or, in the case of tour operators, the selection of agencies and staff, the quality of consultation and the creation of additional services (guide books, information meetings, etc.).

Price policy: The price policy can be market oriented, that means that the price of a product is not determined by considering the costs, but by evaluating the current market situation and competition. Different price policy strategies include price differentiation, high pricing (quality, exclusiveness), low pricing (discount offers) and price balancing (financing the discount on one product through another product which has a high price).

In the tourism sector, price policies are often based on price differentiation of the following factors: time: peak season-off-peak season, weekend-working day, stand-by-offers customer: families, kids, students, seniors volume: rebates for groups, prices for contingents distribution chain: discounts for tour operators point of time of payment: discount for early booking/payment spatial criteria: different prices for different departure points/geographically separated markets commercialisation of "free goods": climate, air, water, location, view, orientation ("ocean view")

Distribution policy: The main decision here is whether the product is purchased directly by the customer or via tour operators. On this decision depends the selection of agencies, booking systems and strategies of motivation and as well as guaranteeing the loyalty of tour operators or agencies (through information meetings and trips, commissions).

Communication policy: The communication policy consists of making the potential customers, tour operators and a wider public aware of the product and guarantee the continuing interest of customers.

The corporate identity (CI) is "the message", philosophy or of the tourism product, the provider or the region. It is a useful starting point for the other parts of communication and helps to position the product in the market.

Public relations (PR) describes the communication of a company with the wider public. It is usually unspecific, giving general information about the product and the provider and it focuses on contact with the media to ensure ongoing and positive media coverage. Advertising transmits specific information to specific target groups. Forms of advertising are TV spots, ads in the press, the internet and elsewhere. Advertising and PR are areas which overlap.

Promotion: The ongoing activities in advertising, sales and public relations are often considered aspects of promotion. The aim of promotion is to keep the product in the customer's and tour operator's mind and to stimulate the demand for the product. Various methods can foster incentives to buy the product. Tour operators which resell the tourism products and journalists can be invited to FAM (familiarization) or press trips. Decoration services, presentations at fairs and direct merchandising like little presents and customer's cards can motivate tourists to buy a product.

Implementation and Control

The implementation takes place after developing the product and other decisions about the presented strategies and it consists of the concrete organization of the marketing measures, considering resources, costs and time. Controlling the outcomes of marketing by comparing the goals with the results is not only required at the end of the process, but also throughout the process through constant monitoring, tests and surveys ensuring appropriateness of the selected strategies.

Tourism Product Development

What is a Tourism Product?

A tourism product is a combination of services, commodities and other material or immaterial items that enable the clients to have a „complex experience", which starts at them leaving their home and ends out their return. The experience consists of what the tourist does and learns during his stay and the individual impressions he gets from visiting the destination.

The so-called original tourism product consists of the natural and cultural attractions of a region. Derived tourism products are developed at a later stage at the destination either to increase tourism or because of an increase in tourism, e.g. transport facilities, hotels, restaurants, information and communication services. The sociocultural environment and the infrastructure of a destination for example politics, education, communication, transport, supply and disposal, can be considered separate or can partially come under both of the above categories. There are a large number of stakeholders (businesses, institutions, people and associations etc.) responsible for the maintenance of the above mentioned tourism attractions categories. Some of them can be seen in the list below:

Accommodation: Hotel managers, private accommodation landlords. Gastronomy: Restaurants, cafes, Kiosks, retailer (tradesmen), farmers. Service: Local authorities, tourism departments & associations, travel agencies.

Infrastructure: the town or regions building authority, the trade promotion office, culture and sport administration etc. The character of the destination: Regional Planning Authorities, Towns building authority, citizen initiatives.

The surroundings: Nature and conservation authorities, planning authorities, farmers, the village citizens, nature conservation initiatives. Transport: road construction administration, communal transport businesses, civil engineering office, national railways, police.

Specific Features of Tourism Products

When compared with other products, a tourism product has a number of specific features: It cannot be produced on stock, it cannot be stored, and it is always prepared for a particular customer and for a certain time. It always consists of items that the product's initiator cannot influence, but that must be considered (e.g. weather, character of landscape, history, etc.). Part of the tourism products are immaterial items such as hospitality, customs and traditions. Tourism products are bound to a particular territory – it is not possible to transport them elsewhere. A tourist buys a product even though he hasn't seen/ experienced it. Finally, the product user-the tourist-has an impact on its quality. He/she can decide about the content and form of the product, even when it is being used.

The Structure of the Tourism Products

It consists of a number of basic elements: preparation, travel to, stay at, travel back from the destination and activities to be completed after returning home. The topic of this lecture deals mainly with one of these elements – the stay in the region, therefore, the term regional product will be used. From a practical point of view, the product consists of four basic parts: the itinerary, lodging, eating and additional services (e.g. travel, money exchange, purchase of maps and camera films etc.). These items are not products themselves but when they are combined they become a part of a regional product.

Who can Produce a Regional Product?

In principle, three basic „producers" can be identified: Individual service providers (e.g. hotels, restaurants, tour guiding) coordinate their products and each of them tries to sell their own service, which is supplemented by the service of other partners. They generate profit mainly by selling the primary service that they provide.

Travel agencies and tour-operators sell a tourism product which is a combination of services from other providers, mainly providers and organizers of itineraries, lodging and catering. The tour operator then sells this product under its own name (or in cooperation with vendors). The income of the travel agency/tour operator is generated from percentages received from providers of individual primary services or by increasing the total price of individual products, or by the combination of both methods. Destination management organizations (DMOs) (e.g. tourism association, tourist information centres, tourism department of the local administration), similarly to a tour operator, create products from services of other providers.

They do not, however, sell this product but provide it for vendors. The profit is generated from the percentages received from the vendor (who generates his income based on percentages received from primary service providers) and/or from percentage gained from the income of primary service providers.

Packages

A tourism package is a form or even a synonym of a tourism product, for the package is what is sold to the customer by the vendor. Producing a package involves a number of steps:

Offer Inventory

A detailed summary of everything that the region can offer the client. It is important that existing attractions and activities are included in the list, not the potential ones. The inventory should not, for example, include "folk customs", if there is nobody to present them to the client; "good traditional cuisine", if no restaurant offers local dishes or "gothic churches" if it is not possible to visit them. For the purpose of a creating a tourism package, each of its elements should be an independent service with a clear provider, price and conditions.

Combining Offers to a Package and its Organisation

When the list of existing offers of the region is completed, its individual elements need to be combined. It is usually necessary to create a balanced composition, where the following features of the individual elements should be included: Focus – the product should have a certain character, a unifying element (e.g. mining history of the region, active relaxation in nature, etc.). From this perspective, the product items should be combined so that they compliment each other– e.g. noisy discos should not be included in a relaxation programme for seniors, highly technical tours of architectural monuments should not be a part of a programme of active relaxation in natural surroundings, etc.

Quality – the individual items should be of similar quality. For example an old bus which hardly works should not be used for rich clients with high purchasing power who are accustomed to high standards. Equally it would not be correct to organize a seminar for them in a noisy restaurant, etc. Length – particular items of a tourism package should have an appropriate and complementary lengths. A client should be given enough time to experience the "full flavour" of everything that is part of the product. A perfectly prepared programme also leaves a certain amount of time for the client to do activities on his/her own (e.g. going for walks, spending time in cafes, taking naps, etc.). It is important that the itinerary is planned realistically so the clients do not need to be rushed or stressed.

This can give them a negative impression of the package they have paid for. Variability – even though each package has its own focus, a certain level of variability also needs to be included, e.g. alternating between active parts and parts for relaxation, indoor and outdoor activities, etc. Morning activities should be differ from the afternoon programme, places to eat should vary and so should the character of activities. Appropriateness of activities – the client's wishes, habits and values need to be respected. Someone who appreciates good food should not be taken to a fast-food restaurant, a nature conservationist should not be offered a colourful plastic aqua park, a Muslim client should not receive pork for lunch, etc.

Marketing of the Package

When the package is ready, it is necessary to find the proper market for it. Identification of the market segments, communication channels, sale methods, etc. is necessary.

More attention is given to this topic. The above described procedure is obviously subject to change. The points 2 and 3 are often interchanged, i.e. appropriate market segments for a region are identified first, and then the available attractions are used to make a package for the identified market segments.

Frequent Mistakes of Product-making

Services that cannot be guaranteed are included in the package – a typical example is when churches are advertised as a great attraction of a region but entries into them are not always possible.

Tight programme – too many activities are planned for one day. This can result in late arrivals, nervousness and a bad impression of the product. On the other hand, long and boring periods of time whilst waiting for the next point of the programme (e.g. waiting too long to enter a museum), also needs to be avoided. Good knowledge of local services and ability to foresee and solve complications are therefore required.

Too much organization – effort is made to arrange the entire programme for the client and he does not get the chance to experience the magic of wandering in quiet historical streets, sitting in cafes, talking to local people, etc.

Improperly set price – tour-operator is afraid to include an appropriate price for their service (for making the product and organization work) in the total price. As a result, they do not generate sufficient profit for future work.

Unequal offer – in an effort to satisfy the customer as much as possible, things that were not part of the original package are offered to him as a surprise. Such additional and operative products are all right if provided to each client. Problems may occur if this is not possible because a client may find out about the new product and, if he did not receive it and paid the same price as those who did, his satisfaction is at risk. Extra services need to be guaranteed for all clients, or each client has to pay for them additionally.

SWOT Analysis

Meaning and Goal of a SWOT Analysis

* S – Strengths.
* W – Weaknesses.
* O – Opportunities.
* T – Threats.

The SWOT Analysis is an effective tool for assessing the current situation. It is necessary for developing a master plan, a strategy or operation programme for a distinct region, town or any other location. It helps to determine existing gaps, potentials and risks as well as to identify the desired direction of future development. It serves as a foundation for further planning and development in any sector. This applies to business and town management as well as tourism development.

When implementing the SWOT method, four basic groups of factors can be identified.

These can be put in two main groups: Internal factors (strengths and weaknesses): Factors that are inherent to a region, society, project or other units; they can be influenced or changed, they are present in a given territory, their owners are identifiable, etc.

External factors (opportunities and threats): Factors that are outside of an analysed region (organization, project or feature), we cannot influence. They can however have an effect on any of the areas examined.

General proceeding of a SWOT Analysis:

1. Taking the inventory: determining the current situation by carrying out surveys and investigations; gathering all accessible facts and information.
2. Drawing the SWOT Chart: evaluation of the current situation by identifying the strengths, weaknesses, opportunities and threats. Include any of the acquired facts in one of the above described groups of factors.
3. Outlining a further strategy (plan, procedure, programme) with the aim to: Promote strengths and/or use them Eliminate weaknesses Use the opportunities offered Eliminate threats.

The procedure of a SWOT Analysis is simple and highly effective, which makes the analysis a convenient tool to be used not only by experts but also by the general public. It can be used in several stages of tourism development, e.g. at the beginning of a process to find out what the properties are, the potentials and needs of a region, and how these should be developed further. The SWOT Analysis can be also be used for the evaluation of the existing situation and methods and thus to find out if it is satisfactory and if the most effective solution was proposed for the given environment and objectives. Carrying out a SWOT Analysis remains the same for every purpose. Only the thematic areas to be evaluated change depending on the field you are working for.

Thematic Areas for Tourism Planning

Frequent Errors when Realising a SWOT

Not distinguishing between the strengths and opportunities, or between weaknesses and threats. This means that the authors do not follow the essential principle. This is that the strengths and weaknesses should refer to the internal features of the analysed object, while the opportunities and threats refer to the external situation, in which the analysed object is situated.

Steps to be Taken Instead of Opportunities: It is wrong to believe that opportunities are in fact possibilities or steps that should be taken to improve the analysed object.

SWOT Without Participation of Residents: The involvement of the local population is important in all steps of tourism planning. They are the most eligible persons for the analysis of the region, because they have an inside view of what activities and services are missing. In addition, they should get involved in the strategy preparation, thus increasing the sense of "public ownership" of the strategy.

Recent Development in Tourism Industry

Tourism is the act of travel for the purpose of recreation, and the provision of services for this act. A tourist is someone who travels at least eighty kilometres from home for the purpose of recreation, as defined by the World Tourism Organization. A more comprehensive definition would be that tourism is a service industry, comprising a number of tangible and intangible components. The tangible elements include transport systems; Air, Rail, road, Water and now, space; hospitality services, accommodation, foods and beverages, tours, souvenirs; and related services such as banking, insurance and safety and security. The intangible elements include: rest and relaxation, culture, escape, adventure, new and different experiences. Sometimes *Tourism* and *Travel* are used interchangeably. In this context travel has a similar definition to tourism, but implies a more purposeful journey.

Health tourism & leisure travel; It was not until the 19th century that cultural tourism developed into leisure and health tourism. Some English travellers, after visiting the warm lands of the south of Europe, decided to stay there either for the cold season or for the rest of their lives. Others began to visit places with supposedly health-giving mineral waters, in hopes of relieving a whole variety of diseases. Leisure travel was a British creation due to sociological factors. Britain was the first European country to industrialize, and the industrial society was the first society to offer time for leisure to a growing number of people. Initially, this did not apply to the working masses.

Winter Tourism; Winter sports were largely invented by the British leisured classes. Organized sport was well established in Britain before it reached other countries. The vocabulary of sport bears witness to this: rugby, football, and boxing all originated in Britain, and even Tennis, originally a French sport, was formalized and codified by the British, who hosted the first national championship in the nineteenth century, at Wimbledon. Winter sports were a natural answer for a leisured class looking for amusement during the oldest season.

Mass travel; The father of modern mass tourism was Thomas Cook who, on 5 July 1841, organized the first package tour in history by chartering a train to take a temperance campaigners from Leicester to a rally in Loughborough, some twenty miles away. Cook immediately saw the potential for business development in the sector, and became the world's first tour operator. He was soon followed by others, with the result that the tourist industry developed rapidly in early Victorian Britain. Initially it was supported by the growing middle classes, who had time off from their work, and who could afford the luxury of travel and possibly even staying for periods of time in boarding houses. For a century, domestic tourism was the norm, with foreign travel being reserved for the rich or the culturally curious. *International mass tourism;* Increasing speed on railways meant that the tourist industry could develop internationally. By 1901, the number of people crossing the English Channel from England to France or Belgium had passed 0.5 million per year.

Attempts to move towards "quality tourism" are difficult given competition from cheaper, unspoilt holiday destinations on the one hand and the legacy of decades of over-exploitation on the other. Receptive tourism is now growing at a very rapid rate in many developing countries. In recent years, second holidays or vacations have become more popular as people's disposable income increases. Typical combinations are a package to the typical mass tourist resort, with a winter skiing holiday.

Special Forms of Tourism;

* Medical tourism.
* Disaster tourism.
* Virtual tourism.
* Bookstore Tourism.
* Vacilando.
* Ecotourism.
* Educational tourism.
* Health tourism.
* Space tourism.
* Adventure Tourism.
* Cultural tourism.
* Agritourism.
* Heritage tourism.

Future Trend of Tourism Industry; The World Tourism Organization forecasts that international tourism will continue growing at the average annual rate of 4 percent. By 2020 Europe will remain the most popular destination, but its share will drop from 60 percent in 1995 to 46 percent. Space tourism is expected to "take off" in the first quarter of the 21st century, although compared with traditional destinations the number of tourists in orbit will remain low until technologies such as space elevator make space travel cheap. On the ocean tourists will be welcomed by ever larger cruise ships and perhaps floating cities.

World Tourism Day

Since 1980, September 27 is celebrated by the World Trade Organization as World Tourism Day. The purpose of this day is to display awareness that tourism is vital to the international community and to show how it affects the social, cultural, political and economic values worldwide. The adoption of the statutes is considered to be a milestone in global tourism.

Water Recreation and Disease

Background

Recreational use of inland and marine waters is increasing in many countries. It is estimated that foreign and local tourists together spend around two billion days annually at coastal recreational resorts. The World Tourism Organization predicts that by 2026, 346 million tourists will visit Mediterranean destinations annually, representing about 22% of all arrivals worldwide (WTO 2001).

It has been estimated that 129 million people visited the beach or waterside in the United States of America between 2000 and 2001, an increase of 6% from 1995 (NOAA 2004). In the United Kingdom it is estimated that over 20 million people use the British coast each year, in addition to inland waters and their surrounding areas, for a variety of reasons. The National Centre for Social Research (1998) reported there were 241 million day visits to the sea/coast in Great Britain in 1998, with people prepared to travel an average of 43 miles to reach the coast. However, perceived risks involving recreational water use may have important economic repercussions in areas that depend to a large extent on recreational tourism as a source of income. An example is the decline in tourists visiting Lake Malawi in South Africa because of news reports about schistosomiasis cases (WHO 2003a).

Indoor water recreation is also hugely popular. Pools may be private (domestic), semi-public (hotels, schools, health clubs, cruise ships) or public (municipal or governmental). Pools may be supplied with fresh, marine or thermal water. Specialist pools, such as hot tubs are used for both pleasure and medicinal purposes and are generally filled with water at temperatures over 32°C (WHO 2005). 'Natural spa' is the term used to refer to facilities containing thermal and/or mineral water, some of which may be perceived to have therapeutic value and, because of certain water characteristics, may receive minimal water treatment (WHO 2005). Water-based recreation and tourism can expose individuals to a variety of health hazards, including pathogenic microorganisms.

Sports which involve intimate contact with the water such as surfing, windsurfing and scuba diving are growing in popularity, and technology is changing the behaviour of recreational water users – the use of wet suits for example, now encouraging prolonged immersion in water even in temperate or cool areas. The type, design and use of pools may predispose the user to certain hazards. Indoor pools, for example, may be subject to higher bather-loads relative to the volume of water. Where there are high water temperatures and rapid agitation of water, it may become difficult to maintain microbiological quality, adequate disinfectant residual and a satisfactory pH (WHO 2005).

The vast majority of research to date in the field of recreational water quality and health has focused on microbial hazards, in particular gastroenteric outcomes arising from contamination of water by sewage and excreta. Mild gastroenteric symptoms are widespread and common amongst recreational water users. A cause effect relationship between bather-derived pollution or faecal pollution and acute febrile respiratory illness (AFRI) is biologically plausible, and a significant exposure response relationship (between AFRI and faecal streptococci) has been reported by Fleisher *et al.* (1996). AFRI is a more severe health outcome than self-limiting gastro-intestinal symptoms, but probabilities of contracting AFRI are generally lower and the threshold at which the illness is observed is higher (WHO 2003a).

Despite the acknowledged constraints of current bathing water quality monitoring practices, considerable information has become available to recreational water users in recent years concerning the microbial quality of the water they are using for recreation. The relatively minor illnesses associated with poor microbial quality of water and non-microbial hazards have been identified in the WHO *Guidelines for Safe Recreational Water Environments* (WHO 2003a; WHO 2005). Less information is available on the more severe potential health outcomes encountered by recreational water users resulting in symptoms which are not self-limiting and require medical attention. Waterborne microbial pathogens are capable of causing illness depending on the dose and the physical condition of the individuals exposed. It should be stressed that exposure to waterborne pathogens does not always result in infection, nor does infection always lead to clinical illness.

The total global health impact of human infectious diseases associated with pathogenic microorganisms from land-based wastewater pollution of coastal areas has been estimated at about three million disability-adjusted life years (DALYs) per year, with an estimated economic loss of around 12 billion dollars per year. Researchers in the United States have estimated that the health burden of swimming-related illnesses at two popular beaches in California, USA exceeds US $3.3 million per year. The annual costs for each type of swimming-related illness at the two beaches were estimated to be: gastro-intestinal illnesses, US $1,345,339; acute respiratory disease, US $951,378; ear complaints, US $767,221; eye complaints, US $304,335.

Although most illnesses contracted through recreational water contact are mild (e.g., self-limiting diarrhoea) diseases with a range of severities may also occur. A number of viruses, bacteria and protozoa associated with more severe health outcomes may plausibly be transmitted through use of contaminated recreational water. Bacteria and protozoa may induce illnesses with a wide range of severity. Bacteria may cause life-threatening diseases such as typhoid, cholera and leptospirosis. Viruses can cause serious diseases such as aseptic meningitis, encephalitis, poliomyelitis, hepatitis, myocarditis and diabetes. Protozoa may cause primary amoebic meningo-encephalitis (PAM) and schistosomiasis is caused by a flatworm (trematode). In addition, gastro-intestinal disorders are amongst a number of illnesses that may be attributed to unidentified or unspecified microorganisms.

These hazards to human health should be weighed against the benefits of using water as a medium for relaxation and aerobic, non-weight bearing exercise. Physical exercise has been shown to positively affect certain cardiovascular risk factors such as insulin resistance, glucose metabolism, blood pressure and body fat composition, which are closely associated with diabetes and heart disease. With increasingly sedentary life styles in many societies, routine daily exercise of moderate intensity is highly recommended to reduce cardiovascular risk. Swimming is often recommended by the medical profession because of its potentially beneficial effect on the joints and indeed on people's general sense of wellbeing. For example, non-swimming dynamic exercises in heated water have been shown to have a positive impact on individuals with late effects of polio, with a decreased heart rate at exercise, less pain, and a subjective positive experience. Although it is difficult to quantify the psychological benefits of exercise, Van de Vliet *et al.* (2004) have shown that fitness training embedded in a cognitive-behavioural treatment programme is associated with positive changes in clinically depressed patients. This includes enhanced coping strategies, sustained efforts to continue activities, and improved awareness of physical wellbeing.

Evidence for Adverse Health Outcomes Associated with Recreational Water Use

The first reviews of the incidence of disease associated with the use of recreational waters were undertaken by the American Public Health Association in the early 1920s. Simons *et al.* (1922) attempted to determine the prevalence of infectious diseases which may be transmitted by recreational water contact. Major epidemiological studies were conducted between 1948 and 1950 by the United States Public Health Service to investigate the link between bathing and illness. The findings concluded that there was an appreciably higher overall illness incidence rate in people who swam in Lake Michigan, Chicago, the United States, in 1948 and on the Ohio River at Dayton, Kentucky, the United States, in 1949 compared with nonswimmers, regardless of the levels of coliform bacteria found in the water quality tests. It was concluded by Stevenson (1953) that, based upon the results of this study, the stricter bacterial quality requirements could be relaxed without a detrimental effect on the health of bathers.

Moore (1959) undertook a similar study in the United Kingdom. His study was based on five years of investigation of 43 beaches in the United Kingdom and concluded that there was only a 'negligible risk to health' of bathing in sewage polluted sea water even when beaches were 'aesthetically very unsatisfactory' and that a serious risk would only exist if the water was so fouled as to be revolting to the senses. Moore insisted that pathogenic bacteria which were isolated from sewage contaminated sea water were more important as indicators of the disease in the population than as evidence of a health risk in the waters.

The subject became one of controversy for many years. It was acknowledged in 1972 by the United States Environmental Protection Agency (US EPA) that there was a lack of valid epidemiological data with which to set guideline standards for recreational waters. There followed a number of epidemiological studies throughout the world. In many of the studies identified, the occurrence of certain symptoms or symptom groups was found to be significantly related to the count of faecal indicator bacteria or bacterial pathogens. Credible associations were found between gastro-intestinal symptoms (including 'highly credible' or 'objective' symptoms) and indicators such as enterococci, faecal streptococci, thermotolerant coliforms and *E. coli*.

The WHO *Guidelines for Safe Recreational Water Environments* reviewed the scientific evidence concerning the health issues associated with using waters for recreational purposes and concluded that enteric illness, such as self-limiting gastroenteritis, and AFRI are the most frequently investigated and reported adverse health outcomes in the published literature. The *Guidelines* also concluded that there is an association between gastro-intestinal symptoms, AFRI and indicator-bacteria concentrations in recreational waters (WHO 2003a; WHO 2005). The *Guidelines* represent a consensus view and assessment among experts of the health hazards encountered during recreational water use. It includes the derivation of guideline values and explains the basis for the decision to derive or not to derive them.

There are relatively few studies which report associations between indicators and other symptoms although there is limited evidence of an association between ear, eye and skin ailments with swimming. Evidence suggests that bathing, regardless of water quality, compromises the eye's immune defences leading to increased reporting of symptoms after bathing in marine waters. Infection could also be due to person to-person transmission. In addition, the statistical probability of contracting an ear infection has been found to be generally lower than for gastro-intestinal illnesses which are associated with higher thermotolerant coliform concentrations (WHO 2003a). Several studies have found that symptom rates were more frequent in lower age groups.

The main focus of effort concerning the health implications of the recreational use of water focuses on the effects of faecal contamination of bathing waters and the incidence of gastro-intestinal diseases and other transmissible diseases to participants in water recreation. The data concerning some of the other hazards is weaker. There are very few epidemiological studies which have considered special interest activities. Evans *et al.* (1983) found no evidence of any particular health risk from short-term immersion in Bristol City Docks, UK. However, Philipp *et al.* (1985) studied the health of snorkel swimmers in the same body of water who were immersed for 40 minutes and revealed that statistically significantly more swimmers reported gastro-intestinal symptoms compared with the control group, even though the water complied with the European Union (EU) bathing water standards.

Medema *et al.* (1995) investigating the risk of gastroenteritis in triathlete swimmers estimated that the exposure of triathletes during a competition was between 15 and 40 minutes and exposure was relatively intense; 75% of all triathletes in his study were comapred with biathletes and it was reported that although the health risks for triathletes were not significantly higher than for run-bike-runners (biathletes) symptoms were higher in the week after the event in those athletes that had been exposed to water. (6.8%) than those that did not (3.8%). The percentage of triathletes swallowing water was 72%.

Dwight *et al.* (2004) compared rates of reported health symptoms among surfers during two winters. Their findings showed that for every 2.5 hours of weekly water exposure, surfers experienced a 10% increase in probability of illness (a variety of different symptoms were tracked including highly credible gastro-intestinal illness, stomach pain, vomiting, diarrhoea, and others). These activities are important to consider since the difference in risk between the various uses of recreational waters lies primarily with the duration of exposure and the quantity of water ingested.

Different behaviours of different populations of swimmers are an important risk factor for infection. For example, swimming in unchlorinated open waters is much more common in warmer climates and this may increase the risk of illnessto swimmers. For several reasons, children are at particular risk of contracting recreational waterborne illness. Children have greater opportunities for exposure; they tend to be more frequent users of recreational waters for longer periods of time compared to older age groups, and their activities, which may involve play, often increase exposure to contaminated water through accidental ingestion. The documented health risks posed by poor quality bathing waters usually relate to acute infections acquired whilst bathing. Most of the epidemiological studies conducted to establish a link between bathing and illness do not address the more severe health outcomes or possible sequelae. This is probably due to the low occurrence of severe health outcomes in recent decades in the temperate regions where the majority of studies have been conducted, and because investigations of rarer outcomes usually require larger study groups.

Severe Outcomes

For the purposes of this review, consideration of whether an illness is severe or not is based on three factors:

- acute symptoms of the disease which are debilitating;

- the ability and probability that the illness will lead to sequelae; and
- the effect of the disease on certain susceptible subpopulations.

Each factor can be considered in its own right or in combination with one or both of the other factors. WHO microbial guideline values for safe recreational water environments are in fact based on evidence of the transmission of relatively mild gastro-intestinal illness and AFRI. However, the guidelines make provision for adjustment where there is more severe disease plausibly associated with recreational water use circulating in the population. The use of DALYs is suggested as a useful approach to do this. Management approaches developed in the WHO *Guidelines* when implemented as suggested will help to mitigate both mild and severe infectious illnesses transmitted through recreational water.

Infections with Potentially Severe Acute Symptoms

Although the majority of illnesses transmitted through recreational water use arerelatively mild and often self-limiting, there are a number of waterborne pathogens that can cause illnesses with severe outcomes even in average populations.

These include: *Campylobacter* spp., *E. coli* O157, *Salmonella typhi*, *Shigella* spp., *Leptospira icterohaemorrhagiae*, HAV, *Cryptosporidium parvum* and a number of others described throughout this review. Some of these have been known for many years; others, such as *Helicobacter pylori*, are emerging as new pathogens or re-emerging after many years (WHO 2003b). Although not always severe, infection by these pathogens can result in hospitalisation, surgery and death. For example, leptospirosis has been found to have a case-fatality rate as high as 22% if left untreated and a hospitalisation rate of 30–50%. The primary disease symptoms caused by infections with these pathogens.

Evidence for Sequelae of Waterborne Diseases

Sequelae are increasingly important to food and drinking-water risk assessment. It has been estimated that around 5% of waterborne diseases result in sequelae. There has been little agreement over a scientific definition for sequelae. The Oxford English Dictionary defines a sequela as 'a morbid affection occurring as a result of previous disease'. Parkin *et al.* (2000) reviewed scientific publications for definitions of chronic sequelae and developed a definition as follows: 'the secondary health outcome that (1) occurs as a result of a previous infection by a microbial pathogen; (2) is clearly distinguishable from the health events that initially result from the causative infection and (3) lasts three months or more after recognition'. The sequelae symptoms may be completely different from the symptoms of the acute illness and may occur even if the immune system successfully manages to eliminate the primary infection. The action of the immune system may initiate the condition as a result of an auto-immune response. However, it is also possible that the initial infection may not have passed when the secondary symptoms appear. For the purposes of this review, sequelae which may last less than three months are also included and, therefore, according to Parkin's definition are not chronic.

The evidence that microorganisms or their products are directly or indirectly associated with sequelae ranges from convincing to circumstantial, due to the fact that it is unlikely that such complications are identified or epidemiologically linked to the initial illness because the data are not systematically collected. In addition, host symptoms caused by a specific pathogen or product of a pathogen are often wide-ranging and difficult to link with a specific incident, particularly as the time of onset of sequelae may vary.

Typically, for example, if symptoms of Reiter's syndrome (reactive arthritis) appear then it will be one to three weeks after initial infection with *Salmonella* spp. Symptoms of haemolytic uraemic syndrome (HUS), if they are to appear, are usually seen within 15 days of infection with *E. coli* O157:H7. However, sequelae such as hypertension and renal failure may not manifest themselves until 15 years later. Leptospires, the bacteria causing leptospirosis, may persist in the brain — in one report, 4 out of 11 patients had persistent headaches for between 6 and 34 years post-infection; ophthalmic involvement with blurred vision has been reported to persist for decades following acute infection. Where there is a long time-period between the initial symptoms and the sequelae, it becomes more difficult to prove an association between the initial disease and the delayed sequelae. A summary of sequelae associated with some microorganisms which may be found in recreational waters. These will be discussed in more detail throughout this review. It is stressed that the development of a sequela is incidental to exposure to recreational water, i.e. the sequelae described in this section result from infection with certain pathogens.

Lindsay (1997) raises a further issue which is not widely discussed in the literature: the effect of chronic disease on human personality factors as a result of symptoms such as continual pain from arthritis, irritable bowel or other conditions such as chronic diarrhoea. However, these will not be discussed in this review.

Severe Outcomes in Special Populations

Diseases that are normally mild and self-limiting in the general population can have severe manifestations in susceptible sub-populations with certain attributes. A variety of host factors impact susceptibility to severe disease outcomes. Human immune status can be affected by diseases (HIV, cancer), age, medications taken (e.g., chemotherapy treatment of cancer weakens the immune system), pregnancy, nutritional status, genetics and other factors. Host factors can influence both the severity of the acute symptoms and the propensity to develop sequelae.

The population of immuno compromised individuals is growing. This population is more susceptible to water-borne infections and tend to experience more severe outcomes (e.g., debilitating illness, death) following infection. A number of studies have shown that enteric diseases are the most common and serious problems that affect persons with acquired immunodeficiency syndrome (AIDS). Between 50% and 90% of people with HIV/AIDS suffer from chronic diarrheal illness, and the effects can be fatal. People with reduced immune function due to cancer treatment have been shown to have a case-fatality rate for adenovirus infection of 53%. Likewise, in the 1993 *Cryptosporidium* outbreak in Milwaukee, Wisconsin, USA, 85% of the deaths occurred in people with HIV/AIDS. People with liver diseases are at particularly high risk of fatal septicaemia after ingestion of, or percutaneous exposure to, *Vibrio vulnificus.* The case-fatality observed for enteric pathogens in nursing home patients in the USA who are more susceptible to infection compared with the general population.

Management of Severe Illnesses

The possible adverse health outcomes associated with recreational water result in the need for guidelines that can be converted into locally appropriate standards and associated management of sites to ensure a safe, healthy and aesthetically pleasing environment (WHO 2003a). The management interventions that may be required to ensure a safe recreational water environment are outside the scope of this publication but include compliance and enforcement measures, water quality monitoring, sanitary surveys, animal waste control measures, wastewater treatment, risk communication and information dissemination to increase public awareness. The reader is referred to the WHO *Guidelines for Safe Recreational Water Environments, Volumes 1 and 2* (WHO 2003a; 2005) which illustrates how this can be best achieved through an integrated framework for assessment and management of risk for water-related infectious diseases.

Summary

There are many unanswered questions regarding the severity and frequency of illness associated with recreational water use. The difficulties associated with attributing an infection to recreational water use are numerous and the majority of research in this field has focused on infections associated with the use of recreational waters resulting in minor, self-limiting symptoms. However, it is plausible that more serious illnesses could result from the recreational use of water and this association has not yet been investigated to any great extent. It is also increasingly apparent that a number of microorganisms or their products are directly or indirectly associated with secondary health outcomes or sequelae and a number of these sequelae may result from water-borne infections. The acute diseases attributable to water-borne pathogens and their epidemiology have been well described, but the sequelae that can result from these diseases have not. Assessing potential sequelae of water-borne infections is a critical part of microbial risk assessment and the formulation of public policy.

Tourism-History

Wealthy people have always travelled to distant parts of the world to see great buildings or other works of art; to learn new languages; or to taste new cuisine. As long ago as the time of the Roman Republic places such as Baiae were popular coastal resorts for the rich. The terms *tourist* and *tourism* were first used as official terms in 1937 by the League of Nations. Tourism was defined as people travelling abroad for periods of over 24 hours.

Tourism-Health Tourism & Leisure Travel

It was not until the 19th century that cultural tourism developed into leisure and health tourism. Some English travellers, after visiting the warm lands of the south of Europe, decided to stay there either for the cold season or for the rest of their lives. Others began to visit places with supposedly health-giving mineral waters, in hopes of relieving a whole variety of diseases from gout to liver disorders and bronchitis.

Leisure travel was a British invention due to sociological factors. Britain was the first European country to industrialize, and the industrial society was the first society to offer time for leisure to a growing number of people. Initially, this did not apply to the working masses, but rather to the owners of the machinery of production, the economic oligarchy, the factory owners, and the traders.

These comprised the new middle class. The British origin of this new industry is reflected in many place names. At Nice, one of the first and best-established holiday resorts on the French Riviera, the long esplanade along the seafront is known to this day as the *Promenade des Anglais*; in many other historic resorts in continental Europe, old well-established palace hotels have names like the *Hotel Bristol*, the *Hotel Carlton* or the *Hotel Majestic*-reflecting the dominance of English customers.

Tourism-Winter Tourism

Winter sports were largely invented by the British leisured classes initially at the Swiss village of Zermatt (Valais), and St. Moritz in 1864. The first packaged winter sports holidays (vacations) followed in 1903, to Adelboden, also in Switzerland.

Organized sport was well established in Britain before it reached other countries. The vocabulary of sport bears witness to this: rugby, football, and boxing all originated in Britain, and even Tennis, originally a French sport, was formalized and codified by the British, who hosted the first national championship in the nineteenth century, at Wimbledon. Winter sports were a natural answer for a leisured class looking for amusement during the oldest season.

Tourism-Mass Travel

Mass travel could not really begin to develop until two things occurred:

- improvements in technology allowed the transport of large numbers of people in a short space of time to places of leisure interest, and
- greater numbers of people began to enjoy the benefits of leisure time.

A major development was the invention of the railways, which brought many of Britain's seaside towns within easy distance of Britain's urban centres. The father of modern mass tourism was Thomas Cook who, on 5 July 1841, organized the first package tour in history, by chartering a train to take a group of temperance campaigners from Leicester to a rally in Loughborough, some twenty miles away. Cook immediately saw the potential for business development in the sector, and became the world's first tour operator.

He was soon followed by others, with the result that the tourist industry developed rapidly in early Victorian Britain. Initially it was supported by the growing middle classes, who had time off from their work, and who could afford the luxury of travel and possibly even staying for periods of time in boarding houses. However, the Bank Holiday Act 1871 introduced a statutory right for workers to take holidays, even if they were not paid at the time.

The combination of short holiday periods, travel facilities and distances meant that the first holiday resorts to develop in Britain were towns on the seaside, situated as close as possible to the growing industrial conurbations.For those in the industrial north, there were Blackpool in Lancashire, and Scarborough in Yorkshire. For those in the Midlands, there were Weston-super-Mare in Somerset and Skegness in Lincolnshire, for those in London there were Southend-on-Sea, Broadstairs, Brighton, Eastbourne and many others.

In travelling to the coast, the population was following in the steps of Royalty. King George III is widely acknowledged as popularising the seaside holiday, due to his regular visits to Weymouth when in poor health. For a century, domestic tourism was the norm, with foreign travel being reserved for the rich or the culturally curious. A minority of resorts, such as Bath, Harrogate and Matlock, emerged inland. After World War II holiday villages such as Butlins and Pontins emerged, but their popularity waned with the rise of package tours and the increasing comforts to which visitors became accustomed at home. Towards the end of the 20th century the market was revived by the upmarket inland resorts of Dutch company Centre Parcs.

Other phenomena that helped develop the travel industry were paid holidays:

- 1.5 million manual workers in Britain had paid holidays by 1925,

- 11 million by 1939 (30% of the population in families with paid holidays),

Similar processes occurred in other countries, though at a slower rate, given that nineteenth century Britain was far ahead of any other nation in the world in the process of industrialisation. In the USA, the first great seaside resort, in the European style, was Atlantic City, New Jersey. In Continental Europe, early resorts included Ostend (for the people of Brussels), and Boulogne-sur-Mer (Pas-de-Calais) and Deauville (Calvados) (for Parisians).

History of Recreational Tourism

The earliest forms of leisure tourism can be traced as far back as the Babylonian and Egyptian empires. A museum of "historic antiquities" was open to the public in the sixth century BC in Babylon, while the Egyptians held many religious festivals attracting not only the devout, but many who came to see the famous buildings and works of art in the cities. The local towns accommodated tourists by providing services such as: vendors of food and drink, guides, hawkers of souvenirs, touts and prostitutes. From around the same date, Greek tourists travelled to visit the sites of healing gods. Because the independent city-states of ancient Greece had no central authority to order the construction of roads, most of these tourists travelled by water, hence seaports prospered. The lands of the Mediterranean Sea produced a remarkable evolution in travel. People travel for trade, commerce, religious purposes, festivals, medical treatment, or education developed at an early date.

Guidebooks became available as early as the fourth century BC, covering a vast area of destinations, i.e. Athens, Sparta and Troy. Pausanias, a Greek travel writer, produced a noted "description of Greece" between AD 160 and 180, which, in its critical evaluation of facilities and destinations, acted as a model for later writers. Advertisements, in the form of signs directing visitors to wayside inns, are also known from this period. However, under Romans rule is where international travel became first important. With no foreign borders between England and Syria, and with the seas safe from piracy due to the Roman patrols, conditions favouring travel had arrived. Roman coinage was acceptable everywhere, and Latin was the common language. Romans travelled to Sicily, Greece, Rhodes, and Troy, Egypt and from the third century AD, to the Holy Land.

Domestic tourism also flourished within the Roman Empire. Second homes were built by the wealthy within easy travelling distance of Rome, occupied particularly during the springtime social season. Naples attracted the retired and the intellectuals. Before the sixteenth century, those who sought to travel had three modes in which to do so. They could walk, ride a horse or they could be carried, either on a little or on a carrier's wagon. The development of the sprung coach was a huge advance for those who regularly travelled, and by the mid 1600's, coaches were operating regularly in Britain. In the eighteenth century the introduction of turnpike roads, which provided improved surfaces for which tolls would be charged. The later introduction of the metal, leaf spring suspension also added to comfort.

Travel also requires accommodation, and at that time, it was basic. To accommodate the new demand for travel inns was provided. They provided fresh horses, and lodgings were available for rent to visitors when they arrived at their destination. From the early seventeenth century, a new form of tourism developed as a direct outcome of the freedom and quest for learning heralded by the Renaissance. Young men who wanted positions at court were encouraged to travel to the Continent to finish their education. Others soon adopted this practice in the upper echelons of society, and it soon became customary for the education of a gentleman to be completed by a "Grand tour" of major cultural centres of Europe, accompanied by a tutor and often-lasting three years or more. The appeal soon became social, and leisure seeking young men travelled, predominantly to France and Italy, to enjoy the rival cultures and social life of cities such as Paris, Venice, or Florence. By the end of the eighteenth century, the custom had become institutionalised for the gentry.

Passports have their origins in the medieval testimonial. A letter from an ecclesiastical superior given to a pilgrim to avoid the latter's possible arrest on charges of vagrancy. Later, papers of authority to travel were more widely issued by the state, particularly during periods of warfare with neighbouring European countries. Spas were already well established during the time of the Roman Empire, but their popularity, based on the supposed medical benefits of the waters, lapsed in the subsequent centuries. Renewed interest in the therapeutic qualities of mineral waters has been ascribed to the influence of the Renaissance in Britain, and elsewhere in Europe.

4

Economic Determinants of Demand: Introduction and Definitions

Introduction

While the economies of many rural areas in the United States have been sluggish in recent years, rural communities that have stressed recreation and tourism have experienced significant growth. This has not gone unnoticed by local officials and development organizations, which have increasingly turned to recreation and tourism as a vehicle for development.

However, not all observers are convinced that the benefits of this approach are worth the costs. There are concerns about the quality of the jobs created, rising housing costs, and potential adverse impacts on poverty, crime, and other social conditions. This report assesses the validity of these concerns by analyzing recent data on a wide range of socioeconomic conditions and trends in U.S. rural recreation areas. The purpose is to gain a better understanding of how recreation and tourism development affects rural wellbeing.

Recreation and tourism development has potential advantages and disadvantages for rural communities. Among the advantages, recreation and tourism can add to business growth and profitability. Landowners can benefit from rising land values. Growth can create jobs for those who are unemployed or underemployed, and this can help raise some of them out of poverty. Recreation and tourism can help diversify an economy, making the economy less cyclical and less dependent on the ups and downs of one or two industries.

It also gives underemployed manufacturing workers and farmers a way to supplement their incomes and remain in the community. Benefiting from growing tax revenues and growth-induced economies of scale, local governments may be able to improve public services. In addition, local residents may gain access to a broader array of private sector goods and services, such as medical care, shopping, and entertainment. While other types of growth can have similar benefits, rural recreation and tourism development may provide greater diversification, and, for many places, it may be easier to achieve than other kinds of development—such as high-tech development—because it does not require a highly educated work force.

Many of the potential disadvantages of recreation-related development are associated with the rapid growth that these counties often experience; on average, "recreation counties" grew by 20 percent during the 1990s, nearly three times as fast as other rural counties. Rapid growth from any cause can erode local natural amenities, for example, by despoiling scenic views.

Cultural amenities, such as historic sites, can also be threatened. Growth can lead to pollution and related health problems, higher housing costs, road congestion, and more crowded schools, and it may strain the capacity of public services. Small businesses can be threatened by growth-induced "big-box" commercial development, and farms can be burdened by increased property taxes. In addition, newcomers might have different values than existing residents, leading to conflicts over land use and public policies.

Growth can also erode residents' sense of place, which might reduce support for local institutions, schools, and public services. Aside from these general growth-related issues, some specific problems have been linked to tourism and recreation industries. These include the potential for higher poverty rates associated with low-wage, unskilled workers who are attracted to the area to work in hotels, restaurants, and In this report, "tourism" and recreation sites. Higher poverty rates could lead to various other social problems, including higher crime rates, lower levels of education, more health problems, and higher costs of providing public services.

With this mix of positive and negative impacts, it is understandable why experts on development policy may be uncertain about the value of rural tourism and recreation development strategies. Hence, it is important that policy makers have access to information about the nature and extent of the socioeconomic impacts of this type of development. Past research has examined some of the impacts. Much of that research, however, is in the form of case studies, with only a few empirical studies examining nationwide rural impacts, such as the articles by English et al. (2000) and Deller et al. (2001). English et al. examined the impact of tourism on a variety of measures of local socioeconomic conditions (local income, employment, housing, economic structure, and demographic characteristics). Deller and his colleagues examined recreational amenities (including recreational infrastructure), local government finances, labour supply characteristics, and demographic demand characteristics, estimating their effects upon the growth of local population, employment, and income.

Our research used an approach similar to that of English and his colleagues, which identified a group of tourism-dependent counties and then used regression analysis to estimate the effect of tourism on various indicators of local rural conditions. Using the new ERS typology of rural recreation counties developed by Kenneth Johnson and Calvin Beale (2002), we identified differences between rural recreation counties and other nonmetro counties for various indicators of economic and social wellbeing. We also examined socioeconomic variations by type of recreation county. We then used regression analysis to test statistically for the effect that dependence on recreation (including tourism and seasonal resident recreation) has on local socioeconomic conditions. Details about the regression analysis are provided in the appendix.

* We hoped to shed light on several important questions about this development strategy. Among these are:
* How does rural recreation development affect residents' ability to find jobs?
* How are local wages and incomes affected?
* How does recreation development affect housing costs and local cost of living?
* What effect does recreation development have on local social problems such as crime, congestion, and poverty?
* How are education and health affected?

* How do various types of recreation areas differ in socioeconomic characteristics?

What Is a Recreation County?

In 1998, Beale and Johnson identified 285 nonmetropolitan recreation counties based on empirical measures of recreation activity, including levels of employment and income in tourism-related industries and the presence of seasonal housing. They modified and expanded their typology a few years later. Their 2002 typology identified 329 recreation counties that fell into 11 categories, varying by geographic location, natural amenities, and form of recreation. It is this typology that ERS has adopted as its recreation county typology. We used the 2002 typology, which covered only nonmetropolitan counties. To simplify our analysis, we excluded Alaska and Hawaii. This reduced the number of recreation counties in our study to 311.

One of the advantages of this typology is that it includes not only places with significant tourism-related activity but also those with a significant number of seasonal residents. Like tourists, most seasonal residents are attracted by opportunities for recreation, including some who come simply to relax in a scenic rural setting. In theory, seasonal residents should have a bigger economic impact on the local community than tourists because they stimulate the housing industry and their season-long presence significantly increases the demand for a wide range of local goods and services.

In addition, seasonal residents often later become permanent residents. Because many seasonal residents first came to the area as tourists, it is difficult, if not impossible, to separate the long-term impact of tourists from seasonal residents. Our use of the ERS typology, which covers both tourism and seasonal recreational/residential development, thus seems ideal for estimating the long-term, overall impacts of tourism and recreation combined.

Another advantage of this typology is that it is derived from a continuous variable—a weighted average of tourism and seasonal housing dependence. In theory, this continuous variable may be used more effectively to estimate impacts than a simple recreation/other nonmetro dichotomous variable because it allows us to examine variations in the extent of recreation. Similarly, the different types of recreation counties in the Johnson/Beale typology can be used to further elucidate and estimate the impacts of recreational activity on local socioeconomic conditions.

General Characteristics of Recreation Counties

The 311 recreation counties in our study are located in 43 States, but tend to be concentrated in the West, the Upper Great Lakes, and the Northeast. In the West, this reflects the ample opportunities for hiking, mountain climbing, fishing, and wintertime sports found in the many national parks and ski resorts there. By contrast, the high concentration of recreation counties in the Upper Great Lakes and Northeast—especially in New England and Upstate New York—is largely due to the popularity of long-established second homes in areas with lakes. Many of these areas also have significant wintertime recreation activities, including snowmobiling and skiing. Not surprisingly, recreation counties score higher (4.25) on ERS' natural amenities index than other nonmetro counties. The ERS natural amenities index ranges from 1 to 7, encompassing six measures of natural amenities, covering climate (temperature and humidity), topographic variation. Data from the 2000 Census reveal that recreation and other nonmetro counties average similar population sizes. However, during the last decade, the population of recreation counties has grown almost three times as fast. Recreation counties also have relatively low population densities, and more of their residents tend to live in rural parts of the county (those with less than 2,500 population).

Using the ERS 1993 county economic and policy typologies, we found that the economies in recreational counties were generally more diverse than in other nonmetro counties. For example, only 30 percent of recreation counties were highly dependent on a single major industry (agriculture, mining, or manufacturing), while 58 percent of other nonmetro counties were highly dependent on just one of these industries. Recreation counties also were slightly less dependent on neighbouring counties for employment; only 13 percent of recreation counties were identified as commuting counties (with a high percentage of their resident work force commuting outside the county for employment), compared with 17 percent of other nonmetro counties.

We also found that about a third (32 percent) of recreation counties were retirement-destination places vs. only 4 percent of other nonmetro counties.

How Were Recreation Counties Identified?

The 2002 Johnson/Beale typology covered only nonmetropolitan counties, using the 1993 Office of Management and Budget (OMB) definitions of metropolitan areas. Johnson and Beale began by examining a sample of wellknown recreation areas to determine which economic indicators were most appropriate for identifying other such counties. They then computed the percentage share of wage and salary employment from the Census Bureau's 1999 County Business Patterns data and personal income from Bureau of Economic Analysis data as these data apply to recreation-related industries, i.e., entertainment and recreation, accommodations, eating and drinking places, and real estate. They also computed a third measure: the percentage share of housing units of seasonal or occasional use, from 2000 Census data.

They then constructed a weighted average of the standardized Z-scores of these three main indicators (0.3 employment + 0.3 income + 0.4 seasonal homes). Counties scoring greater than 0.67 on this recreation dependency measure were considered recreation counties. Next, they added several large nonmetro counties that did not make the cut but had relatively high hotel and motel receipts from 1997 Census of Business data. Additional counties were accepted if the weighted average of the three combined indicators exceeded the mean and at least 25 percent of the county's housing was seasonal. Then Johnson and Beale deleted 14 counties that lacked any known recreational function but appeared to qualify "either because they were very small in population with inadequate and misleading County Business Patterns coverage or because they reflected high travel activity without recreational purpose, i.e., overnight motel and eating place clusters on major highways." These calculations produced their final set of 329 recreation counties. In 2004, ERS established these recreation counties as one of its county typologies. By 2004, some of these counties had changed their metropolitan status based on the new 2003 OMB definitions of metropolitan areas.

The averages shown in this report are "unweighted" averages (simple means). In most cases, these averages appear to represent fairly the typical county in the group being reported. In some cases, however, the average (mean) may be unrepresentative in that it differs significantly from the median. We will point out such instances in the text or in a footnote. Many recreation counties (38 percent) were Federal land counties, meaning that at least 30 percent of the county's land was federally owned; only 7 percent of other nonmetro counties had that much Federal land. In addition, relatively few recreation counties (10 percent) had experienced persistently high levels of poverty (from 1950 to 1990), whereas about a fourth (26 percent) of other nonmetro counties fell into this category. Because recreation counties are not homogeneous with respect to these and other characteristics, the averages we present for all recreation counties mask considerable variation.

Economic Impacts

The conventional wisdom among researchers in recent years has been that recreation and tourism have both positive and negative economic impacts for recreation areas. On the positive side, recreation development helps to diversify the local economy, and it generates economic growth. It achieves this partly by acting as a kind of export industry, attracting money from the outside to spend on goods and services produced locally. It also stimulates the local economy through other means. Infrastructure, such as airports and highways and water systems, often must be upgraded to meet the needs of tourists, and such improvements can help foster the growth of nonrecreation industries in the area by attracting entrepreneurs and labour and by providing direct inputs to these industries. Recreation development can involve significant economic leakages, however, in that many of the goods and services it requires come from outside the community—for example, temporary foreign workers often are drawn to the area to fill jobs in hotels, ski resorts, etc.—and many of the recreation-related establishments (restaurants, hotels, tour and travel companies) are owned by national or regional companies that export the profits.

Thus, part of the money from tourists and seasonal residents ends up leaving the locality. Another economic drawback involves the seasonality of recreation activities, which can create problems for workers and businesses during off-seasons, though this may actually be a plus for places where seasonal recreation jobs are timely, coming when farmers and other workers normally have an off-season.

The greatest economic concern is that recreation development may be less desirable than traditional forms of rural development because it increases the incidence of service employment with relatively low wages. According to Deller et al. (2001), "There is a perception that substituting traditional jobs in resource-extractive industries and manufacturing with more service oriented jobs yields inferior earning power, benefits, and advancement potential" and that this may lead to "higher levels of local underemployment, lower income levels, and generally lower overall economic wellbeing." In addition, many researchers are concerned that recreation may result in a less equitable distribution of income. These problems may be compounded by the higher housing costs in some recreation areas.

These concerns reflect findings from individual case studies. Only a few studies have attempted to estimate how rural recreation areas nationwide differ on economic measures. Deller et al. (2001) found that rural tourism and amenity-based development contributed to growth in per capita income and employment, and concluded that as a result of the positive impact on income "the concern expressed about the quality of jobs created ... appears to be misplaced."

English et al. (2000) also found that rural tourism was associated with higher per capita incomes, and with a higher percent increase in per capita income, although they found no significant relationship for household income. English and his colleagues also found housing costs and the change in housing costs over time to be significantly related to rural tourism. On the other hand, they found no evidence that the distribution of income was less equal due to rural tourism. To address these economic issues, we examined a variety of indicators reflecting employment, earnings, income, and housing costs.

Employment

Two employment measures, the local employment growth rate (percent increase during the 1990s) and the local employment-population ratio (percentage of working-age resident population employed in 2000) are particularly illuminating.

Recreation counties, on average, had more than double the rate of employment growth of other rural areas during the 1990s: 24 percent vs. 10 percent. The regression analysis, moreover, indicated that the extent to which a recreation county was dependent on recreation was positively and significantly related to the rate of local employment growth. Employment growth generally offers residents more job opportunities, enabling some unemployed residents to find jobs and employed residents to find better jobs. However, job growth does not necessarily improve job conditions for current residents. If too many people come into the area seeking employment, and if those newcomers aggressively compete with locally unemployed (or underemployed) residents, the resident job seekers may end up having greater difficulty gaining employment. Thus, we need to look closely at employment data to determine how recreation affects the local ability to find jobs.

To measure the ability of residents to find jobs, we examined the percentage of the working-age population that was employed. For our study, we broke this into three separate rates covering three groups of the working-age population: ages 18-24, 25-64, and 65 and over. We hypothesized that recreation counties might be particularly advantageous for younger and older populations that may have a harder time competing in places with less job growth.

In addition, younger and older groups may find it more convenient to work in recreation counties, which are thought to provide more part-time and seasonal jobs than most other places. As expected, we found higher employment-population rates in recreation counties for both the younger and older age groups. However, the difference was less than 1 percentage point.

The main working-age employment rate (ages 25-64) was roughly the same for both recreation and other nonmetro counties in 2000.[9] However, for each of these age groups, the upward trend in the employment-population rate during the 1990s favoured recreation counties. Our regression analysis indicates that recreation had a positive and statistically significant impact on the employment rates for all three age categories in 2000. Recreation also had a positive and statistically significant impact on the increase in the employment rate during the 1990s, except for the older age group.

Earnings

Conventional wisdom suggests that a main drawback of tourism is that many of the jobs it creates are in restaurants, motels, and other businesses that tend to offer relatively low wages and few fringe benefits. But does this mean that rural recreation development generally leads to low-paying jobs? To address this question, we examined average annual earnings per job (which include wages and salaries and other labour and proprietor income, but exclude unearned income and fringe benefits). We found that average earnings per job were $22,334 in 2000 for recreation counties—about $450 less than in other rural counties. The difference, though only about 2 percent, is consistent with the low-wage hypothesis. On the other hand, our finding that earnings per job increased faster in recreation counties than in other rural counties in the 1990s was not consistent with the conventional wisdom, but again, the difference was relatively small ($200). Our regression analysis, however, found no statistically significant relationship between earnings per job and recreation dependency, at least no simple linear relationship. With regard to change in earnings per job during the 1990s, the regression analysis found that recreation had a positive and statistically significant impact on earnings per job. So these findings do not support the conventional wisdom that recreation results in generally lowpaying jobs.

The data on earnings per job covered all jobs in the county, including those filled by nonresidents. A different picture emerges when we look only at earnings per resident worker. Aside from excluding nonresidents employed in the county (who, in theory, might be lowering the average earnings per job in recreation counties), this measure totals the income workers receive from all the jobs they have. This is important because recreation counties often provide numerous part-time and seasonal jobs, potentially allowing more of their residents to have multiple jobs than the residents of other counties. The average worker's earnings from multiple jobs exceeded the average earnings per job. In recreation counties, earnings amounted to $29,593 per resident worker (16 years or older) in 1999—about $2,000 more than in other rural counties—an 8-percent difference. Our regression analysis found recreation had a positive and statistically significant effect on earnings per resident worker. Thus, some residents may work more hours in recreation counties, but on average they end up earning more than residents of other nonmetro counties.

Income

Earnings are only one source of income. Other sources include interest receipts, capital gains, and retirement benefits like social security. Because many recreation areas have attracted wealthy individuals—including retirees, whose earnings are only a small part of their incomes—we expected recreation county income levels to be higher than in other rural areas. Consistent with this expectation, we found average per capita income was 10 percent higher in recreation counties than in other nonmetro counties. Moreover, per capita income levels were growing more rapidly during the 1990s in recreation counties than in other nonmetro counties. These findings were reflected in our regression analysis, which found recreation had a positive and statistically significant effect on both the level of per capita income and the change in per capita income over time. This should also benefit the community as a whole, because higher incomes mean an increase in demand for local goods and services, as well as increased local government tax collections and contributions to local charities and other social organizations. One problem in interpreting per capita incomes is that they average together the incomes of the wealthiest and the poorest individuals. Thus, a small number of extremely wealthy people could make the community seem much better off than with other measures, for instance, the income of the typical (or median) person in the county. If recreation counties had more wealthy individuals than other rural counties, the per capita measure might be a misleading indicator of how the average family or household in each of these counties differed in income. For this reason, we include a second income measure: median household income in the county in 1999. Using this measure, we found that median household income was 10 percent higher in recreation counties than in other rural counties. The recreation county advantage amounted to $3,185 per year for the median house-hold. The regression analysis reflected this finding, showing a positive and statistically significant relationship between recreation and both the level and change in median family income.

Housing Costs

One of the main complaints about recreation areas is that the cost of living in them is often higher, offsetting much of the advantage that residents might obtain from their higher incomes. Of particular concern is that high living costs could become a significant hardship for people struggling to raise families on minimum-wage jobs. A high cost of living could force some lower paid workers (including some long-time residents) to look for housing outside the area.

The cost of housing is one of the most important contributors to the cost of living. According to Census data in 2000, median monthly rents for housing averaged $474 in recreation counties, 23 percent higher than the $384 median rent in other nonmetro counties. Our regression analysis also found a positive and statistically significant effect of recreation on median rent. Rents also increased faster during the 1990s in recreation counties, with the extent of recreation positively and significantly related to the extent of rent increase.

Though recreation counties had higher rents than other nonmetro counties, over the course of a year this amounted to a difference of only $1,080 per household—about a third of the $3,185 advantage we found in median household income in recreation counties. So after deducting for their higher rents, we found that households in recreation counties still had a significant income advantage over those in other rural counties.

It is difficult to draw conclusions from this kind of information, for several reasons. First, rents show only part of the housing cost picture. Most housing units in the nonmetro counties we studied (in both recreation and other nonmetro counties) are owner-occupied rather than rented. Assuming that higher rents reflect higher home prices and greater equity in homes, higher home prices should increase the wealth of homeowners in recreation counties. In addition, higher rents and home prices may reflect better housing quality in recreation counties, rather than simply higher costs. This might be expected because more of the housing in these rapidly growing places is likely to be relatively new (and hence more valuable), and recreation county residents, having generally higher incomes, may demand better housing than residents of other nonmetro counties. Higher home values also increase the local tax base, which may lead to higher tax collections, enabling local governments to increase public services. Thus, on balance, it is unclear whether these higher housing costs are a plus or minus for the community.

Social Impacts

Various researchers have examined the relationship between nonmetro recreation and social conditions in a community. Page et al. (2001) note that rapid population growth in nonmetro recreation counties has resulted in overcrowded conditions and traffic congestion. Recreation may also affect local poverty rates. Some authors have argued that recreation activity creates new sources of employment, helping to raise the poor from poverty (Gibson, 1993; Patton, 1985). Others have pointed to the low-wage, seasonal, and part-time nature of many tourism jobs, arguing that tourism may actually add to the number of poor in the community (Galston and Baehler, 1995; Smith, 1989). Recreation affects social conditions in other ways. For example, Page et al. argue that tourism and recreation activity may help to maintain or improve local services, such as health facilities, entertainment, banking, and public transportation, because of the increased demand that tourists generate for these activities. The relationship between recreation and crime has also been explored by a number of researchers, with a popular question being whether casinos increase criminal activity.

To address social impact concerns, we identified eight social indicators. Two involve conditions associated with rapid population growth; one identifies a population subgroup (persons in poverty) that may present special challenges; two relate to education; two deal with health-related concerns; and one measures crime.

Population Growth

The first social variable we examined was the county population growth rate during the 1990s. Population growth can be beneficial for stagnant or declining rural areas looking for new sources of employment and income, but in some places it can bring problems. This is particularly true if growth occurs rapidly and haphazardly, contributing to sprawl, traffic congestion, environmental degradation, increased housing costs, school overcrowding, a decrease in open land, and loss of a "sense of place" for local residents. Perhaps because of their natural amenities and tourist attractions, recreation counties experienced a 20.2-percent rate of population growth between 1990-2000, nearly triple the 6.9-percent rate for other nonmetro counties during the same period. These results are consistent with our linear regression analysis, which found a positive and statistically significant relationship between recreation and the county population growth rate. Further analysis revealed an apparent curvilinear relationship, in which recreation counties with moderate recreation dependencies experienced higher growth rates than those with smaller and larger recreation dependencies.

Travel Time to Work

This variable was included to test the hypothesis that growth in recreation counties may lead to increasing traffic congestion. We found that mean commute times for recreation and other rural counties were not significantly different in 2000. Moreover, during the 1990s, commute times increased at roughly the same rate (4.4 percent for recreation counties vs. 4.3 percent for other rural counties). The regression analysis, however, revealed a significant negative relationship between recreation dependence and change in travel time to work during the 1990s. One explanation may be that expanded economic opportunities in recreation counties during the 1990s meant that residents had to travel shorter distances for jobs.

Poverty Rate

Poverty poses a problem for communities by increasing the costs of providing public services and contributing to crime rates, health problems, and neighbourhood blight. Previous research has found that an expanding tourist industry is linked with a decreasing rate of poverty. Given that many recreation counties have attracted well-off retirees and that average income levels have risen in recreation counties, the counties might, on average, be expected to have fewer individuals living in poverty than other nonmetro counties. However, as noted earlier, some have argued that tourism, by expanding the number of low-paying, part-time jobs, could increase the number of individuals living in poverty in these counties. We found that the poverty rate was substantially lower in recreation counties than in other rural counties. In 1999, 13.2 percent of all residents in recreation counties were living in poverty, compared with 15.7 percent in other nonmetro counties. Mirroring the national trend of declining poverty rates during the 1990s, the proportion of residents living in poverty during the decade declined (at approximately the same rate) in both recreation and other rural counties. Our regression analysis also found a significantly negative relationship between recreation and the poverty rate. In addition, the regression analysis found a statistically significant negative relationship between recreation and the change in the poverty rate.

Educational Attainment

Previous research has identified the central role that education plays in rural poverty. Education is important, not only because it contributes to the economy, but also because it can affect the quality of life in rural communities and can help raise people out of poverty. Nonmetro areas with lower levels of education tend to be poorer and offer fewer economic opportunities for their residents. Migration (movement to another area) tends to increase with higher levels of education. Hence, recreation counties, which have had many in-migrants in recent years, may be expected to have higher levels of educational attainment than other nonmetro counties. English et al. (2000) found rural tourism to be associated with higher levels of educational attainment. We examined educational attainment at two levels: high school and college.

Our results show that residents in recreation counties have higher levels of education than other nonmetro residents. Recreation counties have both a smaller share of residents 25 years or older without a high school education, and a higher share of those with at least a bachelor's degree, than residents of other nonmetro counties. In 2000, 18.4 percent of residents age 25 or older in recreation counties did not have a high school diploma, compared with 25 percent in other nonmetro counties. For the same year, 19.2 percent of recreation county residents age 25 or older had a 4-year college degree or higher, compared with 13.6 percent in other nonmetro counties.

During the 1990s, educational attainment on both measures improved in recreation as well as other nonmetro counties. These findings are supported by our regression analysis, which found that recreation had a significant negative correlation with the share of residents without a high school diploma and a significant positive correlation with the share of residents with a bachelor's degree or higher. In addition, a statistically significant relationship was found between recreation and an increase in the share of college-educated residents during the 1990s. However, the change in the share of high school graduates during the 1990s, although positive, was not significantly related to recreation.

Health Measures

Health is important for quality of life. In some recreation counties, many individuals moving in are retirees who demand more from health services than younger people; this could result in improved health services in these places.

Many recreation counties are in pristine locations with clean air and water, which might also lead to better overall health. In addition, residents in recreation areas are probably more likely to be involved in outdoor activities than individuals in other nonmetro areas, which may also promote better overall health.

Our indicators of local health conditions—the number of physicians available and the age-adjusted mortality rate—support the view that recreation county residents have better health and health services than other nonmetro residents. In 2003, recreation counties had 123 physicians per 100,000 residents, compared with 83.4 per 100,000 residents in other nonmetro counties. The analysis also shows that the age-adjusted death rate (computed as a 3-year average) was almost 10 percent lower in recreation than in other nonmetro counties.

Our regression results show that recreation had a significantly negative correlation with the age-adjusted death rate. However, the relationship between recreation and the number of physicians, although positive, was statistically insignificant.

Crime Rate

Many researchers have looked at the link between recreation activity and crime. Some types of recreation counties attract criminals who prey on tourists in-season and rob unoccupied houses during the off-season. Also, some low-income residents of these counties may commit crimes of opportunity, taking advantage of the influx of well-off outsiders. Some researchers have argued that crime may be particularly associated with casinos.

The results of our analysis indicate that recreation counties had nearly a 17-percent higher rate of serious crime (murder and non-negligent manslaughter, forcible rape, robbery, and aggravated assault) than other nonmetro counties. In 1999, the overall rate of serious crime in recreation counties was 2.8 incidents per 100 residents, compared with 2.4 incidents per 100 residents in other nonmetro counties, a statistically significant difference. These results are consistent with our regression analysis, which found that a significantly positive relationship exists between recreation and the crime rate.

However, the meaning of this finding is not clear because the crime rate is a biased measure in recreation areas, due to the fact that crimes committed against tourists and seasonal residents are included in the total number of crimes (the numerator of the crime rate), while tourists and seasonal residents are not included in the base number of residents (the denominator of the crime rate). So the crime rate is expected to be higher in recreation areas, even if residents of these areas are not more likely to be crime victims than residents of other rural areas.

Variations by Type of Recreation County

As noted, Johnson and Beale (2002) categorized each recreation county as belonging to 1 of 11 mutually exclusive recreational groupings, a classification that provides greater insight into the recreational component of each county. The single most common category is the Midwest Lake and Second Home, accounting for 70 counties and overwhelmingly concentrated in central and northern Michigan, Minnesota, and Wisconsin. The Northeast Mountain, Lake, and Second Home group, a closely related category, is mainly concentrated in northern New England (Maine, New Hampshire, and Vermont) and in portions of New York and Pennsylvania. Together, these two similar categories account for more than a quarter of all recreation counties. Both categories are relatively prosperous: North-east counties had the highest level of earnings per job among all recreation types, and the Midwest category experienced sharp increases in household income during the 1990s. Both regions had rates of poverty among the lowest of all recreation categories. Although almost every type of recreation county registered at least double-digit population growth during the 1990s (the exception being the Northeast Mountain, Lake, and Second Home), Ski Resort counties grew the fastest (increasing 38 percent), continuing a trend from the 1980s. Other recreation categories in the West (West Mountain and Other Mountain) also experienced rapid population growth. Ski Resort counties stand out in other ways, measuring substantially higher than other recreation counties on a number of economic variables, including ratio of employment to population, earnings per job, earnings per worker, per capita income, and median household income. Ski Resorts also had the lowest poverty rate among all recreation categories, but had substantially higher housing costs—nearly 40 percent higher than the average for other nonmetro counties—which grew rapidly during the 1990s. Ski Resort counties also stand out in terms of social indicators, having the highest levels of educational attainment, the largest number of doctors, the lowest death rates, and the highest rate of crime among all recreation categories.

In contrast, Reservoir Lake counties and South Appalachian Mountain Resort counties are among the most economically challenged recreation county types. Reservoir Lake counties, which are mainly located in the Midwest and Great Plains regions, and South Appalachian

Mountain Resort counties—in the upland areas of Georgia, North Carolina, Virginia, West Virginia, and Maryland—have among the lowest earnings per worker and lowest median household income levels. They also have among the lowest rents. Both of these regions have among the lowest levels of educational attainment. Further, they have higher-than-average age-adjusted death rates, but relatively low crime rates. The South Appalachian Mountain Resort category also has a significantly longer commute than other nonmetro counties, possibly a reflection of its mountainous topography.

Casino counties also have relatively low levels of economic development, with the highest rate of poverty—over 40 percent higher than for all recreation counties—as well as below-average levels of per capita income, median household income, and earnings per worker. Still, during the 1990s, Casino counties, which are mainly located in the Upper Midwest, the Dakotas, the Mississippi Delta region, and Nevada, collectively had sharp employment growth (a third faster than the average for all recreation counties). Casino counties, which benefited from the establishment of gambling on Native American reservations during the 1990s, had a lower level of educational attainment, fewer physicians, a higher-than-average age adjusted death rate, and a significantly higher rate of crime than most other recreation counties.

Conclusions

This study provides quantitative information on how tourism and recreation development affects socioeconomic conditions in rural areas. Specifically, we wanted to address economic issues related to employment, income, earnings, and cost of living, and social issues such as poverty, education, health, and crime. A summary follows of our main findings on the socioeconomic impacts of rural recreation and tourism development.

Employment: Our regression analysis found a positive and statistically significant association between recreation dependency and the percentage of working-age population with jobs. We also found that, with the exception of the older (65 and over) population, recreation dependency positively affected the change in this employment measure during the 1990s.

Earnings: We examined earnings per job and earnings per resident to measure the value of the jobs associated with rural recreation development. We found that the average earnings per job in recreation counties were not significantly different than in other nonmetro counties, and we found no direct (linear) relationship between local dependency on recreation and local earnings per job in our recreation counties.

However: our regression analysis found a positive relationship between recreation and growth in earnings per job during the 1990s. Thus, the trend seems to favour the pay levels for jobs in these recreation counties. These findings concern earnings of all who work in the county, including nonresidents. They report earnings per job, not per worker—an important distinction because workers may have more than one job, and the availability of second jobs (part-time and seasonal) may be greater in recreation counties than elsewhere. When we focused on total job earnings for residents of recreation counties, we found these earnings were significantly higher ($2,000 more per worker) than for residents of other rural counties.

The regression analysis also found a significant positive relationship between recreation and resident-worker earnings. So the earnings picture for recreation counties appears positive for the average resident. Cost of living. Our research suggests recreation development leads to higher living costs, at least with respect to housing. We found that the average rent was 23 percent higher in recreation counties, and it was positively and significantly associated with the degree of recreation dependency in our regression analysis. While this may reduce some of the economic advantages for residents of recreation counties, it does so only partially. Median household incomes, on average, were $3,185 higher in recreation counties than in other rural counties. Annual costs associated with rent were $1,080 higher in recreation counties, offsetting only about a third of the recreation county income advantage.

Growth strains: We found recreation led to significantly higher rates of population growth. In theory, this can aggravate social problems, such as school crowding, housing shortages, pollution, and loss of identification with the community. The one growth-related social problem we addressed was road congestion. Examining the time it takes to commute to work, we found little evidence that congestion was presenting undue problems for residents in recreation counties. Moreover, our regression analysis found that recreation was associated with smaller increases in average commute times in the 1990s than in other rural counties.

Poverty: Another social problem that appeared to be reduced in recreation counties was poverty. Our regression analysis found recreation was associated with lower poverty rates and with larger declines in the poverty rate during the 1990s. Crime. There may be some cause for concern with regard to crime. We found crime rates (for serious crimes) were higher in recreation counties than in other rural counties, and our regression analysis also found a statistically significant positive relationship between crime rates and recreation dependency. However, crime statistics may be biased in recreation areas because crimes against tourists and seasonal residents are counted in the crime rate, while tourists and seasonal residents are not counted as part of the population base upon which the rate is calculated. Thus, even if people in recreation areas do not face a higher chance of becoming victims of crimes, the crime rates of these areas will appear higher than elsewhere. Nonetheless, one may still argue that recreation-related crime adds to the local cost of policing and incarcerating criminals, just as recreation-related traffic—even though it may not create congestion—adds to the cost of maintaining roads.

Education and health: Our analysis found that recreation is associated with a more educated population, particularly with a higher percentage of college-educated people. We also found relatively good health conditions (measured by age-adjusted death rates) in recreation counties.

This might be expected from the higher numbers of physicians per 100,000 residents that we found in recreation counties. However, our regression analysis did not find a statistically significant relationship between recreation dependence and the local supply of physicians. So some other explanation must be posited for the general good health in recreation counties, such as greater opportunities for physical exercise or residents who are more health-conscious.

Variations by county type: Conditions vary significantly by recreation county type. For example, Ski Resort counties have among the wealthiest, best educated, and healthiest populations of all recreation county types. Ski Resort counties also have relatively high rates of crime. In contrast, Reservoir Lake counties and South Appalachian Mountain Resort counties have among the poorest and least educated residents of all recreation county types, along with relatively high age-adjusted death rates, but they have relatively low crime rates. Casino counties—which had among the highest rates of job growth and the largest absolute increases in earnings per job during the 1990s—also had among the highest rates of growth in employment per person for seniors, perhaps reflecting the greater need for jobs among those over age 65 in these relatively high-poverty communities.

Ideas for Future Research

We focused mainly on conditions facing residents of mature rural recreation counties, that is, places that already have a substantial amount of recreation. Additional insights may come from expanding the analysis to include emerging recreation areas and neighbouring places that may be affected by spillover impacts from recreation areas.

Future research might also address issues related to specific population subgroups, such as low-paid workers, who may face more significant problems related to the high cost of housing in recreation areas. The analysis might also be expanded to examine recreation impacts on other aspects of community wellbeing, such as the environment, public services, institutions like churches and charitable foundations, and small business formation and entrepreneurial activity. Our knowledge of rural recreation impacts might also benefit from different formulations of the regression model.

For example, models could be finetuned to focus on individual indicators, or they could be estimated separately for individual regions and types of recreation areas. Feedback effects might be incorporated into the model—for example, recreation can lead to higher housing costs, which in turn can lead to reduced tourism and recreation development. More sophisticated models may be able to separate out these two effects.

The models might also be examined over different time periods to test for cyclical effects and robustness over time. Research might also measure the effects of specific State and local policies, along with other factors thought to affect the level of rural recreation and tourism (such as the availability of natural amenities and proximity and access to nonmetro areas). This might help State and local officials assess their potential for recreation and tourism development and identify strategies to further this development.

Social Determinants of Demand

The tourism demand is characterized by many factors. The great role among them play the macro determinants of demand. There four of them: social factors, technological factors, economic factors and political factors.

The social factors are connected with the growth of the population which affects the increase of travel tendencies. The population every year develops and seeks the new ways of expression. The people try to find the time and the possibility to travel and to visit different countries and in this way they increase the quality of the life.

The social changes after the Second World War also influenced the travel demand. Since the war the population became older because of the death and a slowing of the birth amount.

The older age groups prefer the more calm and quiet rest and have some special requests to the service and accommodation. The important factor of the tourist demand is the technology. For example the development of transport system, entertainment technologies make possible to extend the amount of travellers and lower the costs for the travelling. These factors make the travelling more available.

The next factor is the economy. During the last years the services bring the largest part of national incomes. The tourism services became more qualitative and it attracts more and more consumers. As more countries have very attractive and potentially profitable but yet not very developed resorts, the good way to get more money is to invest costs into foreign economy.

Politics affects travel propensity activity in different ways, such as: the government involvement into the advertising and promoting of the tourist possibilities; the national support of free market and the protecting of the environment, that provide the independence for the foreign visitors.

There are four main policy instruments, which government bodies use to govern and manage the tourist demand: the control, marketing and promotion, information and provision pricing.

Ann Sammers is a member of a support team at Custom Writing Services. Having completed a number of Practice courseworks himself,

Ann uses her knowledge to provide individualized customer support to students, who order Informative essay.

Theory, Concepts and Methods in Tourism Climate Research

Tourism is one of the world's biggest industries. It is also the fastest growing. For many regions tourism is the most important source of income, for others the potential economic returns from tourism development are enormous.

In these places it is generally accepted that climate is an important part of the region's tourism resource base, but the role of climate in determining the suitability of a region for tourism or outdoor recreation is often assumed to be self evident and therefore to require no elaboration.

Relatively little is known, other than in very general terms, about the effects of climate on tourism and outdoor recreation or the role it plays. And even less is known about the economic impact or significance of climate on commercial prospects for tourism.

The whole area involving which criteria, including climate related-criteria, people use to make decisions about tourism and recreation choices is largely unresearched, but highly relevant to a variety of applications.

Thus far, much of the research specifically on climate reported in the journal literature has been superficial, in that relationships between climate and tourism are assumed rather than observed and seldom objectively tested. Moreover, the research is largely devoid of any clearly structured conceptual framework or frameworks that embrace important theory, paradigms, processes and interactions.

These theoretical frameworks are important because they provide a basis for data generation, hypothesis testing and further theory generation. Without this, it is difficult to develop a coherent set of research methods; and perhaps more importantly, develop models that constitute a bridge between the observational and theoretical levels that can assist is building a coherent knowledge base for understanding, explanation and prediction. This paper reviews the work so far on climate and tourism with a view to identifying what concepts and theoretical frameworks may already exist and looks to ways these may be drawn together in future research.

Concepts and Terms

Definitions

The study area labelled *tourism climatology* deals with the concepts of "climate" and "tourism" in the broadest sense. Climate invokes the concept of "weather" in that it is defined as the accumulation of daily and seasonal weather events over a long period of time, where weather is the condition of the atmosphere at any particular time and place. "Tourism" embraces the concept of "recreation" in that it is the practice of travelling for recreation, where recreation is defined as an activity in which individuals voluntarily engage for personal satisfaction or pleasure.

Thus, in broad terms, there are elements of equivalence in the dual terms *weather* and *climate* on the one hand, and *tourism* and *recreation* on the other. They are often used interchangeably in tourism climate research, which may be broadly defined as the study of interrelationships of tourism and recreation with climate and weather.

Weather and Climate as a Natural Resource

Together with geographical location, topography, landscape, flora and fauna, weather and climate constitute the natural resource-base of a place for recreation and tourism. The concept of tourism climate recognises a climatically controlled resource, which along with weather, according to Hibbs (1966), can be viewed as a recreational resource which at various times and locations may be classified along a favourable-to-unfavourable spectrum.

Thus climate is a resource exploited by tourism, and the resource can be measured. In this way climate can be treated as an economic asset for tourism. The asset can be measured and the resource is capable of being assessed. But there are numerous problems.

One major problem is selection of meteorological or climatological criteria. For example, what exactly are the criteria for *ideal*, *suitable*, *acceptable*, or *unacceptable* conditions?

Only after appropriate climatological criteria have been clearly identified can key questions be answered. When is the best time to visit? What clothing equipment is needed? What are the weather hazards or climate extremes likely to be?

Weather and Climate as Limiting Factors in Tourism

The characteristics of weather and climate are not necessarily determinants of tourism but constitute an important factor in both financial terms for tourism operators and the personal experiences of tourists.

Various places in the world have a "tourism potential" and weather and climate set limits. For example, tourism administrators do not promote places with a little potential or appeal, as this would not be profitable.

On the other hand, the tourist who chooses to visit such places would suffer inconvenience (e.g. transport costs) or discomfort (e.g. heat or cold stress). Financial loses can also result from weather variations and changes. Rainy summers or less snowy winters can have significant impacts on tourism.

Climate Data

The type of climatic data and manner it is presented in tourism climate research depends on the purpose of the work. Information can be used by 1) the tourist planner, 2) the tourist operator and 3) the individual tourist.

For example, a ski facility planner needs information on the length of snow season, whereas skier wants seasonal distribution of probabilities that a skiable depth of snow will exist at a particular location and time. A planner for a tropical island resort planner needs to know the length period of acceptable weather for tourists.

Prospective tourists need to know when and where conditions will be optimal, acceptable, tolerable, or unacceptable. Climate data must be presented in a form that relates to the individuals response to weather or climate conditions.

That is *events* rather than *averages*. Average have no physiological or psychological meaning. Data should give an impression of the likelihood of occurrence of the climate/weather conditions (events). Data should reflect the fact that individuals respond to the integrated, combined effects of weather elements (thermal, physical, aesthetic etc.). Equal importance should be given to the nature and form of output data. It should be presented in a form that can be readily interpreted and understood by the user. Often we have to rely on standard meteorological or climate station data, which may not be representative of the recreational area-valleys, peaks, hills, coast, beach etc. Climate station-data are intended to be representative of the bottom of atmospheric column rather than a particular microclimate or location such as beach, park or ski slope.

Weather and Climate as Factors in Tourism and Recreation 'Demand'

Given that recreation is an activity in which individuals freely engage for personal satisfaction or pleasure, recreation is voluntary behaviour proceeding from one's own free choice. As a result, participation will only occur if the potential participant perceives the climate condition to be suitable.

The voluntary and discretionary nature of recreation means that participation will decrease as discomfort and dissatisfaction increase. Thus satisfaction affects participation, which can be taken as a measure of demand for the climatic resource, the called "demand factor." Examples of indicators of demand in this context are visitation or attendance numbers and hotel/motel occupancy or hotel "tourist nights".

The climate or weather circumstances to which the recreationist or tourist may react or respond (i.e. those that affect decisions) are:

1) conditions anticipated by the tourist (say, gleaned from weather climate forecasts, travel brochures etc.) and
2) on-site weather. These are collectively referred to as human responses to weather and climate. They can be identified and assessed using "demand indicators".

There are two categories of methods for assembling data on human response to climate and thus the demand for the climate resource.

1) Assess conditional behaviour, such as by using questionnaires and images to determine how people may react or think, which includes assessing influence or role of weather or climate forecasts.
2) Examine on-site experience.

Since individuals are experiencing conditions first hand, the latter is more reliable. Ideally, the approach must be activity specific. And it is best not to lump all tourism together, but deal with specific categories of activities, either a) *active* or b) *passive*. Sightseeing (touring) is regarded to be the most common tourist activity.

Approaches to Tourism Climatology

Most research on tourism climate appears to be motivated by the potential usefulness of climatological information within planning processes for tourism and recreation. The research addresses the theme of tourism climate as an adjunct to a variety of decision making processes ranging from those related to such things as the development and location appropriate recreational facilities, or determining the length of the recreation season during which a facility will operate, to those as specific as planning future activities involving personal decisions of when and where to go for a holiday.

There has also been interest in the indirect effects of climate. For example, Perry (1972) suggested that people leave swimming pools and golf courses on wet days and converge on nearby towns in search of amusement indoors. Therefore, depending on the weather sensitivity of the recreational activity, climatic information can help in the planning, scheduling and promoting of alternative indoor entertainment facilities. Perry (1972) also describes the use of climatic information in publicity campaigns to condition tourists' expectations of climate at a certain locations.

In this context, considerable effort has gone into devising numerical indices of climate that summarise the significance of climate for tourism. This is because of the multivariable nature of climate and the complex way they come together to give meaning to a particular weather or climate condition in terms of recreation or tourism.

These indices facilitate interpretation of the integrated effects of various atmospheric elements and permit places to be compared. The problem is all of these is climate ratings are arbitrary as non have been empirically tested, with the exception of study by Harlfinger (1991).

It is clear, however, that if climatic information is to be useful in decision-making, it needs to be presented in a form appropriate to the problem. Tourists respond to the integrated effects of the atmospheric environment rather than to climatic averages. It is generally accepted, therefore, that standard weather data or even secondary climatic variables are not always reliable indicators of the significance of atmospheric conditions.

At any given air temperature, for example, the thermal conditions experienced will vary depending on the relative influence and often offsetting effects of wind, humidity, solar radiation and level of a person's activity. Moreover, the design of a particular thermal assessment scheme will depend on the intended use as well as on the nature of the thermal climatic conditions to which the scheme is to be applied.

For example, schemes have been devised for groups of runners, survival in climates of extreme cold and for general purposes of human climate classification. The importance of this has been recognised in climate-recreation research, but so far there have been few convincing studies aimed at to identify optimal or preferred conditions for various outdoor recreational activities. There have been even fewer that examine the sensitivity of tourism to atmospheric conditions generally.

Several writers have described tourism climate in terms of human response in preference to traditional taxonomic methods of portraying regional climates. In some cases, as in the work of Paul (1972), simple climatic indices such as the Thom Discomfort Index and the Wind Chill Index have been computed from climatological data and, in the case of Green (1967), generalised quantitative summations of weather variables arbitrarily weighted have been employed.

Other researchers such as Terjung (1968), Danilova (1974), Bauer (1976) and Yapp and MacDonald (1978) have used more sophisticated measures of tourism climate based on the body's thermal exchanges with the environment. Mieczkowski (1985) has devised a broadly based climatic index for evaluating world climates for tourism. However, meaning attached to these measures has been secondarily derived and interpreted without field investigation.

It was with the above in mind that the work by de Freitas (1990) set out to examine, by way of a case study in Australia, methods capable of giving information that can be used to appraise and rate recreational climates in terms of user sensitivity and satisfaction. Ideally, given the complexity of the problem of addressing the amenity role of climate, the research should concentrate initially on a well-defined human activity; preferably one that is clearly linked with amenity resource attributes of the atmospheric environment. These requirements are fulfilled by a variety of outdoor recreational activities of which beach recreation appeared to be the most appropriate.

There are several reasons for this.

1) Beach recreation is an activity in which the human body is usually lightly clad and therefore directly exposed to atmospheric elements.
2) Beach users in Australia are normally clustered in a relatively small area (patrolled by lifeguards). Therefore, sample populations can be readily observed, and the compact area facilitates on-site monitoring of atmospheric and associated environmental variables representative of ambient conditions.
3) For the beach user, individual recreational aims or objectives of the occasion are similar. From a research standpoint these characteristics offer a relatively controlled situation.
4) Beach use is among the most popular of outdoor recreational activities in Australia and elsewhere as measured by beach attendance figures.

Thus, greater knowledge of the influence of climate on beach recreation is likely to be economically important to the coastal recreation industry.

Two broad categories of questions exist around which the investigation was built. Since the heat balance of the body is fundamental to assessments of human climates, the first category involves specification of the thermal environment.

1) Given methods of body-environment energy budgeting, how are outdoor thermal conditions best quantified?
2) How should thermal index values be interpreted?

The second category of questions centres on assessing the atmospheric resource generally in terms of recreation:

1) What thermal atmospheric conditions are those most preferred for (beach) recreation?
2) To what extent is the level of (beach) user satisfaction influenced by non-thermal atmospheric conditions?
3) What are the relationships between atmospheric conditions and participant satisfaction?

Conceptual Frameworks

Human response to climate is largely a matter of perception, with the exception of the thermal component. Thus some climate variables are entirely *physical* (e.g. rain), some are *physiological* (e.g. air temperature), some are *psychological* (e.g. clear blue skies) and some are *combinations of all three.*

Many writers on the subject of tourism climate single out the thermal component of climate as the most important element. But within a broad range of moderate or "non-extreme" thermal conditions, other factors assume relatively greater importance in determining the pleasantness rating of a given weather or climate condition.

The nature of the relationship between the atmospheric environment and the enjoyable pursuit of outdoor recreational activity may be seen to be a function of facets of on-site atmospheric conditions.

The *facets of tourism climate* given at the top of Figure 1 are 1) *thermal,* 2) *physical,* and 3) *aesthetic.*

1) Treatment of the *thermal* characteristics of on-site conditions involves four steps.

   a) Integrate the physical factors influencing the body-atmosphere thermal state, The method used must include both the attributes of those exposed and the functional attributes of the environment as well as the complete range of atmospheric variables. For the atmospheric environment these include air temperature, humidity, wind, solar and longwave radiation and nature of the physical surroundings, and for the body, metabolic rate, posture and clothing.

   b) Provide a rational index with sound physiological bases that adequately describes the net thermal effect on the human body.

   c) Identify relationships between the thermal state of the body and the condition of mind that expresses the thermal sensation associated with this state.

   d) Provide a rating of the perceived thermal sensation and corresponding calorific index according to the level of satisfaction experienced. This means identifying subjective reaction classified on a favourable-to-unfavourable spectrum as a measure of desirability of conditions.

2) The *physical* category is identified in recognition of the existence of specific meteorological elements such as rain and high wind that directly or indirectly affect participant satisfaction other than in a thermal sense. The occurrence of high wind, for example, can have either a direct mechanical effect on the vacationer, causing inconvenience (personal belongings having to be secured or weighted down) or an indirect effect such as blowing sand causing annoyance. Others things that fall into physical category are rain (duration), rain days (frequency), ice, snow, severe weather, air quality and ultraviolet radiation.

3) The aesthetic aspects relate to the climatically controlled resource attributes of the recreation environment, which Crowe, McKay and Baker (1973) have termed the atmospheric component of the 'aesthetic natural milieu'. Included within this category are 'weather' factors such as visibility, sunshine or cloud associated with the prevailing synoptic condition (for example, 'a nice, clear, sunny day'), day length and visibility.

By employing, independently, separate indicators of the on-site experience, the reliability of each was examined and interpreted by comparison and apparent threshold conditions verified.

Little is known about the effects of climate on human behaviour, but it is clear that in some cases behaviour is a response that modifies or enhances the effects of the atmosphere.

Behaviour can be used as a measure of human sensitivity and satisfaction. Role and significance of behaviour is that an individual can adapt/adjust in five ways:

1) Passive acceptance;
2) Avoid of areas of unfavourable weather or climate determined condition;
3) Change activity to suit weather condition so as to maximise enjoyment of outdoor experience;
4) Use structural or mechanical aids; and
5) Adjust thermal insulation of body (clothing).

The results of the research showed that body-atmosphere energy balance indices are reliable indicators of on-site thermal conditions. Thermal component is main factor determining the desirability of weather Behaviour is a reliable indicator of the significance of weather conditions. Use of shade and clothing are best indicators of heat and cold stress, respectively. Change of posture related to on-site conditions, to a greater degree than expected. Duration of visit is best behavioural indicator of overall significance of recreation climate.

Certain behavioural adjustments (use of shade umbrellas, windbreaks and possibly increased frequency of swims) serve to reduce the beach user's sensitivity to on-site atmospheric conditions, although stated preferences as regards beach weather remain the same. In the absence of ideal conditions, an individual can create, to a point, a personal microclimate that is acceptable.

Surprisingly, attendance is a poor measure of demand (i.e. user response to varying on-site atmospheric conditions). Attendance only reflects the outer limits of acceptability. The work suggested that time spent on site per visit (duration of visit) is a more accurate measure of user response and preferences. Furthermore the findings of the research indicated that atmospheric conditions within the broad zone of acceptability are those that the beach user can readily cope with or effectively modify. Optimum thermal conditions are those requiring no specific adjustment or behavioural fine-tuning.

Future Directions

Thus far, most work in tourism climatology has been based on subjective criteria and unverified perceptions of tourists. More field studies are required along with work that assembles observational data to determine the actual responses, perceptions, needs, reactions and expectations of vacationers. Anderssen and Colberg (1973) have shown that of factors that affect tourism demand, the dominant attributes of a tourist destination are cost, climate and scenery. Research is needed to assess the relative importance and role of the climate attribute as a component of the tourist destination image.

There a number of studies are in the tourism climatology literature that identify potentially useful areas for future research. For example, Ross (1992) has shown that climate, as a component of destination image, does strongly influence tourist behaviour. Hunt (1975) pointed out that images and expectations of a destination may have as much as, or more, to do with an area's tourist image projection than the more tangible recreation resources. Publicity about climate to be expected in an area can also modify a tourist's expectations and thus their degree of satisfaction with the outcome of the experience. There is the often-quoted example of the Irish Tourist Board, which shrewdly promoted the delights of a cool and rainy Irish summer. It was thought to have influenced the expectations of tourists, thus reducing their disappointment.

Ross (1992) has also explored the influence of a variety of climatic conditions on both ideal holiday destinations and on perceptions of the wet tropics area of Far North Queensland.

Given that distinct patterns were found, these results have implications for those involved in the tourism/hospitality industry, as it should influence the way the area is marketed to potential visitors to Far North Queensland as a holiday destination. There is also the question of forecasting tourist travel overseas based on climate. Palutikof (1999) and Agnew and Palutik of (2001) have explored this area.

They found that: a) outward and inward visitor movement is a response to both weather during the year and travel and weather the previous year; b) rainfall is a better indicator of outward travel than inward, with wetter conditions encouraging more visits abroad; and c) autumn temperatures and sunshine have the greatest influence on inward travel. Predictions of tourist travel based on these findings could be important to the travel industry and justify further research.

There are costs to both tourists and tourism operators resulting from the occurrence of unexpected less than satisfactory climate. These need to be fully documented and methods and approaches to studying these require attention. Even now tourists and tourist operators can take out insurance on likelihood of "bad" weather conditions occurring while on vacation. The question arises as to how insurance companies define "bad weather" and the extent to which this is accurate or appropriate, and how this compares to perceptions of the "quality" of conditions experienced by tourists themselves on the one hand, and how it varies with different recreational activities on the other.

The popularity of Mieczkowski's Tourism Climate Index (TCI) shows that there is demand for this type of unitary indicator of climate. What is now required is research that tests the accuracy of such an index or devises a similar index using systematic surveys to interpret it, rather than relying on arbitrary and subjective value judgements of the researcher, as in the case of TCI. An ideal tourism climate model would:

- Rely only on standard climate data.
- Minimise use of average values and maximises use of actual (real) observations.
- Use as input all attributes of the atmospheric environment.
- Use an integrated body-atmosphere energy balance assessment of the thermal component of climate
- Includes all three attributes of tourism climate: thermal, aesthetic and physical/mechanical.
- As an added feature, recognise the notion of climate as a limiting factor, or climate limits to tourism, with focus on thresholds or limitations; for example, times when climate unsuitable or unappealing to the vacationer.

In all of this, the aim should be to adopt standard methods and indices as far as possible. There is also a need to provide potential tourists with probabilistic information on climate to be expected at various destinations. This will lead to improved information and improved choice. Clearly, much work remains to be done.

5

Environmental Impacts: Hills and Mountains

Introduction

Tourism has become one of the most important aspects of man's spatial behaviour in modern times. It is, as some say, the most important civil industry in the world growing at a phenomenal annual growth rate of 10-15%. According to some estimates it contributes around 10% of the global GDP and 7% of the work force. According to World Travel and Tourism Council, the total global capital investments, worldwide consumer spending (10.9%) and world's international trade in goods and services make tourism as one of the top three categories of trade.

In India also the 'white industry' is growing at a good pace thanks to the 'leisure revolution' and abundance of discretionary income. However, money making is not and has never been the best part of tourism. The social and cultural aspects, though less perceptible have more for reaching consequences. For a country like India endowed with vast natural wealth and human resources, tourism acquires a place of special importance. However, one should not turn a blind eye to ecological and environmental changes brought about by the increasing tourist traffic.

Tourism is normally seen as a money minting industry. With the kind of growth rate and the income generation abilities, it assumes a particular significance in India. In the absence of a trade surplus or a sound foreign exchange reserve, tourism is making a phenomenal though unplanned growth. But the returns of tourism should not obscure the long-term impacts of this smokeless industry on the local environment. In this Unit, we shall talk about the various aspects of hill tourism and try and analyse its impact on the environment. We will also try to explore the possible ingredients of a suitable management strategy. The present Unit is an attempt to analyse the varied impacts of tourism in the context of hills' and mountains' environment.

Mountains and Hills: Spiritual Abodes to Tourist Destinations

Hills and mountains have occupied an important place since ancient times, when they were considered abodes of gods. Sages and hermits would meditate and hence lot of reverence and divinity was attached to them in the Indian context. Some like Kailash, Meru, Kishkindha, Govardhan, Vaikuntha were particularly sacred. The modern concept of hill stations which transcends religious connotations and makes them commonly accessible owes much to British endeavours. It arose with the expansion of European imperialism in the Orient in the nineteenth century. The French established Da Lat in Indo-China, the Spanish built Bagnio in Manila and the Dutch founded several similar centres in Indonesia. But no colonising power built more stations than the British in India. Their rapid growth was due to the real relief they provided from the heat and disease of the plains in summer, while later, after the struggle of 1857, they offered a place of refuge from the reality of life on the plains below.

Not all hill stations were established in a uniform manner. Most of the earliest stations were originally built as army cantonments and were meant to give European troops a breather from the pre-monsoon heat. Some of the more remote cantonments like Chakrata and Jalapahar lingered on in isolation while other more accessible ones attracted civilian attention and soon flourished as social and educational centres. The resorts nearer to large administrative centres also usually attracted local patronage. Thus, Ooty was summer capital for Madras, Murree for Rawalpindi, Nainital for Lucknow, etc. Others were popular with a particular clientele, e.g., Kotagiri acted as a magnet for planters and box-wallahs, Mussoorie attracted high-spirited young military cadets out for a good time, and Shimla was the preserve of the top military and civilian personnel. Even the down-market stations enjoyed specialised patronage as Ranikhet catered principally to the signals and armoured corps and Almora drew survey, railway and telegraph staff. Madanapalle attracted mainly pensioned native officials, while Matheran served as a destination for wealthy Parshi merchants. Kodaikanal was not established by the British but by ailing American missionaries. But two things were particularly there – firstly, hill stations attracted people from nearby or surrounding areas, maybe due to transport problems and secondly, that they had a loyal devoted clientele in the sense that visitors would visit the same place year after year.

The change, from hills catering to the affluent and the influential few to regular holidaymakers, was in part, a product of improved transport and communication networks. Other factors like increasing knowledge and awareness of hill stations, aggressive marketing by tourist agents, leisure time and availability of disposable income also played an important part.

Why Hills and Mountains?

Hills and mountains are unique ecosystems; their ecological and cultural attributes make them favourite tourist destinations. As 'zones of refugia' they offer ideal conditions for the three R's – rest, relaxation and recreation. They cater to the varied demands of a vast segment of society. Some of the main reasons behind hill tourism are:

a. Summer retreat – with their climatic and geomorphic conditions they offer ideal summer retreats from the scorching heat of the plains.
b. Natural surroundings – confluence of various ecosystems; hills, forests, snow, rocks and varied relief and ecological features attract naturalists, bio-scientists, academicians, poets, sightseers, photographers.
c. Pilgrimage centres – Some of the hill stations also happen to be major pilgrim centres thus attracting huge tourist traffic. Vaishno Devi, Amarnath, Kedarnath, Badrinath, Gangotri, Yamunotri, are just a significant few.
d. Mountain sports – like mountaineering, trekking as in Leh, skiing, ice skating (as in Kufri, Patnitop), helicopter skiing, river rafting (as in Manali), gliding etc. attract sports enthusiasts.
e. Floral and faunal diversity – Wildlife and diversity of plant species make them ideal destinations for wildlife lovers. Bioprospectors have of late become a significant tourist component. Nanda Devi Sanctuary would be an example.

f. Adventurists and Explorers – The mountaneous terrain often lure many adventurers or explorers. Wanderlust accounts for but a small proportion of tourist traffic.

g. Miscellaneous – factors would include recreation, leave after work, desire to visit friends, relatives, honeymoons, etc.

Tourist Movements

G.R. Gruber primarily working in the context of Alps explains tourist movement through the following flow charts. As tourism is the movement of people – from say source 'A' to 'B' and then back, four kinds of movements are possible. Although 'A' and 'B' can be locations anywhere in the world for our purposes, let us assume 'B' as places in the highlands. Generally, tourist movement goes on throughout the year but there are two distinct phases of tourist movement.

a. When the summers are on their peak.

b. Early snowfall.

In additions, the Christmas and other long holidays also at times govern movement of tourist traffic.

Geographical Spread

The Indian subcontinent is dotted by mountain ranges all across; the Himalayas and the associated ranges in the north and northwest, Purvanchal groups in the northeast, the Aravalis in the northwest, the Satpuras, Vindhyas, Eastern and Western Ghats in the peninsular region. There is thus an abundance of hill stations, some of which are not so well known. Graeme D. Westlake, "An Introduction to Hill Stations of India", divides them into four groups; the Himalayan, Central Western and Southern group for a convenient study.

Distribution of Indian Hill Stations and Cantonments

Himalayan Group

1. Ziarat	2. Sheikh Budin
3. Cherat	4. Murree
5. Khaira Gali	6. Nathia Gali
7. Dunga Gali	8. Gulmarg
9. Bakloh	10 Balun
11. Dalhousie	12. Dharmsala

13. Bharwain
14. Chail
15. Shimla
16. Jutogh
17. Sabathu
18. Solon
19. Dagshai
20. Kasauli
21. Chakrata
22. Mussoorie
23. Landour
24. Lansdowne
25. Nainital
26. Ranikhet
27. Almora
28. Chaubattia
29. Darjeeling
30. Lebong
31. Jabalpur
32. Kurseong
33. Shillong
34. Haflang

Central Group

35. Mount Abu
36. Chikalda
37. Panchmarhi
38. Ranchi
39. Hazaribagh
40. Parasnath

Western Group

41. Saputara
42. Khuldabad
43. Matheran
44. Lonavala
45. Khandala
46. Pune
47. Purandhar
48. Mahableshwar
49. Panchgani
50. Amboli

Southern Group

51. Ramandurg
52. Horsley Hill
53. Nandidurg
54. Bangalore
55. Madanapalle
56. Yeracaud
58. Ootacamund (Ooty)
59. Wellington
60. Coonoor
61. Coimbatore
62. Palmaner
63. Kodaikanal
65. Courtallam
66. Ponmudi

Ceylon

67. Nuwara Eliya

Burma

68. Maymo

Westlake's map shows pre-1947 India and some additions might have been there nevertheless it serves as a useful tool for the distribution of hill stations.

The Himalayan resorts, at an average altitude of 6000 feet, offer magnificent views and range after range of jagged snowy peaks. The Western stations are not much over 2000 feet with the highest, Mahabaleshwar, reaching a modest 4700 feet above sea level. They do, however, provide scenic vies and pleasurable walking, not trekking though. These stations perch on the Western Ghats, a long ridge of volcanic rock running north to south and are full of snowfalls and rarely experience frost. At their southern extreme, the Ghats suddenly descend down into rolling downs and then rise again to plateaux of surprising height. Ootacamund (Ooty) and Kodaikanal are higher than almost any other hill station save the Himalayan group and have a climate almost European in coolness and damp.

Impacts of Tourism on Mountain Environment

While dealing with the impacts certain things should be borne in mind:

a. Tourism does not necessarily have a negative impact, in many cases particularly in the economic field, it promises a huge growth potential. Having said that any analysis of the impacts has to be done with a long term agenda. In an strictly cost-benefit analysis the short term gains of tourism might be neutralised by long term losses.

b. Environment primarily does connote the physical ecological environment but a comprehensive analysis of the possible impacts would also involve treatment of the local society and economy of the region. The impacts thus generated are overlapping, e.g., ecological impact could well spill into the sociocultural or economic impact.

c. Generally speaking, however, it is the unrestrained mass tourism which leaves a trail of disasters. Ecotourism or sustainable tourism on the contrary, are being projected as having positive ramifications.

d. There are certain determinants (discussed subsequently) which influence the tourist-impact relationship. Purpose, profile, duration, etc. condition the possible impacts of tourism on the local environment.

Impact Determinants

The impact of tourism on hills and mountains is to a great extent conditioned by the following factors:

a. The number and duration of stay of the tourists; this is particularly true in the context of 'mass' or 'exploitative' tourism. Thus, the duration of stay in some cases becomes directly proportional to the impact on local environment.
b. The sphere of interests of the tourists: sports, relaxation, nature-watch, pilgrimage.
c. The fragility of the local environment, the accessibility of the region, the geo-morphological features and the nature of terrain.
d. The standard of living and the income of the tourists as well as the areas visited by the tourists (e.g., socioeconomic disparity).
e. The extent and type of infrastructural facilities, i.e., transport, accommodation, etc.
f. The tourists' awareness of the sociocultural and ecological environment and the resultant behaviour.
g. Existing government policies, regulations and guidelines.

While discussing the impacts of tourism on mountain environment another thing that has to be borne in mind is that the word mountain environment does not only connote the physical or the natural landscape, i.e., forests, rocks, ice, climate, but also the cultivated landscape (houses, villages, fields, infrastructural facilities) and the people as well (behaviour, customs, traditions). The net impact of tourism is different in different regions depending on the relative interplay of the factors discussed above. Let us now discuss some major impacts of tourism, both direct and induced on the hills and mountains. For the sake of convenience, let us divide these into three parts.

a. Ecological impacts.
b. Sociocultural impact.
c. Economic impact.

Ecological Impacts

Tourism's impact vis-a-vis physical environment has come in for a lot of debate. People are becoming ecologically more conscious day by day. Many humanists and sociologists like Elzeard Bouffier of France, Toyohiko Kagawa of Japan, Sunder Lal Bahuguna of India to name just very few have been raising environmental issues vigorously. Many reports, both national and international have also come up documenting tourism's impact on environment. The German Alpine Club's International Symposium in Munich (1983), and OECD Report on Impacts (1981) merely reflect some early attempts in this direction.

While there may be a difference on the degree or intensity of the resultant problems, it is generally agreed that unregulated tourism tends to destroy forests, consume firewood, creates pollution and over-crowding, endangers ecological balance, threatens the floral and faunal diversity, produces garbage trails, overburdens environment with tourist structures and roads, causes at times natural hazards as also withdraws labour from agriculture, changes the land use pattern, etc. Let us analyse some of these impacts in greater details.

Forestation – By way of building of infrastructural and accommodation facilities or industrial requirements or grazing or firewood collection has led to reduction in forest cover in the hills and mountains. Rich forested slopes have been converted into barren rocks in the name of development activities like roads, hotels, tourist huts, and trekking trails. Compare this situation with National Forest Policy recommendations which envisages 60% of the mountain areas to be covered with forests, whereas in the case of Himalayas, less than one fifth of the region is under snow cover, 3.7% under high meadow (Bugyals) and nearly 42.3% of the land is denuded of any vegetal cover. It is to be noted that only 4% of forest land comprises good quality trees. The best coniferous forests are degenerating fast, there is a shrinkage in natural habitats and extermination of many plants and animal species. Musk deer, snow leopard, barasingha, etc. are becoming extinct. The dwindling Dal, Manasbal, Wular, Kounsernag Lakes and high incidence of floods in the rivers Jhelum, Sindh and Chenabl coupled with apparent change in marco and micro climatic conditions are some visible manifestations of misuse and mismanagement of various habitat types. Degraded landscapes, ranging from glacial and peri-glacial areas with depleting snowfields to hill-slopes, foot hills and valleys are also reflective of the human interference. Recent studies of geo-ecosystems in Dhauladhar range and the adjoining areas south of the Punjab Himalayas as also in Uttar Pradesh and Eastern Himalayas have revealed 'erosion damage'. Owing to litho logical, structural, climatological and relief conditions, such areas are highly susceptible to erosional processes, being induced or accelerated by human activities such as over-grazing, tree logging, fuel wood-collection and improper constructions.

Loss of flora and fauna – Very much associated with deforestation (in fact it has been mentioned in passing earlier) increasing tourist menace is auguring danger for the floral and faunal wealth. In Nepal, several species like Rhododendron arboreum, Mynica esculenta, Cedrus deodaea, etc. are on the verge of extinction, whereas species like Akies spectabilis, Tsuga dumosa, Rhododendron nivale, etc. are under intense economic pressure. In Nepal mountaineering expeditions primarily account for decimation of biological wealth. In the Uttarakhand part of Himalayas, the soils, biomass, flora and fauna and water have suffered a lot due to unplanned encroachment. Tourism and associated projects have been major destroyers. The Ramaganga dam has submerged a vast area falling under the natural habitat of tiger and other animal species. Tehri and Jamrani dams have also produced similar effects. Increasing construction at Gangotri is causing great loss to a number of plant species like Chir, Fur, Birch, etc. Heavy utilisation of open tracts adversely affects the biomass. Trampling directly kills plants and causes soil compaction. Increased used of an area changes the microclimate and water balance and thus kills plants. These changes in the local biotic community can lead to eventual loss of the species. Plants are also lost by plucking of wild flowers and leaves by wanderers. Brahmakamal is one such greatly affected variety. Valley of flowers has been at the receiving end. In the case of animals, as has already been said, shrinkage in natural habitats, flourishing souvenir industry, contamination of ecosystems as well as in some places actual hunting have been primary decimating factors.

Garbage trails and pollution – Waste generation especially solid waste by the hotels like food, vegetable, paper, rags, clothes, bottles or the hospitals like glass, bottles, polythene, gloves, bandage, cotton, plastics, etc. is causing major damage to the local ecosystems. Most of the hill stations lack sewerage and waste disposal facilities. Of particular importance here is the fact that while some wastes are biodegradable others like soft drink bottles, polythene are non-biodegradable and cause immense harm to the environment. Surveys carried out in Kullu Manali Tourist Complex (KMTC) suggest huge amount of daily waste generation. Valley of Flowers also suffers from a similar problem. In many cases water bodies are choked. Lakes, rivers and ponds become polluted. Dal Lake in Srinagar is heavily polluted, weeded and eutrophied thanks to release of an incredible amount of faecal matter and pathogenic materials from the houseboats. In addition, atmospheric pollution through motor vehicles, aircrafts, road and rail transportation, coal fuel, oil, natural gas, wood fuel and forest fires is also becoming increasingly prevalent. Of late, noise pollution is otherwise silent, serene ecosystems is also a problem to be taken into account.

Increasing instances of natural hazards due to disturbances in the fragile ecosystems of the hills and mountains are not unknown. A study conducted by James S. Gardner in Shimla is very illustrative. Increasing tourist traffic in Manali combined with the vulnerability of it's ecosystem has produced natural disasters. In recent increase in the number of high density multi-storeyed hotels, constructions of buildings in the flood and erosion susceptible areas adjacent to Beas, the development of road network and winter recreation activities has elevated risks from natural hazards like snow avalanches, earthquakes, flash floods, rock slides, slope failures, etc. The Manali case shares many characteristics with similar situations elsewhere in India.

Mountain sports – like trekking, skiing, ice-skating, etc. are producing many undesirous results. Studies conducted in Nepal suggest that trekking and trekker related activities are leading to accelerating rate of deforestation in the Sagarmatha area, thereby destroying the habitat of numerous wild animals and high altitude plants. In India, this has led to the need to close down the Nanda Devi Sanctuary for trekkers and shepherds. Markha valley in Laddakh has also borne the pressure of tourist menace. Likewise, water sports, involving diesel-powered speedboats and motor boats contribute to surface water pollution in many areas.

Deviations in land-use patterns are becoming common on many hill stations. The desire for 'quick gains' has led to regression of agricultural activities. In many cases tourism has overlapped agriculture thus creating a tourist monoculture. This is disastrous both, in the long run, both to the economy and ecology of the region. Likewise overcrowding, urban sprawl, shortage of civic amenities when incongruent with the carrying capacity of the region tend to produce harmful effects on the environment.

However, in many cases tourism has also served as a tool for conservation and environmental regeneration. If conducted properly tourism awakens ecological consciousness and the need for introducing measures of conservation in sensitive areas of nature monuments and wilderness. Retreat from hillside farming in the most marginal and dangerous areas is another gain.

Socio-Cultural Impacts

While dealing with sociocultural impacts let us first discuss the mechanisms of tourist-culture interface and then examine case studies if any. Local society and it's customs constitute an important tourism resource. Village lifestyle, traditional ceremonies and religious processions, arts and crafts are vigorously marketed by tourist organisations. There is, however, much evidence to demonstrate that traditions and quality of life of the host society can be eroded by mass tourism. In one of the better known frameworks, Doxey has developed an irritation index which traces the local community's reaction, beginning with a level of euphoria associated with early tourist arrivals through to antagonism when a place becomes saturated with tourists. Doxey suggests that the level of irritation was correlated with the degree of compatibility between host community and the visitors, the location of tourist accommodation and how much the locals directly benefit through employment and associated perks of the tourist industry. Also important in this regard is the configuration of the tourists. Mass package holiday-makers demanding facilities and levels of service matching metropolitan cities have little interest in understanding of local culture and history. Such tourists have little interaction with local residents. Studies have shown that tourism at many hill stations has been accompanied by higher prices for craft goods, greed and crime in societies. In addition, the so-called demonstration effect involving the adoption by local residents, particularly younger people, of aspects of tourist life styles, is becoming increasingly common. High levels of expatriate ownership and management, together with resort development that has created private areas for tourists further alienates the local population receiving only limited benefits. Unregulated and insensitive tourism can also lead to dissolution of social cohesion, youth social conflicts, criminality, prostitution and immorality in the host society. Loss of cultural identity promoting commercialisation of tradition selling of antiques, vandalism and materialistic thinking also afflict the host society.

Tourism, however, also has a positive side when it comes to the host society. It entails behaviouristic change in the host society when the residents seek to improve their 'image'. It also, in many cases, delays out migration and provides motivation for learning. Preservation of cultural monuments, rediscovery of lost traditions, promotion of current culture, training of new craftsmen and contact with the outside world by way of infrastructure modernisation and urbanisation are other positive entailments of tourism development. Let us now have a look at 'Leh' an important tourist destination in order to get a better picture of the state of affairs.

Leh in Laddakh was a forbidden land upto 1974. Subsequently it was marketed as 'The Little Tibet'. It is a classic example of how a unique cultural heritage could be ravaged by sudden tourist invasion. It goes on to show how tourism induced development in a backward economy can only result in marginal economic gains with major sociocultural losses. Proliferation of external entrepreneurs has led to economic dislocation of the local residents.

Some good work has been done by the way of restoration and renovation of monasteries and revival of some art traditions but otherwise Leh has paid a heavy price for the development of tourism. Only a small part of tourist earnings remain inside the region, the rest being siphoned either to the valley or the lowlands.

The sociological cultural front has borne the flood of tourist invasion in a major way. Lamas are increasingly coming under the influence of western culture. The younger generation has been uprooted from their age old tradition, and local pilgrims are discriminated against the better paying foreigners. Many religious olyeets have become 'wares' for sale and cultural assets and art olyeets have got commercialised and are either being sold or smuggled. In Tibetan culture, 'art' is not a saleable commodity. Leh's example clearly depicts the contradiction between tourism and tradition.

Economic Impacts

Recreational tourism induces growth at three levels – national, regional and local, although the quantum of this growth may be different at different levels. Let us have a look at some of the possible mechanisms through which tourism affects the economy of a region.

Tourism Related Industries and Employment Potential

Tourism is not a single industry but a loose confederation of number of these. It is usually classified in the tertiary sector, mainly a service sector. Geographers call it a 'landscape industry' since the products of tourism are made of natural beauty, dramatic landscape and cultural heritage. The development of various segments of tourist industry depends upon the importance and popularity of the tourist places.

Laying down of transport networks like roads, railway tracks, trek routes, rope ways all require a huge labour force for this construction and upkeep. Provision of better accommodation facilities by way of construction of classified hotels, indigenous hotels, tourist bunglows or other state establishments and other types specially tent houses, dharmasalas, etc. is another major responsibility of tourism industry. Souvenir making is another significant component of a good tourism policy. Thus, tourism, we see, is a labour intensive industry. A large number of seasonal works can seek employment such as the masons, carpenters, porters, rickshaw pullers, hotel guides, waiters, tourist guides, escorts, boatmen, pony owners, candi carriers, etc. These job opportunities sustain the hill economy to a great extent.

Income Aspects and Multiplier Effect

Tourism circulates existing wealth among social groups and geographic regions. The money spent by the tourists goes to the local business in a number of ways. This money in turn is spent on provision of goods and services to the tourists. Thus, through this multiplier effect one can explain the additional spending or job creation caused by a given level of tourist expenditure. However, the scope of multiplier effect is greatly reduced because of various leakages in the form of import of foreign goods, interest on foreign investments, etc.

Infrastructure and Regional Development

Tourism is an important mechanism to initiate and generate

infrastructure development and improvement. The construction of roads, railway lines, airports, electricity and gas supplies, sanitation, water supply etc. which are mainly undertaken to attract the tourists benefit the local residents also by way of provision of civic amenities. Besides, the development of infrastructure prepares the basis for diversification of other economic activities. Thus, regional development is a natural corollary of development of tourism in a region. Foreign exchange, taxi revenues, impetus to local arts, economic diversification – are other accompaniments of development of tourist destinations.

However, there are certain negative aspects of tourism development which should not be ignored. It creates inflationary tendencies and seasonal dependency besides uneven economic development. Domination of external entrepreneurs, burden on commercial services and over-utilisation of scarce resources come along naturally.

What Needs to be Done?

While talking about possible remedial measures and suitable management strategies one could go on endlessly talking about the do's and the don'ts. Thanks to absence of preventing planning in India, we have reached a stage where things have become precarious. All the major hill stations are under tremendous ecological-cultural stress. The present state of affairs do not augur well for the long-term sustenance of this growing industry.

The basic dilemma with tourism and in particular mountain tourism is that the basic capital is landscape. Once it is degraded or damaged, it can hardly be repaired or redressed. The tragedy with mountain tourism is that as the mountainous regions are trying to emerge from their subsistence economy, they are seized up by modern exploitative forces causing rupture in the ecosystem. Tourism, which in a way was brought to mitigate socioeconomic disparities between highlands and the lowlands, has on the contrary widened the gap for the same region. In fact, market mechanism tends to destroy it's own resource. As it is rightly said "Tourism destroys tourism". The irony of the situation as Bilting says is that while the next of the landscape is being paid for, the long-term costs of presentation are not.

The need of the hour is to address the issue with urgent sincerity. There could be many possible suggestions in this direction like devising a tourism management plan for every region; a plan that encompasses all-important aspects and is interactive in nature. Such a plan should take into account:

(i) the ecological aspects, the nature of the terrain, the relative fragility of the ecosystem and the geo-morphic features.

(ii) the macro level tourism development plans should be integrated with the socioeconomic development at the micro-level. Integrated rural development schemes, non-conventional energy development, self-employment programmes conservation programmes and tourism development plane should work together as an integrated whole towards a common goal of development without sustainability disturbing the lives of the local people.

(iii) Building laws should be made more stringent in the mountainous areas. Multi-storeyed building unsuitable to the local landscape should not be allowed. All the buildings must be built on passive heating designs, so that the spare heating reliance on fuel-wood and imported fuels comes down. Solar waters could be encouraged.

(iv) Local people or their representatives should be involved while making tourism plans or administrative boards. Their wishes, aspirations, cultural values and economic necessities should necessarily be taken into consideration.

(v) The quantitative and qualitative aspects of tourism should be addressed sincerely. Controlling the number of tourists visiting a place could be a good starting point. Khajiar in Himachal Pradesh, the mini Switzerland of India is one good example in this regard. The formation of tourists boards on the lines of Vaishno Devi Management or Amarnath Shrine Boards could possibly regulate the tourist traffic. The quality aspect of tourism is equally important. Awareness generation and sensitisation of the tourists to local ecology, culture, economy, etc. could be useful. In fact, the tourist complexes could and should be used for diffusing information both to the tourists and the local populace. Another component of awareness generation could be orientation programmes. Mountaineering courses to promote expedition and the studies of glacial retreats, depleting snowfields, deforestation are being organised by Geological Survey of India and institutes like Wadia Institute of Himalayan Ecology. Such attempts need to be streamlined. Audiovisual media could also be used in enlightening the tourists.

(vi) A crucial link between the tourists and the local populace and ecosystems are the guides or escorts. Only trained tourist guides should be allowed to entertain tourists.

(vii) Diversion of tourist traffic to less frequented sites on a policy level could be of immense help. Development of alternative tourist spots on the likes of Laddakh Sarai near Leh or Span Resorts in Katrain between Kullu and Manali could be very fruitful.

(viii) At times regulations and legislations should supplement the efforts taken by other agencies.

Thus, any successful management strategy has to be very comprehensive in scope and address all possible ramifications of tourism development. The tourism industry has to take a serious view of this regard not merely through resolutions but through actual practice in their operations.

Nepal: A Case Study

Nepal is one of the dream tourist destinations. Ideal for trekking, wildlife, mountaineering, scientific expeditions geography, climatology, anthropology, sociology and linguistic archaeology, Nepal has a lot to offer. Tourism, thus, experienced a boom in this Himalayan kingdom. According to an ADB Report (1982) it took five years of tourist traffic to loose 15% of Nepal's forests. The impact of tourism has been analysed through a series of impactograms by T.K. Shrestha.

Let us Sum up

Mountain tourism has a good potential for growth in India. Efforts should be taken to mitigate the harmful effects of tourism on the hill environment. In fact, mountain tourism needs to be carefully organised. A proper planning focusing on the vital infrastructural areas will go a long way in harnessing its potential. We have noticed above the antiquity of hills as areas visited by pilgrims. We have also noticed the gradual shift from pilgrimage to modern day tourism in these hilly regions. But we also understand that an unbridled growth of tourism activity in these regions is replete with serious harmful consequences. Our hilly regions are eco-fragile and cannot sustain tourism activity beyond a certain point. Therefore, planning tourism activity in these regions in such manner as to take care of the harmful impact on the region is vitally necessary. Macro-planning for the region must account for ecological and sociocultural concerns of the people of the region. Possibly then we shall be in a position to adequately utilise this vast and valuable natural resource for tourism purposes.

Motivation for Holidaying

A review of tourism literature reveals an abundance of studies on motivation and satisfaction, however there is an apparent lack of research into the motivational factors which influence event tourists. Event tourism is globally important in terms of its popular appeal and ability to generate travel and tourism related benefits to destinations. Although research has been undertaken into the internal and external forces of the destinations attributes (i.e. climate, culture) and how they motivate travellers and the fact that there has been an increased interest in discovering what motivates tourists behaviour there has been an apparent lack of focus into defining what motivates event tourists. Hence the aim of this paper is to analyse the motivational factors which influence event tourists to attend an event.

What are Motivations?

To be motivated means *to be moved* to do something. A person who has no stimulus to act, is considered to be unmotivated. On the other hand a person who is moved to act is seen as motivated. Motivation can vary from the levels of motivation (how much motivation) and also the orientation of the motivation (what type of motivation). Underlying all behaviour are needs and motivations grounded in the basic physiological and socio-psychological wants of all humans. The standard theories of motivation applied to understanding leisure and tourism behaviour are (Murray's (1938) Needs Theory of Personality, Maslow's (1943) Hierarchical Theory of Needs and Berlyne's (1960) concept of optimal level of stimulation.

Murray (1938) explained that "A need is a stimulus – a force pushing an individual in a certain direction or to behave in a certain way' and identified 12 physiological needs which are viewed as primary needs, and include air, water, food and security, and also identified 28 psychological needs which are considered secondary needs and are connected to mental or emotional satisfaction. Murray postulated that needs are changeable and that they gain or lose importance as they are satisfied and in fact, suggested that there is a 'need cycle' and that needs can be dormant during the non-stimulated period, and are susceptible to stimuli during the ready period and so determine an individuals behaviour during the active period and also suggested that these needs work in combination with each other. A more structured approach was adopted in Maslows (1943) Hierarchical Theory of Needs which suggested that peoples behaviour is driven by both physiological and socio-psychological needs. However, Maslow had a more structured hierarchical order to the needs of activation and satisfaction. He believed that the lower-order needs (psychological needs followed by safety needs) had to be satisfied before an individual could work on the higher-order needs of love, belongingness and self-esteem. At the top of the hierarchy of needs is self-actualisation which is an opportunity for individuals to 'become everything that one is capable of becoming (Maslow, 1943).

Dispite this apparent difference Maslow (1970) agreed with the research by Murray (1938) that behaviour may be motivated by one or more needs and suggested that the hierarchy of needs may not be as rigid as it first implies. Research using both theories into tourism and leisure have found that the relationship between needs and activity choice is quite complex. This research has lea to the belief that behaviour is multidimensional and that the same activity may be motivated by a variety of needs at different times for the one individual or that one activity may have different meanings to another person at the same time. No matter how complex the relationships may be, the motivation theory still provides insights into why people choose to take part in certain events or activities i.e. being an event tourist.

Further research has indicated that motivation can be referred to as biological/psychological needs and wants, including forces that arouse, direct and integrate a person's behaviour and activity. Various disciplines have been used to explain the phenomena and characteristics related to motivation. However, they are very complex as they relate to human beings and human nature, which in itself is complex. Whilst in the disciplines of sociology and psychology, motivation is often directed towards cognitive and emotional motives or internal and external motives. Such internal motives are associated with feelings, instincts and drives whereas external motives involve mental representations such as beliefs or knowledge. MacCannell (1977) notes that from an anthropological viewpoint, tourists are motivated to escape the routine of daily life and seek authentic experiences. Whereas from a socio-psychological point of view, motivation is classified as seeking and avoidance behaviour.

Event tourists may relate to one or many of the areas mentioned above. They may be escaping their daily routine by seeking an authentic experience at a 'Sing Sing' (traditional song and dance) in the South Pacific. Or they may be attending a week long health clinic event to restore there inner strength.

What are Events?

Events range from small local events or festivals to what are known as mega events. As there several types of events and there may be different motivations for attending each type of event. Motivations may include 'keeping up with the Jones' to being the 'first on the block to attend an event' or just to escape the daily routine. One type of event is a special event and McDonnell, Allen & O'Toole (2002) considers a special event to usually be one-off or infrequent by nature. The special event could then be considered as a mega or hall mark event. Getz (1997) defines mega events as:

Their volume should exceed 1 million visits, their capital costs should be at least $500 million, and their reputation should be of a 'must see' event. Mega events, by way of their size or significance, are those that yield extraordinarily high levels of tourism, media coverage, prestige or economic impact for the host community or destination.

An example of a mega event would be the Olympic Games which fulfils all of the criteria to which Getz (1997) refers. The Olympics are significant as they yield extraordinary high levels of tourism and prestige and obtain a great deal of media coverage which in turn has further economic impacts on the host community and destination in general.

On the other hand, a hallmark event is considered to be smaller in scale than the mega event and generally has a special meaning or significance for a region or community. Allen, O'Toole, McDonnell & Harris (2002) defines hallmark events as:

> *A major one-time or recurring event of limited duration and often developed to enhance awareness, appeal or profitability of a tourism destination over a short time. However, Ritchie (1984) enlarges this definition viz: A major one-time or recurring event of limited duration, developed primarily to enhance awareness, appeal and profitability of a tourism destination in the short term and/or long term. Such events rely their success on uniqueness, status, and or timely significance to create interest and attract attention.*

The major point which both these definitions have in common is that they include a reason to celebrate, to bring various groups or individuals together to experience what the event has to offer. The event may last over several weeks or just a day. It may be a one time or recurring event and it may be a public or private sector event. Whichever type of event it is, there is the need to motivate people to take action to attend. Getz (1997) takes the general approach that people attend events to satisfy various personal needs.

Motivations to Attend an Event

There are several groups of motives proposed by McDonnell et al. (1999). The four main groups proposed by McDonnell et al. (1999) are *social motives, organisational motives, physiological motives and personal motives. Social motives* may include the opportunity to experience social interaction with others or of being part of the community spirit which takes place during an event. The event attendee may feel so moved by their social motives that they want to partake of good deeds and may become a volunteer at the event.

The second group are *organisational motives.* These generally include the need for status or recognition that they have been a participant at the event. For example, there is status and/or prestige connected with attending an event such as the Olympic Games. Organisational motives also include sponsorship or community support. For example, organisations want to appear to be supporting the community through their commitment to the event.

Physiological motives are the third group and these include the need for relaxation and or exercise depending on the type of event. An attendee at an event expects to eat, drink and to be entertained as part of the event process.

The final group are *personal motives*. These motives can be different for each attendee. Some of the personal motives could include the need to seek new experiences from the mundane. Or to fulfil an ambition i.e. to attend the Passion Play in Oberammergau, Germany. On the other hand it may related to personal development.

Actual attendance itself may be attributed to multiple motives or just a single motive.

Motivations of a Tourist

A review of the literature on tourism motivation shows that people travel because they are 'pushed' into making a travel decision by internal psychological forces, and 'pulled' by the external forces of the destination attributes. Tourists obviously have their own internal and external reasons for travelling. However, theses reasons could have positive or negative impacts on travel satisfaction which has as been used as a tool to assess the outcome of the travel experience. This concept of motivation can be divided into two groups which indicate that people travel because they are either pushed or pulled to do so by forces or factors. These factors illustrate how tourists are pushed by motivation variables into making travel decisions and then how they are pulled or attracted by a destination attributes. Whilst push motivations are related to the tourists' desire, the pull factors or motivations are aliened with the attributes of the destination choice. Put simply the push motivations are related to internal or emotional factors whilst pull motivations are connected to the external, cognitive or situational factors.

Crompton (1979) found that push motivations could be grouped into the following areas; escapism, rest and relaxation, prestige, health and fitness, adventure and social interaction, family togetherness and excitement. Tourists may travel to escape the monotony of their every day lives and for authentic experiences. The pull motivations are attributed to the overall attractiveness of the destination. Pull factors may include; beaches, cultural attractions, natural scenery, shopping and so forth. However, these push and pull factors may work in tandem and the destination attributes may stimulate and reinforce inherent push factors. Several research studies have been undertaken using these perspectives.

Further research by Iso-Ahola (1982) suggested that individuals perceive a leisure activity as having the potential to produce satisfaction for two reasons. The first reason is that the leisure activity may provide intrinsic rewards (such as mastery and competence) and secondly to escape from routine. In 1987 Kippendorf conducted similar research and found that tourists are motivated by 'going away from rather than going toward something' and that tourist motivation is generally self oriented.

Research into the needs, motivations and expectations of tourists has been conducted for several years. Whilst it does several researchers who have delved into this field. It is generally accepted that push and pull factors (as motivations) have generally been used in studying tourist behaviour. These studies have played a useful role in understanding the different needs and wants which motivate and influence the behaviour of tourists.

Although past explanations of tourist behaviour has been based on a unidementional approach, many tourism researchers are now moving to more than one motive or need which affects the tourists' behaviour.

Earlier studies acknowledged the following key motivation elements in relation to tourism. They are; the need to escape (for example a dreary home life) and to seek (new and exciting experiences). There is still acceptance of the undimentional approach to motivation on the understanding that a variety of behaviours can be explained as a response of a small number of motivational 'needs'. This appears to be the main view despite suggestions that motivation may be outdated since the decision process is a result of many experiences and knowledge of destinations. Gnoth (1997) suggests that motivation's two dimensions are lasting dispositions and object-specific elements. The interaction between motivation and the symbolic consumption of tourism experiences for its social or hedonic value, rather than functional utility was identified by Brown (1992).

Tourism Motivations Versus Event Motivations

Dann (1977; 1981) and Crompton (1979) have written extensively on 'push' and 'pull' tourist motivations noting that 'push' motivations are internal or emotional factors i.e. the tourists' desires. On the other hand they stressed that 'pull' motivations refer to the destination attributes i.e. external cognitive or situational factors. For example a tourist may want to visit great Grandmothers birth place in Ireland (push) and the airfares are two for the price of one (pull).

However, McDonnell et al. (1999) researched event motivations and divided them into four groups; social motivation (interaction), organisational motivation (status/recognition), physiological motives (relaxation/exercise), personal motives (new experiences/personal achievement). This approach provides a broader explanatory capacity. When comparing the tourism motivations as postulated by Dann (1977; 1981) and Crompton (1979) and the event motivations put forward by McDonnell et al. (1999) it appears that no pull motivates have been applied to event motivations. In other words, the importance of beaches, cultural attractions, natural scenery and shopping (to name a few) have not been considered a motivational factor for event attendees. The question is then, will this be the case for event tourists or will pull factors play a part in their motivation to attend an event and if so how important will they be?

Developing A Motivational Typology

There are several proposed motivational typologies in the tourism literature for vacationers, tourists and travellers and many of these typologies are based on segmentation criteria which have been used to subdivide the travellers into homogeneous groups to assist in the development of targeting and positioning strategies. These criteria can be used separately or in combination. Often demographic criteria (such as age) is used, the benefits the traveller is seeking and the family life cycle.

Several researchers have studied behavioural variables such as holiday activities which tourists take part in when on holiday. Attention has also been given to researching the amount of expenditure distance travelled, chosen destination and frequency of the journeys. Whereas Swarbrooke & Horner (1999) suggested the more traditional criteria based on geography and economy should be used. Decrop & Snelders (2005) note that socio-psychological typologies offer a more integrated picture of the traveller because they connect descriptive aspects of the traveller with sociological or psychological variables. Decrop & Schnelders (2005) typology of socio-psychological variables with references to various researchers.

Whilst the issue of motivation of tourists has come under some scrutiny the typologies of Dann (1977;1981) and Crompton (1979) which provide the framework for developing an event tourism typology as it includes pull factors together with push factors. The categories include escape, self-exploration, social interaction, prestige, regression, relaxation and improvement in relationships together with external cognitive and situational factors. Recent research by Fairley (2003) noted that nostalgia is also a motivating factor for being an event tourist and should also be considered when developing a typology to define an event tourist.

Summary and Conclusion

In summary this paper has drawn attention to a number of significant gaps which have been identified in the literature in relation to event tourists. These are:

- A general reluctance by researchers to adopt a standardised definition of event tourists,
- A general lack of research examining the motivation of event tourists,
- The general lack of current research in providing relevant and reliable constructs known to predict motivations in relation to event tourism.

The limited published evidence available suggests that this could become a valuable source of insight into further development of the understanding of event tourism. As stated previously, limited research has been conducted into the motivational factors influencing event tourists and as it is a global phenomenon it is considered to be of great importance. More research therefore needs to be conducted into this area which will allow a typology to be developed of event tourists.

6

Motivations for Pleasure Vacation

Introduction

The travel market is often divided into four segments: personal business travel, government or corporate business travel, visiting friends and relatives, and pleasure vacation travel. This study focuses on the pleasure vacation travel segment.

The objectives of the research were to identify motives which directed respondents' selection of destination, and to develop a conceptual framework that would integrate such motives. It was anticipated that the motives might provide a basis for subdividing or segmenting those travelling for pleasure.

The concept of a stable equilibrium state is either stated or implied in most theories of motivation. Disequilibrium or tension in the motivational system occurs when some need arises. Disturbance of equilibrium drives the organism to elicit a course of action which is expected to satisfy the need and to restore equilibrium. The action ceases when equilibrium is restored as the result of the need being met. Hence, satisfactory resolution of the tension state is the criterion against which alternative actions are compared, contrasted,: and evaluated.

In the study reported here, the concern was to identify states of tension or causes of disequilibrium which provoked respondents' decisions to select particular vacation destinations.

It is recognized that motivation is only one of many variables which may contribute to explaining tourist behaviour. To expect motivation to account for a large portion of the variance in tourist behaviour is probably asking too much since there may be many other interrelated influences operating. Nevertheless, motivation is considered a critical variable because it is the impelling and compelling force behind it all.

Just what motivates people What does Florence have over sitting in front of the television? Why the Fjords of Norway over Icing on a beach in the sun? Why Bali-or Acapulco? u — or wherever? Even more interestingly, why do some people choose not to take holidays at all? Are they just poor, or do they have ideological objections?

It has been suggested that it is possible to describe the who, when, where and how of tourism, together with the economic and social characteristics of tourists, but not to answer the question "why". Lundberg (1976) in the most recent edition of his basic text devotes a chapter to "Why Tourists Travel," but prefaces it with the comment:

> Because research and established theory are lacking, the comments included here are necessarily impressionistic and made principally to stimulate investigation...the observations that follow make no claim to validity other than a validity based on observation and reflection.

Most discussions of tourist motivation have tended to revolve around the concepts of "pull" and "push." The push factors for a vacation are socio-psychological motives. The pull factors are motives aroused by the destination rather than emerging exclusively from within the traveller himself. In this study, this latter category of motives is termed "cultural". These motives reflected the influence of the destination in arousing them. Traditionally, push motives have been thought useful for explaining the desire to go on a vacation while pull motives have been thought useful for explaining the choice of destination. For example, Dann (1977) states: While a specific resort may hold a number of attractions for the potential tourist, his actual decision to visit such a destination is consequent on his prior need for travel. An examination of "push" factors is thus logically, and often temporally antecedent to that of "pull" factors.

Prominent among the "pull" studies is the world reported by Williams and Zelinski (1970). They studied international tourism flows and partially explained these flows by the term "heliotropic." Gray (1970) suggested a synonymous term "sunlust" which may be a more descriptive term referring to the same phenomenon. Sunlust characterizes vacations which are motivated by the desire to experience different or better amenities for a specific purpose than are available in the environment in which one normally lives. It is prominent with particular activities such as sports, and literally occurs with the search for the sun. Williams and Zelinski (1970) effectively define this phenomenon when they state:

Specifically in those cases where Country B offers singly or in combination contrasting or desirable climatic characteristics, scenic attractions, cultural and historical features, sports, shopping facilities, night life, and so on, either missing or in short supply in Country A, one might expect a significantly high flow from A to B. Gray (1970) suggested that an alternate appeal to sunlust, that destinations may satisfy, is wanderlust. He defined wanderlust as: That basic trait in human nature that causes some individuals to want to experience different existing cultures and places, or the relics of past cultures in places famous for their historical associations, ruins and monuments.

Tourism researchers and writers have displayed a preference towards "cultural" motives in seeking to explain why tourists travel. Similarly, the tourist industry generally has focused on cultural factors in seeking to attract tourists. As a result, a review of the published literature reporting why people select one destination rather than another reveals that relatively little empirical research has been undertaken into socio-psychological motives. It is these motives which emerged as being of prime importance in the study reported here.

The most comprehensive empirical studies reported in the literature which are concerned with socio-psychological motives of tourists are those undertaken by Hill (1965), Plog (1976), and Dann (1977). The studies by Hill and Plog, like the study reported here, both used unstructured interviews to collect their data, focusing upon interpretation of individual responses in search of qualitative insights and understanding. Hill's (1965) study, which was commissioned by the Irish Tourist Board, identified some underlying motives for going on a vacation. These were used by the Irish Tourist Board as primary themes upon which to base its advertising and promotional efforts. Plog (1976) empirically derived typical vacationer profiles, which included motives, of each stage of the life cycle.

Dann (1977) confirmed his hypotheses that the answer to the question "What makes Tourists Travel" lies primarily in the socio-psychological concepts of "anomie" and "ego enhancement." In addition, both of these motives had a strong fantasy component. Underlying the anomie hypothesis is the need that man has for love and affection and the desire to communicate with his fellow man. Dann suggested that there is a desire to transcend the feeling of isolation obtained in everyday life, and that this need for social interaction can only be fulfilled by the individual getting away from it all on vacation. Similarly, Dann argued that man requires to be recognized, and that travel provides opportunity for ego-enhancement or self recognition.

Hill (1965) concluded:

> *A holiday is undertaken in response to a sense of internal damage or depletion and represents a period of replenishment and restoration. When he goes on holiday, the holiday maker is hoping to taller in and store "internal goods" with which he will return enriched, regenerated and recharged to his own environment.*

This appears to support the assumption of most writers in the field of tourism who generally express the primary motive for taking a pleasure vacation in terms of personal enrichment of one kind or another. However, personal enrichment may not be the exclusive prerogative of the pleasure vacation.

Howard and Sheth (1968) distinguish between specific and non-specific motivation. If motivation is specific, it is uniquely satisfied by the pleasure vacation experience. If it is non-specific it can also be satisfied by alternative opportunities available from other sources. For example, Hill reported that for those respondents who could easily give up the opportunity to go on a pleasure vacation, the same tension reliever or internal refreshment was sought in some other kind of activity:

> *It was noticeable that when alternatives to the holiday were mentioned, there existed a fundamental notion of repair and renovation to internal objects. However, for the majority of Hill's respondents, a pleasure vacation was regarded as a more or less essential period of refreshment. It was regarded as virtually priceless. If it has to be forfeited because of pragmatic constraints, this forfeiture was regarded as only temporary.*

The study explored the contention that socio-psychological motives may be useful not only in explaining the initial arousal, energizing, or "push" to take a vacation, but may also have directive potential to direct the tourist toward a particular destination. This differs from the traditional conceptual framework described earlier, in which the primary utility of socio-psychological motives lies in explaining the initial decision to go on a vacation, and the consequent decision, choice of destination, is conceived to be primarily a function of the cultural pulling power of the destination. Motives were a primary focus and typically recurred at a number of points throughout the interviews. The interviews were tape recorded, subsequently transcribed, classified and their content analysed to isolate all data which pertained to motives. The content analysis yielded patterns of responses which provided the basis for the conceptual framework formulated in this paper.

The respondents consisted of a sample of adults who were conveniently available. They resided either in College Station, Texas or in the Greater Boston area of Massachusetts. Nineteen respondents were female and twenty were male. Thirty were married, four were single, and the spouses of five were deceased. Only five respondents did not have children. The age and occupational profile of the sample. The occupational data suggests that the sample primarily was comprised of middle-class respondents.

It is important to note that the study reported here was essentially a qualitative study. Its objectives were limited to identifying, and obtaining insights into, tourists' motivations. Because of the research design, data collection technique, and the limited sample size, this study was not concerned with identifying the distributions of these motives in a population. An investigation into the distribution of these motives, which builds upon the basic work reported here, is currently being undertaken by the author as a subsequent project.

Analysis

A conceptualization of the role and relationships of respondents' underlying states of disequilibrium which emerged from patterns in the data. It identifies four main components.

First, a state of disequilibrium. Second, a break from routine, which was conceptualized as an initial overt manifestation of disequilibrium. Third, three behavioural alternatives: stay at home, go on a pleasure vacation, or travel for other purposes such as visiting friends and relatives or going on a business trip, each of which may provide a break from routine. Fourth, the particular motives which help determine the nature and destination of the pleasure vacation if that alternative is selected. These are aligned along a continuum as being primarily either socio-psychological or cultural.

The Nature of a Break From Routine

Almost every respondent described the essence of a vacation as being a break from routine. These breaks could generally be classified into two categories, short-term and long-term. These appeared to resolve different types of disequilibrium. Short-term disequilibrium seemed to reflect a particular set of circumstances or events which were temporal disruptions to homeostasis. Typically, these were expressed as "pressures." In this situation, a break from routine was perceived to be a necessary and sufficient condition to restore homeostasis. Long-term states of disequilibrium could not usually be satisfied by a single pleasure vacation. Instead these states of disequilibrium were satisfied through an ongoing program of pleasure vacations. A break from routine was perceived as necessary to facilitate the resolution of long-term disequilibrium states, but the break alone was not sufficiently inclusive to resolve the state of tension. Long-term disequilibrium was perceived by respondents as being ever present but postponable. In contrast, short-term disequilibrium demanded immediate attention. In other words, the data suggested that a two tier system of disequilibrium was operating.

This is hypothesized to have meant continuation of doing the same kinds of things but in a different physical, or social context. The essence of "break from routine" was, in most cases, either locating in a different place, or changing the dominant social context from the world milieu, usually to that of the family group, or doing both of these things. The kinds of activities in which people engaged were generally not different, although they were sometimes more concentrated. Respondents' life styles did not change. A break from routine often involved emphasizing particularly desired elements of the life style rather than changing the life style to incorporate different activities. The mundane elements in the routine were discarded, but the preferred discretionary elements of the normal life style were retained.

Motives Influencing Selection of Type of Pleasure Vacation and Destination

Once a desire to go on a pleasure vacation has been established, concern shifts from the impetus dimension of motivation to its directive dimension which serves to guide the tourist toward the selection of a particular type of vacation or destination in preference to all the alternatives of which the tourist is aware. In most decisions more than one motive is operative. Priorities between alternative destinations are a function of the intensity of the particular combination of motives which are dominant in a hierarchy of motives at a particular moment of time. This hierarchy of motives construct helps to explain divergent reaction at different points in time by the same respondent to the same stimuli.

The data suggested that respondents' motives usefully could be conceptualized as being located along a cultural — socio-psychological disequilibrium continuum. Much of the tourist industry's modus operandi is based upon the assumption that tourists are attracted to a destination by the particular cultural opportunities or special attributes that it offers. However, the findings of this study suggested that for some respondents, the destination itself was relatively unimportant.

Respondents did not go to particular locations to seek cultural insights or artifacts; rather they went for socio-psychological reasons unrelated to any specific destination. The destination served merely as a medium through which these motives could be satisfied. The following sections of the analysis briefly discuss each of the motives empirically identified in this study, and categorize them as being located either toward the socio-psychological or the cultural end of the continuum.

Socio-Psychological Motives

Socio-psychological motives were rarely overtly identified by respondents in early discussion of their pleasure vacation experiences. These motives were difficult for respondents to articulate.

However, as the interview proceeded, it often became apparent that while initial concern and effort had been with selecting a vacation destination, the value, benefits, and satisfactions derived from the vacation were neither related to, nor derived from, a particular destination's attributes. Rather the satisfactions were related to social or psychological factors unique to the particular individual or group involved. In effect, these motives represented a hidden agenda. This suggests that one of the reasons that some people do not take pleasure vacations is unknown. The data suggested seven socio-psychological motives which served to direct pleasure vacation behaviour. These motives were: escape from a perceived mundane environment; exploration and evaluation of self; relaxation; prestige; regression; enhancement of kinship relationships; and facilitation of social interaction.

Escape from a Perceived Mundane Environment

A temporary change of environment was a frequently expressed respondent motive. Even the most prized living environments sometimes became mundane to those living there. For example, one respondent who lived on Cape Cod indicated that when crowds of people descend upon the Cape in the summer, many of the local residents go to Maine, New Hampshire, or Vermont to avoid the crowds. Escape was sought not only from the general residential locale but also from the specific home and job environments. There did not appear to be any single optimum type of environment that facilitated escape.

The critical ingredient was only that the pleasure vacation context should be physically and socially different from the environment in which one normally lives. For some respondents, the escape offered by a pleasure vacation was for a much longer time period than the actual trip. As Clawson and Knetsch (1966) have suggested, anticipation of the trip was an important ingredient of the total experience. One respondent commented that "You are sustained a little through the winter, first by anticipation of Christmas, then by anticipation of the trip in February or March. It is something to which I look forward in the long winter."

Exploration and Evaluation of Self

The data suggested that a pleasure vacation may be viewed by some people as an opportunity for re-evaluating and discovering more about themselves or for acting out self-images and in so doing refining or modifying them. For example, one respondent commented:

> *This trip put a lot of things in perspective for me. It helped me to get a clearer picture of myself because I put myself in different situations. I saw how I interacted with other people in other conditions. I had some constraints come up, some hardships, and I had to deal with that. It gave me a chance to see what is inside of me and how that would come out, without any outside pressures. You don't find this out when you go to the office from eight to five.*

Self-discovery emerged as a result of transposition into a new situation. The novelty of the physical and social context appeared to be an essential ingredient in the process. These insights into the person's self could not be achieved by staying at home or visiting friends and relatives. In the case of the latter there would be outside pressure serving to ameliorate hardship, and hence dilute the value of the experience, because of the accessibility of friendly other people. In the case of the former, there would be less likelihood of finding different situations or conditions.

Exposure to a different milieu sometimes caused a revision of existing perceptions of self-status and enhanced feelings of self-worth. A respondent who was a boat be of low status in that community, but on pleasure vacations, " I see people who are a lot worse off than I am, and I sort of appreciate what we do have." Other respondents stressed that exposure to a different milieu for a period of time served as a reference point re-evaluation of their own life style.

Self-discovery was not confined only to those respondents who went camping or sought inexpensive pleasure vacations. The wealthiest and most widely travelled respondent in the sample expressed similar sentiments. After a cruise vacation in which she found that she was not disposed to the socializing and organized activities which characterized the experience she commented, "I learned a lot about myself on that cruise."

Relaxation

The term relaxation was a constant respondent theme, but its use was often ambivalent. Generally, there was a reluctance on the part of respondents to relax physically. Respondents would say they felt relaxed and then admit that they came home physically exhausted. It was apparent that the term relaxation referred to a mental state rather than a physical relaxation. Given this interpretation it was possible to reconcile physical exhaustion or fatigue as being mentally refreshing and relaxing.

Relaxation meant talking the time to pursue activities of interest. The activities selected were often a reflection of the increased time available at the vacation destination. In the rhythm of the normal routine, the mind was not directed toward these hobbies or interests. These interests were not selectively perceived because they were not pertinent to the prevailing train of thought or dominant motive.

Most respondents indicated that they were fatigued upon their return home from the exertions expended on the vacation and on associated travel. This fatigue factor together with the contribution the vacation has made to ameliorating tension states possibly accounted for the sentiment that respondents frequently expressed, "I am always delighted to go on a vacation, but I am just as delighted to return home again."

Prestige

Although some respondents suggested prestige was a primary motivating factor in other people's trips, few of them accepted that there was any prestige motive involved in their own pleasure vacation decisions. It may be that as travel has become more frequent, it is perceived to be less prestigious. Travel may have become part of the indigenous life style rather than symbolic of a higher life style. Prestige potential disappears with frequency of exposure.

Regression

Some respondents suggested that a pleasure vacation provided an opportunity to do thingswhich were inconceivable within the context of their usual life styles. The things respondents' cited were often puerile, irrational, and more reminiscent of adolescent or child behaviour than mature adult behaviour. The opportunity to engage in this behaviour was facilitated by withdrawal from usual role obligations. On vacation, respondents were freed of the mores that inhibit capacity for this type of enjoyment. One respondent stated, "My life style is free and more relaxed when I go away from home. I let my guard down more than I would at home." While puerility was the prevailing form of regressive behaviour, another form was identified by some respondents. This was the search for the life style of a previous era. This is sometimes referred to as the "nostalgia factor." In essence, the desire was to regress to a less complex, less changeable, less technologically advanced environment. For example, a respondent stated that she and her friends were:

> *Looking for the simple life. We are not looking for big cities, but are looking for peasants of the soil. A lot of us are very romantic. We want to go out and see the fields; to escape Americanism.*

Like the puerile regression state, this search for the life style of a previous era is a transitory, ephemeral tension state, and when homeostasis is restored, return to the routine of life is accepted. The actuality frequently is not congruent with the image, for as the same respondent commented, "It depends where they go, but a lot of people come back not always totally satisfied."

Enhancement of Kinship Relationships

Many respondents perceived the pleasure vacation as a time when family members were brought close together. Hence, the pleasure vacation served as a medium through which family relationships could be enhanced or enriched. This enhancement is often facilitated by long drives in an automobile because family members are physically juxtaposed for long periods and forced to interact with each other. It is inevitable that a much greater exchange and understanding of each other is likely to occur than in the normal routine situation in which family members go in different directions interacting only spasmodically. The essence of this tension state was well expressed by a respondent who stated:

> The important notion is being out of routine. It isn't that you are away from a place anymore than you are at a place. What is different is the act that you are together as a family. You are able to put aside the other kinds of responsibilities that each of you may have that would otherwise be impinging themselves upon that notion of focusing inwards and putting things together.

Facilitation of Social Interaction

It was evident that an important motive for some respondents going on a pleasure vacation was to meet new people in different locations. These trips were people oriented rather than place oriented. Like several of the other motives which were located towards the socio-psychological end of the disequilibrium continuum, respondents often became aware of this motive only after the trip was completed.

A variety of dimensions of this motive emerged from the data. For some respondents, an opportunity for transitory meetings with others from outside familiar reference groups to exchange views, was all that was sought. Others were seeking more permanent relationships that would serve to extend their range of social contacts. Several observed that interaction with non-familiar people was more likely. In some cases, social contact was initiated by children, who were a common ingredient shared by some parties. The physical planning of accommodations was also perceived to be an ameliorating factor, for if the accommodations were closely juxtaposed they facilitated interaction.

Although several respondents expressed a desire to interact with local people in the destination area, they reported that this was frequently difficult to achieve. Most interaction was with other tourists in the area. There was little common identity with local people who were serving as waitresses, and much more with other tourists who were also waiting in line or visiting a particular attraction for the first time. Some respondents suggested that travelling with others may inhibit opportunities for interacting with local people at the destination. The availability of companions provided built-in entertainment and removed the urge to visit with others outside of the group; the natural tendency was to turn inward rather than outward.

The organized tour was a preferred type of vacation for some respondents because it served as a vehicle for facilitating social intercourse as well as being financially expedient. The prime ingredients inducing the camaraderie which respondents reported from tour experiences appeared to be the sharing of many dimensions of the experience and close physical juxtaposition with others. Some participated regularly in group tours which were arranged locally and were comprised of people who knew others in the group from the outset. In essence, these people were taking some of their home social environment with them to a different location. The existence of a nucleus of known people provided a good foundation upon which to establish new social relationships through introductions. In addition, the group often had a common interest which facilitated social interaction. For example, it may be comprised of lawyers, teachers, doctors, rose growers, or home builders.

Cultural Motives

Motives located towards this end of the continuum were concerned with the destination rather than with the social and psychological status of the individual. Most respondents explained their reasons for going on pleasure vacations in terms of cultural motives. In many cases, cultural motives were more apparent than real. In other cases, the data suggested that many respondents did not receive socio-psychological satisfactions, but received almost exclusively cultural benefits.

Two primary cultural motives were expressed. They were novelty and education. These may be related since exposure to new destinations, sights, and experiences is presumably educational. However, respondents did not always perceive this relation ship and hence they are discussed separately.

Novelty

Novelty was defined by respondents in a variety of ways. Synonyms included curiosity, adventure, new and different. Novel meant new experience but it did not necessarily mean entirely new knowledge. Often respondents knew a lot about a place. The novelty resulted from actually seeing something rather than simply knowing of it vicariously.

A prefer*ence for going to a previously unvisited destination was a consistent factor. This* aspect had previously proved satisfactory, rather than to purchase a brand with which they have had no previous experience. Generally, this does not appear to apply to pleasure vacations. Cultural disequilibrium appears to be an on-going state which requires a supply of fresh cultural stimuli to restore homeostasis. In most cases, respondents anticipated that re-experiencing known cultural stimuli would not contribute as much as experiencing new stimuli to reducing the tension state. Hence, when the pleasure vacation product was purchased, a different destination brand was selected by respondents.

At the same time, there were some respondents who returned to a previously visited vacation destination. In some cases, the same destination was selected each year. While the data did not enable the reasons for this to be identified, it may be speculated that three factors account for this phenomenon.

First, habitual destination respondents may be motivated primarily by socio-psychological rather than cultural motives. Second, they may have restricted knowledge of the want satisfying attributes of other places. Returning to a proven destination reduces the risk that an unfamiliar alternative may not be as satisfying as those previously experienced. The third factor may be fear, or anxiety of the unknown, which is removed by revisiting a destination.

The urge for new and adventurous experiences was frequently compromised by the felt need to minimize rises of exposure to novelty which may be threatening. One respondent, who was a travel agent, pointed out that for some people, it was a fearful experience to go into an unknown situation in a country where the people did not speak your language. These people "would like to go away from home but they also have the desire to be taken care of. That is why you get tours and tour conductors, because it is a security blanket." People used organized tours to introduce themselves to travel, its problems and associated fears. Organized tours served to remove any anxiety or exposure to unfamiliar situations that may have been threatening.

An alternative strategy to the organized tour for reducing anxiety and fear was to experience the unknown by starting with the known and using that as a base. For example, a number of respondents indicated that they had visited the Mexican border towns, but had no intention of going further into Mexico. The border towns were close to the perceived safety of the known United States and could thus be experienced relatively quickly with minimal anxiety. Similarly, some of the respondents who had visited Europe indicated that they started in the United Kingdom where they knew the language, or in a country that they had previously visited, so that there was some familiarity. From this relatively familiar base, sorties were made into new areas. When they felt comfortable there, the process was repeated and exploration extended to their new destinations.

Education

The positive influence of pleasure vacations on childrens's' education was exhorted by most respondents and in some cases was the primary consideration in the selection of a destination. Education was perceived as a means of developing a rounded individual. One respondent suggested, "As a generalization, those who have been on vacation, and have travelled, are usually more interesting to talk with than those who have not."

It was perceived as almost a moral obligation to take the opportunity to visit a distinctive phenomenon, particularly if it was reasonably accessible. The sense of "ought" to see and experience a particular place frequently meant that circumstances, especially present location, had been the trigger which initiated selection of a destination. Cultural disequilibrium was not site or destination specific. It did not relate to one particular place, but it was generally applicable to all places. Hence, there was a feeling expressed by several respondents that, "I ought to go because I am here," particularly if it was anticipated that the present residential location was transitory. In this situation, it may have been perceived as the one opportunity in a lifetime to see particular cultural phenomena. If the opportunity was not grasped then educational benefits were lost.

Conclusions and Implications

Delineation of underlying motives offers useful insights into understanding the destination selection decision process. All else equal, preference is likely to be given to a destination which is perceived as most likely to service the dominant motive. Nine motives were identified. Seven of these were located towards the socio-psychological end of the disequilibrium continuum and two towards the cultural end. For ease of exposition, the motives were discussed as separate entities. However, they should not be considered as mutually exclusive, nor should any single tension state be selected as the determinant of behaviour. They operate in tandem or combination, for motives are multidimensional.

Thus, destination decisions were usually energized by several motives acting in tandem. The study suggested that any given destination can in principle attract customers whose motivations are neither homogeneous nor necessarily compatible. While the study gave no indication of the distribution of the two disequilibrium states in the population, it suggested that more attention usefully could be given by the tourist industry to socio-psychological disequilibrium in developing its product and promotion strategies than is presenting the case. The tourist industry's modus operandi is based upon the assumption that people go on vacation to do and see things. The data suggested that, for many respondents, this assumption is challengeable. They have been conditioned to thinking in terms of destination, but a number of motives emerged from the data which were not place specific. Consumers motivated by socio-psychological motives were not looking for uniqueness in the product. That is, some specific attribute it possessed which other destinations did not have. The pleasure vacation destination was not perceived by most respondents as a "speciality good."

There appear to be two directions which could usefully be pursued profitably by the tourist industry if it accepts the significance and role of socio-psychological tension states in pleasure vacation decisions suggested in this study. First, efforts are required to arouse people's awareness of their own real motives. The in-depth interviews caused many respondents to confront for the first time their real motives for going on a pleasure vacation. Several commented similarly to the respondent who stated, "This is interesting, I am learning all these things about myself." They expressed surprise at what they revealed, for the motives which ultimately emerged were often radically different from the reasons they were accustomed to giving for going on a vacation. The interviews proved to be an exercise in self-discovery. The role of the travel agent may be a factor. These details were discovered through interviews, then the counsellor would be in a much better position to recommend the most appropriate type of pleasure vacation and destination. The second direction lies in the development of the destination product and its promotion.

The motives may be used as a basis for market segmentation. They provide cues and insights around which destinations can develop and promote their product to target segments. Supplier efforts have generally focused on unique amenities and facilities of the destination. Socio-psychological tension states suggest that this may not be the most appropriate strategy. For example, the escape from a mundane environment, exploration of self, and regression motives, require only a destination which is physically and socially different from the residential environment. Literally thousands of destinations could meet these criteria and thus serve as direct substitutes. The detailed cultural attractions of a destination are not important in this context. The best promotion strategies for this market segment may be to stress the contribution the destination can make to reducing these disequilibrium states and to stress price advantages.

Those destinations seeking to cater to the relaxation motive may stress familiarity and the availability of facilities to enjoy preferred activities rather than a radically different environment or new activities. Destinations targeting at the prestige market segment may emphasize their unique qualities as a destination, rather than the activities or facilities available. This uniqueness must be fairly widely disseminated so that it is known to peer groups in order that they are able to confer upon members appropriate prestige for visiting it. At the same time it should not be promoted as a popular mass destination. The social interaction motive may be accommodated by physical juxtaposition of parties and organized programming, while enhancement of kinship relationships may be a useful theme for promoting family pleasure vacations.

Cultural disequilibrium referred to the desire to see new places or do things in a different environment. It is this motive to which most tourist supplier effort is presently directed. Two culturally oriented motives were identified. These were novelty and education.

Novelty implied that there was no desire to return to a previously visited destination no matter how successful the vacation. This lack of "brand loyalty" may be ameliorated by establishing a network of cross recommendations. That is, agreement between destinations to recommend satisfied consumers to a destination with similar characteristics in a different location. Chain and franchise organizations offer illustration of this at the individual motel or fast-food facility level. For example, if the vacationer enjoyed Dade County, Florida, they may be recommended to try the Rio Grande Valley region of Texas, or Orange County, California. This offers the credibility accrued by the proven destination that there is a good probability of the vacationer enjoying a similarly satisfying experience in a different cultural context.

To remove the fear inhibition present for some in contemplating a novel pleasure vacation, the organized tour may more prominently promote its anxiety reducing potential, rather than concentrating exclusively on price advantage which is its present tendency. Similarly destinations may stress the attributes with which vacationers were likely to feel familiar, that is their recognizable cultural ties, before pointing out cultural differences. Establishing the known before proceeding to the unknown.

Educational prowess may be useful in attracting vacationers for whom the education motive is dominant. Finally, many respondents changed residential location frequently. Location appeared to be an important ingredient in bringing the education motive state to the head of the hierarchy of motives.

This suggests that people are likely to be susceptible to promotions reminding them that the opportunity to visit a destination in reasonable proximity may not arise again. People went on pleasure vacation to satisfy a variety of different motives. As a result, the attributes which might attract them to a destination differed. The implications suggested in the above paragraphs are intended to be illustrative of how these data may be applied rather than exhaustive. Specific implications appropriate to a particular destination will according to its attributes, environmental niche and goals.

Theoretical Aspects of the Sustainable Tourism Strategies

In order to identify the importance and appropriateness of the sustainable tourism strategy in the growth and development of the industry, it has to identify the theoretical support. The major tourism theories are discussed here for identifying how the CSR concept is relevant in the tourism development and growth.

Tourism theories: Travel and tourism theories are mostly based on travel motivation. The basic factors that influence the travelling decisions are tourist need satisfaction, customer satisfaction and destination loyalty. Tourist motivation factors have higher influence on the tourist behaviour of travellers with regard to their destination choice, needs, goals and preferences. In case of ecotourism, social psychological desire to break out from the habitual ordinary life is the primary push factor. The major pull factors which force travellers to take travel decisions are destination attributes such as natural attractions like wild life and immaculate environment.

As per the theory of Iso-Ahola interpersonal escape and interpersonal seeking motivate tourism and recreation among the individuals. In case of personal seeking and personal escape dimensions, tourism experiences have great role in motivation. Sporting events, beaches, amusement parks, and natural parks improves the motivational levels of tourism and recreational activities to a greater extent. Tourism motivation in holiday trips is the desire to travel for satisfying the internal needs and wants. Incentive tourism is a motivational tool among the employees as well as other organizational personnel.

Most of the weekend travel decisions are related to the intention to take rest and spend the weekend for relaxation. Travel behaviour among individuals can be described as a function of quantifiable aspects such as socio-demographic characteristics and physical characteristics of the region. Most of the travelling decisions are situational in nature.

Travel behaviour of individuals is influenced by individual personality, attitudes and perceptions. Attitude of travellers has influence on beliefs and behaviour in travel decision such as the frequency of use. Novelty seeking is the prime motivating factor that affects the travelling of most of the individuals. The positive and negative feed back from the travel affect their future decision to travel a particular destination.

The motivational factors have a key role in the tourist decision making behaviour. In the motivational factors, push and pull concept was introduced by Crompton and Chon in 1979.

Push factors affect the desire for travel whereas pull factors affect the actual destination choice. In the concept of Crompton 1979, there are nine motive factors influencing the leisure travellers. Seven of them are socio psychological factors and two are cultural motives. Push factors are internal factors whereas pull factors are external The seven push factors include, making a change in the routine life environment, meeting self needs, relaxation, establishing social relationships, prestige and social interaction. Novelty and education are the pull factors. According to Iso-Ahola, 1980, there are mainly two motivational factors in tourist behaviour. The first feature is approach, focusing on recreational opportunities for intrinsic rewards, and the second feature is avoidance which is escape oriented. The increasing trend of shorter holiday breaks is a signal of escape dimension among the tourists behaviour.

The study by Teare (1994) on peoples' motives for selecting hotel leisure breaks in the UK states that there are six factors such as attending a pre arranged event, as a break from personal commitments, as well as employment pressures, to fulfil the desire of relaxation or visit a particular destination and to exploit the seasonal benefits of short breaks. The personal motivation factor may differ as per individual behaviour. When considering the theoretical concepts it revealed that protection of the natural environment is an essential factor for motivating the travellers to visit the destinations.

Through the keeping of novelty of the destination environment, its attraction can be sustained over a longer period of time. Thus the tourism theories better support the appropriateness of sustainable tourism strategy for the sustainable growth of the industry. Motivation for travel is a complex area of tourism research. Sharpley (1994) identifies many factors which motivate people to travel. These include a personal need to escape from daily routines, to visit friends and relatives or to learn about other cultures. To understand an individual's motivation to travel, it is necessary to examine their desires, needs, experience and preferences and social, economic and demographic circumstances as well as prevailing social norms and customs.

Although there is a large amount of literature on what motivates people to undertake travel and tourism, the quantity of research into cultural tourist motivation is limited. In particular, there are few studies or surveys of international visitors' motivations and attitudes to Australia's cultural attractions, events and products, despite considerable interest in the Australian cultural tourism industry. Some people, like the English elite who undertook the Grand Tour in the sixteenth and seventeenth centuries, are motivated to travel because of culture.

Such visitors, therefore, can be termed 'specific' cultural or culturally motivated visitors. However, for most people, culture is not a sole motive for travel. Rather, participation in cultural activities is one potential component of a travel itinerary and may occur if opportunities arise. Visitors for whom this is the case can be called 'general' cultural visitors.

Studies of the Motivations of Cultural Visitors

According to some tourist motivation theories, motivations are developed as a result of 'pull' and 'push' factors. Pull factors relate to the characteristics or attractions of a travel destination. For cultural tourists visiting Australia, they include attractions such as the Sydney Opera House and Aboriginal sites. Push factors relate to the needs and wants of individuals that lead them to 'buy' particular holidays. For cultural tourism and tourism as a whole, they include the desire for social interaction and relaxation, to experience something different and to learn about themselves and the places they visit for participating in cultural activities. Other researchers have identified more specific motivations.

Motivation Theory

"Crompton (1979) notes it is possible to describe the who, when, where, and how of tourism, together with the social and economic characteristics of tourist, but not to answer the question "why," the most interesting question of all tourist behaviour."

While motivation is only one of many variables in explaining tourist behaviour, it is nonetheless a very critical one, as it constitutes the driving force behind all behaviour. Motivation sets the stage for forming people's goals and is reflected in both travel choice and behaviour; as such it influences people's expectations, which in turn determine the perception of experiences. Motivation is therefore a factor in satisfaction formation.

Basic motivation theory suggests a dynamic process of internal psychological factors (needs, wants and goals), causing an uncomfortable level of tension within individuals' minds and bodies, resulting in actions aimed at releasing that tension and satisfying these needs. Motives, implying such an action, require the awareness of needs, as well as objectives, promising to satisfy these now conscious needs in order to create wants and move people to buy. Objectives or goals are presented in the form of products and services, it is therefore the role of marketing to create awareness of needs and suggest appropriate objectives, promising the satisfaction of these.

Several authors suggest that in the Western World free time and holidays are connected to the concept of self-actualisation or self-realisation. The latter defined by Grunow-Lutter (1983.) as *"a person's dynamic relationship between the real and the ideal self, constituting a process of decreasing the distance between these two cognitive systems, themselves subject to continuous change."* It is the individual's aim to achieve a state of stability, or homeostasis, which is disrupted when the person becomes aware of the gap between real and ideal self, or as Goosens calls it a need deficiency. The resulting need to self-actualise represents the motive, which under the constraints of the situation sets the stage for the process of motivation. But to what extent does tourism satisfy the intrinsic need for self-actualisation? Tinsley and Eldredge (1995) summarise 15 years of research into psychological needs, satisfied by leisure activities, and proposed leisure activities clusters such as novelty, sensual enjoyment, cognitive stimulation, self-expression, creativity, vicarious competition, relaxation, agency, belongingness and service. It is questioned however; whether these superficial needs are intrinsically motivated, suggesting that these motivations are merely culturally learned stereotypes or explanations for leisure behaviour. As Fodness (1994) states, a widely accepted integrated theory for needs and goals behind motivation is lacking. The question is of course why this is the case.

Research into motivation can be distinguished into two categories, the behaviourist and the cognivist approach. The discussion has therefore traditionally revolved around either push or pull factors influencing tourist behaviour. Push factors represent lasting dispositions, as they are internally generated drives. The individual, energised by such drives, will then search objects for the promise of drive reduction and develop a motive. The behaviourist view thus emphasises the emotional parameter of decision-making, while the cognivist approach focuses on situational parameters in which motives are expressed, consequently encompassing a certain knowledge which the tourist holds about goal attributes as well as a rational weighing up of situational constraints. This cognitive process results in motivations, which are more object specific than motives, as these only imply a class of objects and may result in a range of different behaviours, depending on the situation.

This unidimensional approach has been criticised however, as push and pull factors influence the consumer simultaneously, integrated by the concept of involvement, an unobservable state of motivation, arousal, or interest, which is evoked by stimulus or situations. This is the case, since pull factors such as marketing stimuli as well as the destination's and service's attributes respond to and reinforce push factors. Consequently research increasingly seeks to integrate emotions and cognition in the individual's decision-making process, indicating a more holistic approach.

As a result it became evident that people's intrinsic needs are influenced by external factors. Rojek (1990) asserts that in post-modern society the superstructure of advertising, television, fashion, lifestyle magazines and designer values increasingly take the role of forming knowledge and beliefs. People's needs are neutral, as motives however, they require an object towards which the need is directed, and when linked to actual situations, cultural and social impacts are also applied. Situations raise motives to the level of values, as such they are evaluations based on learned behaviour and perception.

If a drive is reduced satisfactorily the individual is likely to remember the behaviour and employ the same behaviour again, thus acquiring habits. Tourism experiences may therefore become learned behaviour and acquire the role of habit enforcers. Cognivists argue that knowledge and beliefs in future rewards, anticipatory in nature, are equally a product of formerly encountered situations, and external formation.

It may be concluded that motives merely represent learned behaviour, which are influenced by offered objects or tourism activities, while motivations represent knowledge and beliefs formed by society and culture or tourism marketers. The psychogenic need for self-actualisation, abstract in nature, is therefore operationalised in a learned and practical manner and expressed in values, which are learned strategies to either adapt one's environment to one's needs or adapt one's self to a given environment. Such values equally include effects of enculturation and socialisation. Furthermore the perceived gap between real and ideal self, may indicate both externally and internally controlled evaluations. McCabe therefore asks what researchers can expect to know about individuals' drives, by asking them about their motivations and needs as these may not be available to individuals as part of their consciousness (2000a,). Iso-Ahola (1982) states that *"people do not walk around with numerous leisure needs in their minds and do not rationalise specific causes of participation if their involvement is intrinsically motivated"* (cited in Goosens 2000). Hence it may be assumed that needs are suggested by immediate social peers, and the wider context of particular social realities as well as the influence of the media. Yet as Weissinger and Bandalos (1995) stress, intrinsic leisure motivation, which is a global disposition and describes a tendency to seek intrinsic rewards, is characterised by self-determination, an awareness of internal needs and a strong desire to make free choices based on these needs.

While self-actualisation may be accepted as a need intrinsic to all individuals, society exercises a great deal of influence on the formation of the ideal self and thus perceived needs. However the notion of authentic or true self, determined by way of experience, offers a solution to the predicament. According to Waterman (1984), individualism symbolises four psychological qualities, the first one is a sense of individual identity, based on the knowledge of who one is and what one's goals and values are, as such it is related to the philosophical concept of true self, which indicates what an individual reckons personally expressive and what it is to be actualised. The second is Maslow's self-actualisation, which is the driving to be one's true self. The third quality is Rotter's (1966) internal locus of control, which reflects a willingness to accept personal responsibility for one's life, and finally principles (postconventional), moral reasoning, which involves consistency with general abstract principles.

Consequently, only if tourists become more autonomous and thus aware of intrinsic needs and motives are they able to self-actualise. As McIntosh and Goeldner (1990) explained, order is becoming less important in Western society and a desire for disorder in the tourism experience is becoming more important. Kim and Lee point out that *"opportunities for unplanned action and freedom from institutionalised regulations are distinctive of Western tourists"* (2000). This indicates that tourists exhibit a certain desire to liberate their identities. According to Krippendorf (1984), in order for tourists to cease being just users of holidays, they must come to know themselves, their motives and other cultures. It may therefore be assumed that self-actualisation is an intrinsic need, characteristic of any tourist, but must be understood in terms of true self as opposed to ideal self and as such is independent of societal pressures and involves the transcendence of habitual behaviours and mindstates. This proposition requires further elaboration and must be viewed in the context of modernity, which hinders this process but at the same time brought about its awareness.

The Escape Motivation

Recently, means-end theory has been applied to recreation and leisure settings by using the laddering method to investigate activities such as ski destination selection, spring break destination choice, nature park interpretation and marketing for urban tourism what a product is, what it does and what people get from it.

These form the three main elements of focus in means-end theory, starting with the physical, observable *attributes* (the "means"), *consequences* (benefits or costs) that follow from the attributes, which further lead to personal *values* (the "ends"). Means-end theory focuses on why and how product attributes are important. Attributes! Consequence (benefits or costs)! Value different) at either end based on personal values.

Individuals are attracted to a particular destination based on a variety of factors such as one's personal traits and leisure and travel motivation grounded within a broad conceptual push-pull scenario. Leisure and recreation are important motives for amenity migrants. This model contends that motivation to reside specific to the Bow Valley include a desire to balance a mountain recreation lifestyle with work, to be with a friend or partner, to escape, to purchase a second home, to be in a place suits one's values, to be next to the (aesthetic lifestyle) mountains and to pursue a career in tourism or parks. Factor analysis results revealed two factor components labelled To Live and To Escape. The former included to pursue a career in tourism, hospitality or parks, to start a business, to balance work with a mountain recreation lifestyle and just to be with a friend or partner while the former included to own a second home and to escape.

Lived Experience of Negotiated Leisure. The leisure negotiation process is framed by the human-environment relationship and remains dynamic due to constant evaluations of the one's ability to negotiate aspects of a changing environment with one's personal resources. The lived experience component of the model includes the element of leisure and recreation behaviour.

Behaviour is important as it is postulated here that leisure/recreation behaviour imprints the destination through the expression of demand. For example, the persistent behaviour of mountain biking may result in the development of additional mountain trails, a built mountain bike park, or even the banning of mountain biking from certain or all trails. Likewise, the presence of upper middle class urban dwellers may bring about a perceived demand for up-scale restaurants and cafes. Or the presence of families with children may bring increased demand for traditional recreation facilities such as pools and ice arenas. Recreation behaviour is an expression of demand which is likely to impact supply thereby altering the environment.

Environment: The environment within a high recreation amenity destination can be characterized as having significant natural and cultural resources. It involves a strong social component of community and reference groups. The social element can also include detractions such as crowding, congestion and other forms of conflict such as with recent and long time residents. It also includes structural components such as the economy, housing, roads and health and educational infrastructure which all contribute to the negotiation. Physical, social and structural aspects of the environment are assumed to act both as a facilitator to one's leisure goals, and constraint or stressor at different times. It is also assumed that over time the nature and character of the Environment evolves (dotted line) as the physical and social aspects of the destination evolve.

Negotiation and Coping Strategies: From a leisure and recreation perspective negotiation with one's internal and external constraints is widely understood within the Leisure Constraints model which includes three basic levels of leisure constraint of intra-personal, interpersonal and structural. The Leisure Constraints model is perhaps best suited to understanding what aspect of the internal (personal traits and motivation) and external (physical, social and structural) environments are being negotiated and how. The Recreation Coping model is used to understand the way in which people respond to stressors within a recreation setting.

The Recreation Coping model posits that individuals will respond using one of more of four possible responses to stress within a recreation environment they include two cognitive based responses of rationalization and product shift and two behavioural based responses of displacement and direct action. It is postulated that an individual will begin leisure and recreation negotiations relying on typical leisure constraint negotiations for the selection and pursuit of activities and behaviours. With increased time at the site it is believed that an individual will rely more heavily on recreation coping strategies as various types of stressors persist and complimentary strategies are found. However, it is assumed that despite the shift in emphasis over time both leisure constraint and recreation coping negotiation strategies may be present at any one time.

Amenity Migrant Typology: Resulting from Motivation and the dynamic of the leisure centred human-environment negotiation is a typology of amenity migrants based on the findings of this investigation. The typology is primarily based on the qualitative data analysis and appears in Box A. The typology is a result of different types (what is being negotiated) and levels (intensity) of negotiation within the human environment. Various amenity migrant typologies appear in the literature. Factor analysis results revealed four distinct factor components based on importance of recreation amenities they include; back country, culture, recreation and entertainment.

Amenity Migrant Typology

1. Those who wish to pursue a mountain recreation lifestyle in the Bow Valley rely on it for their livelihood but can not negotiate the costs over the benefits and decide to leave;

2. Those who wish to pursue a mountain recreation lifestyle in the Bow Valley and rely on it for their livelihood but negotiate to overcome the costs for the benefit;
3. Those who live in the Bow Valley to pursue more urban recreation and hospitality & tourism careers within the area;
4. Those who wish to pursue a mountain recreation lifestyle but do not rely on the Bow Valley for their livelihood directly (commute or remote work situations); and
5. Those who wish to escape to the Bow Valley part-time (second home) and do not rely on the valley for their livelihood.

Place Attachment, Dependence, and Identity. The relationship the individual recreationist develops with the place over time can be understood using the concept of place attachment including underlying concepts of place dependence and identity.

Together, as place attachment, it is used to characterize the continuous manifestation of the human-environment negotiation as a relationship with the place. Place attachment, dependence and identity are assumed to be strong predictors of whether an individual will stay or leave a destination. Some will leave and others will remain. Even those who leave the site impact the evolution of the destination as was their behaviour an expression of demand for the tenure of their residency. Those who leave may be seeking other destinations more supportive of their identity, goals and personal resources. Those who remain impact the destination through their behaviour, and in other ways such as policy development, and through on-going, shared discourse that creates a collective understanding of place. Place attachment loops back (dotted line) to motivation as the individual's relationship with the place will be affected by the continuous negotiation process which is assumed to influence one's motivation to engage in future negotiations and in what manner. Place attachment loops back as an antecedent to the continuous negotiation process.

Affect on Destination and Recreation Supply. The final component of the models seeks to provide insight into how the leisure based human-environment relationship physically affects a high recreation amenity destination. It is postulated here that as population increases urban-type recreation supply increases and backcountry (outside of the townsite) generally remains stagnant or decreases. This general pattern has been previously observed. For example Glorioso & Moss (2006) discuss the rapid increase of urban amenities in the Santa Fe region during the 1980s to present in association with amenity migration. Moore, Williams & Gill (2006) report loss of recreation land adjacent to Whistler BC townsite as a result of residential and golf course development coupled with increased urbanization. As the destination evolves including the quantity and quality of urban and recreation supply this will result in an equally evolving image of the destination that will serve to attract different types of individuals. This is a simple displacement process similar the Plog's (2002) model, however based on tourists, whereby a destination evolves and as it does it attracts 'venturerers' at first then 'dependables' later on. Similarly, early, density-crowding-satisfaction models realized that within any one site varying conditions would attract different groups of people more or less comfortable with crowding conditions. The quantitative survey included a 27-item scale to assess whether residents perceived change in their recreation and structural environment in the form of increases or decreases in urban-type recreation, backcountry recreation, tourism activity, and structural elements such as jobs, housing and cost of living.

Factor analysis on the scale revealed seven factor components in accordance to where most change has been perceived (no particular direction of change) they were labelled as crowding, backcountry, urbane, town, outdoor recreation, and urban. A five-cluster solution revealed that overall some factor components were perceived to have increased and others decreased. More specifically, overall factor components 'crowding' (seven crowding related items) and 'urbane' (four items related to cafes, restaurants, and bars) were perceived to have increased while 'outdoor' (four items related to trails, ski areas, festivals), 'backcountry' (four items related to more remote outdoor activity), was perceived to have decreased while 'town' (five items related to structural aspects and public recreation) has remained about the same. The quantitative results generally support the final component of the model whereby in-town recreation supply increases while backcountry recreation increases. The results of cluster analysis on one of the four measures contained within the questionnaire. The sub-scale means for each of the clusters, the composite mean for each cluster, a cluster label and the results of the Scheffe test. The scale for Q8 was a six point scale with the final scale item of 'don't know' recoded as missing therefore it is based on a five point scale whereby 1 has increased greatly 3 is has not changed and 5 is has decreased greatly.

An ANOVA was conducted to determine if there were differences among the means of the clusters which yielded value of for each of the subscale items. A post hoc analysis of a Scheffe Test was conducted to determine which clusters are significantly different from which and in what direction. Numerous significant tests (p=.05) were reported with the direction of difference indicated by the arrow. Additionally Classification Results(a) test reported that 97.2% of the originally grouped cases were classified correctly.

Indicate that overall some factor components are perceived to be increasing and others are perceived to be decreasing for example if a cut off point of 2.5 within the scale is adopted whereby that which is less than 2.5 is perceived to be increasing and that which is over 2.5 is perceived to be decreasing than overall respondents report that 'crowding' and 'urbane' components are perceived to be increasing while 'town' has generally remained the same and 'outdoor', 'backcountry' and 'urban' (only one item) have all decreased. Also, that the five clusters are different however some basic patterns emerge. With respect to the 'crowding' subscale, cluster 1 (nothing is different) is different from the others. Cluster 2 (crowded out) generally differs from the others with respect to the 'urbane', 'outdoor', 'backcountry' and 'urban' subscales.

Overall, cluster 2 (crowded out, N=65) is different from others with respect to perception of change in the Bow Valley. In general, the exploratory findings support the assertion that change is occurring the direction of increased crowding and urban-type recreation amenities and opportunities with a perceived decrease in backcountry-type recreation amenities and opportunities

Relaxation

How Motivations, Constraints, and Demographic Factors Predict Seniors' Overseas Travel Propensity

As the trend in aging societies is growing all over the world, the travel and tourism market for senior citizens has attracted much attention recently from both practitioners and academics. The market shows great potential, not only because of its considerable population proportion, but also because of senior citizens' great contribution to a tourism economy. It is generally accepted that seniors in developed countries on average possess a relatively large share of discretionary income and time and are still in good health. These characteristics enable them to travel more, and many seniors have the time to travel and are willing to spend a significant amount of their savings on travel. In addition, the travel behaviour of seniors is characterized as travelling more frequently, going longer distances, staying away longer, spending more money, and relying more on travel agents. Hence, senior travellers are important to the tourism industry and will grow in importance as their segment grows in size and wealth. Understanding seniors' travel decision behaviour is a crucial issue to travel marketers who compete for this important market.

The theory of tourism demand states that it is influenced by three major determinants: economic factors, socio-psychological factors, and exogenous factors. The economic factors include per capita income, cost of living, exchange rate, tourism prices, and transportation costs, among others. The social-psychological factors are associated with the decision-making of travellers such as demographic factors, travel motivations, constraints, images of destinations, and travel preferences, among others. The exogenous factors are associated with the business environment. The psychological determinants of demand in explaining some reasons why tourists travel and select particular destinations. Motivation is defined as the 'driving force behind all behaviour'. From the perspective of the traveller's decision-making process, travel motivations are seen as the energizers of demand that promote an individual to decide on a holiday. Travel behaviour can be predicted by underlying motivations.

Hence, those who are highly motivated might be those who are most likely to overcome constraints and participate in more leisure activities. The concept of travel motivations is based on the existence of "push" and "pull" factors. This has been extensively discussed and is a generally accepted concept. Push motivation refers to an individual's internal energy and an increase in the desire for people to travel, while pull motivation refers to a force external to an individual that influences where people travel, given the initial desire to travel.

Ryan (1991) finds that tourist travel motivations could be identified as wish fulfilment, shopping, escaping from a mundane environment, rest and relaxation, an opportunity for play, strengthening family bonds, prestige, social interaction, and educational opportunities. The most common motivations identified by related research regarding seniors' travel motivation are rest and relaxation, escaping from a mundane environment, social interaction, physical exercise, learning, nostalgia, visiting friends and relatives, and excitement. Shoemaker (1989) notes that among fourteen motivations, rest and relaxation as well as escaping from a mundane environment are the most salient two motivations, while knowing friends of a different gender and playing golf are the least important two motivations for senior travellers in Pennsylvania.

Interestingly, after ten years, Shoemaker (2000) finds that the main motivations of senior travellers shifted to visiting new places and experiencing new things. Regarding seniors' travel motivation, some main classifications can be identified in the literature such as rest/relaxation, social interaction, health, learning, seeking, escaping, attracting, cost, nostalgia and visiting historical sites.

Huang and Tsai (2003) reported that 'Get rest and relaxation' (35.6%) and 'Meet people and socialization' (20.1%) are found as the main travel motivation of Taiwanese seniors. In addition, considering both push and pull dimensions of Taiwanese senior travel motivations, Jang and Wu (2006) found the push motivations include 'ego-enhancement', 'self-esteem', 'knowledge seeking', 'relaxation', and 'socialization' while the pull motivations encompass 'cleanliness and safety', 'facility, event and cost', and 'natural and historical sites'.

Travel Constraints

Unlike motivations that serve as energizers, constraints towards travelling function as filters for tourism demand, preventing the decision makers from engaging in travel even though the motivation may exist.

Leisure constraints can provide a conceptual framework that may help understand why individuals do not participate in specific tourism activities. The hierarchical model proposed by Crawford and Godbey (1987) and Crawford et al. (1991), is the most accepted theoretical framework of leisure constraints.

Their studies categorize leisure constraints into three hierarchically organized levels: intrapersonal, interpersonal, and structural constraints. Furthermore, participation in leisure activities is seen as a process of overcoming the various constraints. The intrapersonal constraints are defined as individual psychological states and attributes, such as stress, anxiety, attitudes, and perceived self skill, that might inhibit one from participating in leisure activities. They exist when people fail to develop leisure preferences due to problems or misconceptions associated with personality needs, prior socialization, personal ability, and perceptions of reference group attitudes. The interpersonal barriers result from social interactions with friends, family, and others. The structural constraints include factors that block people's intentions from taking actions such as economic resources, availability of time, and accessibility. The most often cited constraints to travel in related research are a lack of time, financial considerations, physical and emotional costs, health status (objective and self-reported), perceived disability, age, security concerns, lack of information, family approval, and family responsibilities.

Regarding the dimensionality of leisure constraint measurement, Jackson (1993) identifies six dimensions of leisure constraints from eight studies: social isolation, accessibility, personal reasons, costs, time commitments, and facilities. The social isolation dimension can be deemed as an interpersonal dimension that is based on characteristics involving interaction between/among people. The accessibility dimension includes factors such as a lack of or limited access to transportation or 'getting there'.

The personal reasons dimension is an intrapersonal dimension that includes items pertaining directly to an individual's abilities or motivations. The cost dimension covers items related to the outlay of money. The time dimension represents a collection of items referred to as reasons that affect levels and intensity of participation among adults. Finally, the facility dimension relates specifically toleisure settings and individuals' perception. Although the theoretical hypothesis assumes a positive impact of travel motivation on travel propensity, it is acceptable to see a negative impact of *socialization* motivation on travel intention in this study.

The decision of whether to travel overseas or to travel domestically involves different decision-making considerations. The push power of travel motivation, such as socialization in general, can motivate seniors to travel in the domestic context due to familiar cultural and/or social customs, languages, etc. However, travelling overseas might be a barrier for seniors due to an unfamiliar or foreign environment. This is indirectly supported by about 70% of retirees choosing group package tours as their overseas travel mode in Taiwan.

The Psychology of Relaxation

The Gospel of Relaxation was the subject of a speech made by Mr. Herbert Spencer at a dinner given in his honour in New York City in 1882. Mr. Spencer called attention to the extreme form of "persistent activity' 3 which characterizes the American people. The energy of the savage, he said, was spasmodic. He could not apply himself persistently to work. He lived in the present and did not worry about the future. Civilized man more and more pursues a future goal and applies himself to work until it becomes a passion.

In America, said Mr. Spencer, this strenuous and high-pressure life has become extreme, and a counterchange a reaction must be imminent. We take our multitudinous responsibilities too seriously. There are too many lines in our faces, our gray hairs appear too early, our nervous breakdowns are too frequent. Damaged constitutions and a damaged posterity are among the results. Emerson, with his saying that the first requisite of a gentleman is to be a perfect animal, is a safer guide for us than Carlyle with his gospel of work.

More recently, Professor James, Annie Payson Call, and other writers 1 have eloquently preached this same gospel of relaxation. We are told that we are too breathless; that we live under too much stress and tension; that we are too intense and carry too much expression in our faces; that we must relax, let go, breathe deeply, and unburden ourselves of many useless contractions.

There seems to be a good deal of truth in this. Some of us manage to escape neu-rasthenia, but few of us are free from fatigue, chronic or acute. We hear with amazement now and again some one say, "I was never tired in my life." Surely under normal conditions we ought not to be so tired as we are, nor tired so often.

Impressed with the strenuous character of American life and the need of more rest and recreation, practical common sense, not waiting upon theory, has turned to discover means for relieving the excessive tension incident to our present habits of living. Some, as we have said, preach the gospel of relaxation, content to tell us that we are too intense. Others have established schools with practical and helpful rules and methods for relaxation and have brought comfort and relief to many. Again, a new and unique interest has suddenly arisen in play. Men and animals have always played; but now we have first become conscious of play and curious about it. We insist on play. If children do not play, we teach them to play. And we are anxious to know about the theory of play.

Finally, a score of movements, perhaps many score, have sprung into notice, whose purpose is to encourage or provide some form of relaxation. We recall the recreation movement; the physical-culture movement; the playground movement; the Boy Scouts; the Camp-Fire girls; the ever-increasing interest in athletics, not only in our colleges, but also in our high schools and grammar schools; the radical change in Young Men's Christian Associations from devotional to hygienic and athletic religion; the renaissance of the gymnasium and the Olympic games; the increased interest in outdoor life of all kinds; the renewed devotion to outdoor sports, like tennis, golf, baseball, and football; the rapid extension of the play motive into almost every branch of education; the new vacation schools and school excursions; finally the supervised playgrounds, supervised folk-dancing, supervised swimming, wading, tramping, gardening, singing, and storytelling. Even with very young children the Montessori system seeks to relieve the tension of the old task methods by making the child's activities natural and interesting as well as useful.

More than twenty-five hundred regularly supervised playgrounds and recreation centres are now maintained in about six hundred and fifty cities in this country. A brand new profession has appeared, that of play leader, employing nearly seven thousand professional workers.

The legislatures of some States have passed laws requiring every city of a certain size to vote on the proposition of maintaining playgrounds. New York City expended more than $15,000,000 on playgrounds previous to 1908.

The city paid $1,811,000 for one playground having about three acres. Chicago spent $11,000,000 on playgrounds and field houses in two years. Formerly the boy could play on the street, in the back alley, in the back yard. Now, the alley and back yard have disappeared, the street is crowded with automobiles, and the few remaining open spaces are given over to the lawn-mower and keep-off-the-grass signs, while more and more the school has encroached on the boy's precious period of growth, filling at least nine of the twelve months of the year and adding the evils of evening study and the dread of examinations.

For reasons which will be shown presently, boys must play. Take away the opportunity for legitimate play, and the play instinct, the instinct of rivalry, of adventure, of initiation, will manifest itself in antisocial ways. Hence the juvenile court and the reform school. "Better, playgrounds without schools," says one writer, "than schools without playgrounds."

Up to the present time this is about as far as we have gone into the subject of relaxation. Its psychology has not really been studied at all. We have simply been impressed by the tense and strenuous character of our manner of life and have connected this with the increase of nervous disorders and nervous breakdowns and perhaps with the increase of insanity, and have felt the need, accordingly, of more recreation and play, and more harmony and poise in our way of living, and have taken, there fore, a few practical steps in this direction. But suddenly within the most recent days things have happened which have caused some of us to begin to think more deeply on the whole subject of work and play, and have suggested that it is not a local American problem at all, but a world problem of the present age, and that perhaps great social questions may be involved. The outbreak of recreation crazes in America was the first of these events, but it was the calamity of the European war which most distinctly called our attention to the need of a more careful study of the psychological conditions of our modern life.

Just as we thought the world to be getting very serious, and settling down to work and to problems of social and individual welfare and to political and moral reform, it has suddenly gone amusement-mad in America and reverted with unparalleled ferocity to primeval bloodshed in Europe. These amusement crazes have taken many forms, but the most virulent form was seen in the dancing mania, which has passed through various stages in North and South America and has been so widespread and so compelling that it has reminded us of the epidemics of the Middle Ages. At its height, according to the newspaper reports, a tribe of Indians in Nevada built a great dance-hall in the midst of their village, and imported a teacher of the tango.

Then came the moving-picture craze, which has seized the world like an obsession. No one can suppose that this colossal social phenomenon is to be explained by the mere fact of the discovery of the cinematograph, and that the people were merely waiting upon the invention in order to flock to the spectacles. The invention was an incident. The real significant fact was the psychological situation. Consider the following editorial from a recent number of the "Nation":

The historian will come to grief if he attempts to describe the cause of frivolity in the New York of 1915 A.D. as historians have depicted the frivolity of Rome under the early emperors, and to compare bread and the circus with lobster a la Newburgh and the cabaret. Going back to Rome, and assuming the grand manner, he will speak of a city that drew to itself the booty of the civilized world, of a population enervated by the largess of politicians doling out the plunder of three continents, of a citizenship lulled into civic indifference by gifts and amusements in other words, an imperial city gone rotten with prosperity.

If the parallel holds for New York, the historian would have to describe a city that went mad over cabarets because it had more money than it could spend wisely, because it had no serious interest in the problems of the civic and social life, because its serenity was undisturbed by wars or the fear of wars, because there was no unemployment problem, no city-budget problem, no workmen's compensation problem, no widows' pension problem, no Mexican problem, no German problem. Else how account for a city gone mad over the fox trot and the white lights? Life was much simpler in imperial Rome than it is in New York today, though even under the early Caesars the picture was not so uniform as the average historian has painted it.

At least we know today that the fact of 400,000 unemployed in New York City does not militate against the prosperity of the "movies," which are the circenses of the masses; and the fact of Wall Street's unemployed has not interfered with the prosperity of the cabarets. Quite the contrary. There is good reason for believing that not all the young men at the afternoon teas are professional idlers and parasites, but that a good many business men and brokers have taken to dancing in the afternoon because there was nothing to do downtown. Perhaps the grasshopper in La Fontaine's fable, who sang all summer, did so because business was rotten, and when the ant told him to go and dance in winter, he was only advising him to do the best possible thing under the circumstances.

To be sure it is no longer possible to dispose of such things as these by referring them to "frivolity" or to "luxury," but neither is it possible to say that they are due to idleness. For instance, a correspondent in a small mining-camp near the Mexican border writes that the Mexican labourers, who comprise six-sevenths of the population, are strictly amusement-mad, spending their last pennies at the "movies" or the merry-go-round or for intoxicants. May it not be that these amusement crazes are a form of reaction against a manner of life that is too serious and tense. May they not be indications of a lack of physiological adjustment. We are making great efforts in these days to secure better social adjustment through the study of social and economic conditions; but is it not possible that the trouble is not in the lack of social adjustment, but in the lack of physiological adjustment in the individual, so that what we have to strive for is not so much improved social conditions, as improved health and improved physical constitutions, to be gained by a different manner of life, a different kind of education, and a different proportion of work and play.

Then there is another cloud which has recently appeared on the social horizon leading us to think that the problem of work and play needs further study. We refer to the remarkable increase in the number of deaths from diseases of degeneration. A few years ago, rejoicing over the discoveries of Pasteur and his followers, we had great hope of increasing the span of human life by the conquest of the devastating parasitic diseases. These diseases have, indeed, to some extent been conquered. We have now less dread of typhoid, tuberculosis, pneumonia, and diseases of this class due to microscopic enemies, but the expected increase in racial stability has not come. Some, therefore, are beginning to ask whether the better way to lengthen human life is to remove the enemies which threaten it, or to increase our power of resistance to these enemies.

According to Mr. E. E. Rittenhouse, president of the Life Extension Institute, there is a marked decline in the power of American workers to withstand the strain of modern life. They wear out sooner than they did a few years ago. The chances of death after reaching the prime of life have increased because of the extraordinary increase in the death-rate from the breaking-down of the heart, arteries, kidneys, and of the nervous and digestive systems. Mr. Rittenhouse's conclusions as to the serious inroads of these diseases in modern life are based not on mortality records of the idle rich and such classes, but upon actual physical examination of a large number of male workers, including officials, clerks, and employees of banks and commercial houses, averaging about thirty years of age. The results show that these diseases of degeneration, so-called diseases of old age, are " reaching down into middle life and below, and increasing there, and apparently at all ages." These diseases, not being so quickly fatal as the parasitic diseases, produce decreased efficiency and increased misery, oftentimes through many working years.

The lesson which investigations such as this teach is that the problem of public health and longevity is not altogether a problem of hygiene in the narrower sense in which this word is commonly used. It is rather the deeper question of vitality, of biological adjustment, of racial stability; and it involves questions of heredity, of mental and physical balance, of manner of life, of physical education, of work and play.

Sociologists are becoming acutely conscious of the fact that our cultured classes are not self-perpetuating. The increasing number of childless marriages and small families in these classes indicates that a process of displacement is taking place in favour of peoples of hardier stock and simpler habits, depriving us at once of the advantages of physical heredity and making progress depend very largely upon social heredity alone. A given stock of people may cultivate its brains to the highest point of intellectual and moral efficiency, but, if it neglect the corresponding development of somatic vitality, if it neglect strength and vigour of muscles, heart, lungs, stomach, and reproductive system, it is doomed to extinction and cannot pass on to posterity the intellectual and moral power which it has itself inherited.

Finally, the increased desire for narcotics in the form of drugs, tobacco, and alcohol, prevalent in all civilized countries, is a further indication of some serious lack of balance between body and brain. There is a lack of adjustment somewhere, and the problem of the day is to find out where it is and how it may be remedied. It is not our purpose in this book to study this great problem, but rather a single phase of it, namely, the relation of work and play and the results both to the individual and to society of excessive work and insufficient relaxation. It is very probable that our modern strenuous life is bringing too heavy a strain upon the brain, particularly those parts of the brain immediately connected with the mental powers which condition that peculiar kind of progress which the world is now making. The tendency of the times is toward a very swift industrial, commercial, professional, and intellectual activity.

It is an age of great effort and endeavour, of stress and tension, of labour and strain, of scientific and inventive ability; an age of great efficiency and striving for efficiency; an age of variegation; a centrifugal age. It is not an age of peace, of calm, of poise, of relaxation, of repose, of measure, of harmony, of conservation. It is not a centripetal age. The spirit of the age is that of Francis Bacon. It is not the spirit of such greater minds as Buddha and Jesus and Sophocles and Plato and St. Francis.

What is likely to be the outcome of such tendencies as these? Our current sociology speaks almost exclusively of the proximate social results. What is perhaps more important is to speak of the immediate physiological and psychological results, because they throw light upon certain ultimate and still more important social consequences.

The immediate social results of an age of such great activity and great expenditure are clearly pointed out, for instance, by Professor Giddings in his "Democracy and Empire." These are, in brief, (1) an increase of wealth, culture, and refinement, followed by a marked increase of population; (2) a movement of the people toward the large cities; and (3) a displacement of the higher types of people by the lower, followed by an increase of crime, vagabondage, suicide, and feeble-mindedness.

These social results we may leave to the sociologist. But what is the effect of such an age of great activity and great expenditure upon the individual? This we believe to be just now the important question, and it is to the answer to this question that we hope the studies in this book may be a contribution.

The result, in a word, is a rapid and extreme fatigue of the higher brain and an unusual and imperative demand for rest and relaxation. Nature has provided various means for rest and relaxation, in sleep, play, sport, laughter, etc. But what will happen when the claims made upon the working brain are in excess of the powers of repair provided by these natural means of relaxation, or when these means themselves are neglected ? There will be increasing irritability and probably reactions more or less violent and spasmodic, and if there are any artificial means of relieving the strain and temporarily restoring the balance, there will be recourse to such aids. The craving for narcotic drugs, tobacco, and alcohol, will be an example of the latter, and the recurrence of recreation crazes will be an illustration of the former. Finally, it is altogether possible that society as a whole may suffer from such excessive mental activity and such excessive tension, and that great social upheavals may follow, such, for instance, as war. Thus we may understand why the psychologist in treating the laws of relaxation may bring together in one volume subjects apparently so unlike as play, sport, laughter, profanity, alcohol, and war.

The principle involved in all the forms of relaxation here studied is relief from tension or release from some form of restraint. Although this tension and restraint on the part of the individual are necessary conditions of all social evolution, they have been greatly intensified by the manner of life which characterizes the nineteenth and twentieth centuries. The repression of primitive impulses to the end of growing social needs is the fundamental law of human progress. Such continual repression necessitates constant effort, constant strain, and constant exercise of voluntary attention. It involves those higher brain centres whose development has conditioned human progress, and brings upon them a severe and constant strain, making rest and relaxation imperative.

When this everlasting urge of progress is excessive, as it has been in recent times, we may say that there is in a way a constant subconscious rebellion against it and a constant disposition to escape from it, and the method of escape is always the temporary reversion to simpler and more primitive forms of behaviour, a return to nature, so to speak. Sudden momentary and unexpected release from this tension, with instinctive reinstatement of primitive forms of expression, is laughter. Daily or periodic systematic return to primitive forms of activity is sport or play. War is a violent social reversion to elemental and natural intertribal relations. Profanity is a resort to primitive forms of vocal expression to relieve a situation which threatens one's wellbeing. Alcohol is an artificial means of relieving mental tension by the narcotizing of the higher brain centres.

Thus the reader may understand why we have associated in a single volume these seemingly diverse kinds of human behaviour they are all forms of relaxation. That which is common to all these phenomena is the relief from the tension of our modern strenuous life by means of a return to nature, or a return to early and elemental forms of behaviour which offer rest or release from the burdens of life. All therefore appear as forms of relaxation, some helpful and normal, others abnormal and brutalizing.

If we should succeed in tracing all of these modes of human behaviour to their psychological sources, we may contribute something to the clearing-up of certain difficult social problems of the day. We may, for instance, be enabled to see very clearly that evil and destructive forms of relaxation cannot be banished except by substituting normal and healthful forms.

The growing worldwide craving for alcohol, tobacco, and other narcotic drugs and the fatal and inevitable recurrence of war, with its fearful toll of human life and its still more fearful toll of hard-earned human savings, perplexing though they are as social problems, nevertheless might become much clearer in the light thrown upon them by the study of the laws of mental relaxation.

In the present stage of human culture, war seems like a species of insanity. It is no longer taken for granted. It no longer fits in as a part of the natural order of events. It seems anomalous and grotesque. It has lost its glory and seems now barbaric. We have been so long accustomed to have our disputes settled by courts of law, whose decisions are based upon principles of justice, that an appeal to mere brute force in the settlement of international disputes appears to us more and more absurd.

Recently the reversionary character of war has been startlingly revealed to us by the reversionary logic and the reversionary morals which accompany it. And yet wars one after another, each more terrible than the last, are flaunted in the face of nineteenth and twentieth century civilization, are flaunted directly in the face of worldwide movements for international conciliation.

In like manner the use of alcohol, from the standpoint of modern science, appears as a kind of insanity. Scientific study has now shown that alcohol has none of the good effects upon the body or mind which formerly it was supposed to have, and that it is not even a stimulant. Yet the consumption of alcohol steadily increases.

Under these circumstances we should welcome any light, however small, which psychology can throw upon these subjects. The desire for alcohol and the instinct for war are phenomena which lie in the field of psychology, and reformers will make little headway against these evils unless they take into account the psychological motives.

We may, if we choose, redouble again our efforts against alcohol, but it would be the part of reason to find out, if we can, the causes of this growing desire in order that they may, if possible, be removed. So we may, if we choose, redouble our efforts toward universal peace, but a more rational method would seem to be to find out the deep-lying causes of war and see whether anything can be done to remove them.

In the chapters which follow, an attempt is made to treat these subjects psychologically and in particular to consider them from the standpoint of phylogenetic experience. We must call to mind not only the animal and savage past from which man has emerged, but also the forces or tendencies which are manifest in his development. It is not sufficient to explain war by recalling that man is a fighting animal, that he has literally fought his way up to manhood. It is far more important to understand that his constant advance has been attended by conditions of tension and stress which have made his periodic and temporary reversion to primitive habits an actual condition of renewed progress. It is still more important to learn how the supreme intelligence with which evolution has finally crowned mankind may be used to devise some means by which these periodic reversions to savagery may be made unnecessary.

Lately we have seemed to forget that human progress is rhythmical, that mankind advances by a series of relapses and recoveries, and that after each recovery there is new ground gained, sometimes very much new ground.

It may be that we have here the explanation of war, and it may be that there are conditions present in the social life of our times which intensify these rhythmical reversionary tendencies, so that no manner of humanitarian effort can withstand the periodic demand for war, just as no manner of prohibitive legislation and no manner of science sermons can stem the desire for alcohol. Especially in the last century has "progress," as it is called, been very rapid, progress in science, in industry, in invention, in everything, and the tension and rapidity of our lives have become correspondingly great. After great tension there must be great relaxation. There is a limit to the strain which the social mind can stand. It is imperative that we study the laws of mental tension and mental relaxation. The psychology of play may throw much light on the psychology of war.

No engineer or architect undertakes to build a bridge or skyscraper without an accurate knowledge of the strength of material. Modern life is a kind of social skyscraper. The minds of the individuals who constitute society are the material. This material is put under too much tension. A collapse necessarily follows. In our social life these collapses appear as reactions or reversions, sometimes cataclysmic, as in the case of the war in Europe, sometimes sporadic, as in the dancing crazes and the amusement crazes in America.

In the following pages an attempt has been made to study the strength of this human material, to study the causes of the social strains and the forms and directions taken by the social reactions. If these studies teach us nothing more, they will at least show that the folly of explaining war by referring it to mere political rivalries is no less than that of referring amusement crazes to "frivolity" and the desire for alcohol to "depravity."

The Psychology of Play

When we think of play, we usually have in mind the play of children. But grown-ups likewise play, and to their plays we sometimes apply the word "sport." Since it is our purpose in this book to study relaxation in its various forms, evidently it is sport, rather than play in its narrower sense, that we are especially interested in, for one could hardly speak of the play of children as a form of relaxation.

Many books have been written about play, and it is the play of children that they usually deal with, a subject indeed of the greatest interest and the most vital importance. Little or no study has been made of the psychology of the play of adults, and this is unfortunate for two reasons: first, because of the importance of the subject itself in its relation to certain fundamental problems of our social life, and, second, because the play of children receives new and valuable light when it is studied in its relation to the play of man in the wider sense.

While our interest, then, in this chapter is primarily in the play of adults considered as a form of relaxation, nevertheless it is very evident that we could make no progress in this study without first examining the nature of play in general and without first considering the theories of play which other writers have proposed. It will be interesting, then, to follow this plan and see whether the old theories of play are satisfactory, and if not, whether it is possible to propose a new theory which shall bring the plays of children and the plays of men into harmony with each other, and at the same time into harmony with the laws of recreation and relaxation in general.

Many theories of play have been offered, but they may all be referred to three principal ones, which have been named the Schiller-Spencer theory, the Groos theory, and the Recapitulation theory. An examination of these theories will no doubt show that none of them are wholly incorrect. They are rather partial views, not necessarily inconsistent with one another, but in need of more careful definition and limitation. Herbert Spencer's theory is that play activities are those which do not directly subserve life processes, but are due to an inner need of using those bodily organs which are over-rested and under-worked. In the lower animals, therefore, the occasion for play would not arise, since all their energies are constantly expended in the maintenance of life; but in the higher animals and in man, time and strength are not wholly absorbed in providing for immediate needs. There is thus a surplus of vigour and this surplus is expended through the usual channels; not, however, in real activities, that is, in work, but in simulations of real activities, that is, in play. Play is thus the dramatizing of real life. Kittens chasing balls and children nursing dolls are illustrations.

Although modern writers might state this in somewhat different form, the theory is essentially sound so far as it goes. The rather hypercritical objection which has often been urged, namely, that we sometimes play when we are tired, is easily answered and need not be considered here. The real weakness of the theory is that it is incomplete.

It explains why people that is, grown people--tend to be active all the time when they are not sleeping.

It explains nothing more than this and this needs no explanation, since it is characteristic of all animal life to be active. To explain how processes of nutrition lead to the accumulation of energy, which results in muscular activity, and that when there is no work to do this takes the form of play, is only a longer way of saying that an animal is alive and necessarily active. To speak of that energy which is not expended in life-serving processes as "surplus energy" is to assume that man exists to work, and that play is something extra, a kind of afterthought, to fill up the time.

A further difficulty with Spencer's theory is that it does not apply to the play of children at all, for the reason that the child is not a working animal, and does not provide his own sustenance. Hence there could be no "surplus energy." His whole life is a play life. Of course, if the theory had been stated a little differently, it would apply perfectly to the play of children. Children are alive and active, and their activity, not being directed to immediate life-serving ends, we call play.

But the most serious difficulty with Spencer's theory is that it does not explain the form taken either by the plays of children or of adults. His view is that men and animals in their surplus-energy moods that is, in their play would simply go on doing in a dramatizing way what they are accustomed seriously to do in their working moods. The horse would run, the tiger would jump, the cat would chase imaginary mice, and the man presumably would plough and reap and dig and write books and give lectures. But this is precisely what the man does not do. He goes fishing, plays golf and baseball, goes to horse-races, and rides in automobiles. The Spencer theory, therefore, misses the whole point. It is true because it is a truism.

The Groos theory of play attempts to supply what the Spencer theory lacks, that is, to account for the actual form taken by the plays of children and young animals. Unfortunately, it gives little attention to the plays of adults.

According to the Groos theory of play, the plays of animals and children are instincts which have arisen through the action of natural selection because of their usefulness as a practice and preparation for life's later serious duties. Professor Groos has written two volumincus books on the play of animals and the play of man containing a wealth of material on these subjects, but the reader cannot fail to be impressed by the lack of connection between the facts and the theory. The author seems, indeed, to have arrived at his theory of play through a purely deductive process. Since play is an instinct, and since, as we cannot admit the inheritance of acquired characters, every instinct has arisen in response to some definite practical need, and since it is evident that play has no immediate life-serving function, it must serve as a practice and preparation for life's serious pursuits.

In this argument the premises may be sound, but the conclusion has no necessary connection with them. Plays, indeed, are instinctive, and no doubt all instinctive reactions have had at some time in our racial history some life-serving meaning. But the fact that natural selection has not yet eliminated the great multitude of old racial habits with which the young child's nervous system teems does not prove that they have been retained because of their usefulness as a practice and preparation for future life. In any animal species, such as man, that lives in a changing environment and has a long period of youth followed by a period of great rational power of transformation, we may expect behaviour to be largely determined by inherited habit.

As Professor Thorndike says: "We fear, not the carriers of malaria and yellow fever, but thunder and the dark; we pity, not the gifted youth debarred from education, but the beggar's bloody sore; we are less excited by a great injustice than by a little blood." We are no longer so impressed by the infallible powers of natural selection as when Professor Groos wrote.

Man's original nature is not so perfect as we once thought. We are more impressed by its "archaic unreason." And even in the case of instincts which are now useful, it does not follow that, if they appear before the time of their life-serving usefulness, they must serve as a practice and preparation for such later use. Nature is not so parsimonious and calculating as that would indicate. It is not necessary to explain the doll plays of little girls as a practice and preparation for their future maternal duties. They may be simply exhibitions of a maternal instinct which sometime in the life of the individual may be useful, as when a tree showers down ten thousand seeds, of which one only may germinate. So the fighting plays of boys may be simply old racial habits, the line of least resistance for boyish activities. In one sense, to be sure, if one should wish to look at the matter ideologically, play, like food or sleep, or like growth itself, is a preparation for manhood. But it is better to regard the child as a playing animal, realizing in him-self his own end. Play, like growth or life itself, belongs to the concept of childhood. Play is just the name we give to the child's activities. In the Groos theory, as in that of Spencer, there seems to lurk the belief that the child is naturally quiescent, and that if he plays, his play must look forward to that particular aspect of life which we call his serious or bread-winning activity.

When we consider what the plays of children actually are, we discover, except in a limited number of imitative plays, but faint resemblance between them and the serious pursuits of adult man. They resemble rather the pursuits of primitive and prehistoric man, and many of them are like the sports of adults of the present day. The plays most dear to the hearts of boys are running, jumping, climbing, coasting, skating, wrestling, wading, swimming, boating, fishing, hunting, shooting with darts, spears, arrows, or guns, building bonfires, robbing birds' nests, gathering nuts, collecting stamps, eggs, beetles or other things, flying kites, digging caves, making tree houses, spinning tops, playing horse, playing marbles, jackstones, numbers, hide-and-seek, tag, blackman, prisoner's base, leap-frog, baseball, football, tennis, cricket, golf, etc. Children of all ages have the greatest interest in pet animals, dogs, cats, rabbits, birds, horses, etc. No small part of the child's life is occupied with playing with these pets and in earlier years with toy animals of all kinds. To these plays should be added, of course, the countless indoor games, such as checkers, chess, cards, dominoes, etc.

These children's plays have so little in common with the later pursuits of adult life that it is evident that some quite other theory is needed to explain them than the practice and preparation theory. When the boy is grown to manhood he will not be found doing these things, except in his hours of relaxation. His serious pursuits will take other forms. He will be found cultivating the soil, harvesting his crops, shoveling dirt, sand, or coal, blasting rocks from quarries and minerals from mines, building houses, buying, selling, manufacturing or transporting goods, teaching school, healing diseases, preaching sermons, practising law, engaging in politics or commercial transactions, giving lectures or conducting scientific research. This is the "serious" life of today and the life of the ancient Greeks and Romans was much the same, and it is all far removed from the play life of the child, which likewise is much the same in ancient and modern times, and involves altogether simpler forms of response. If the serious life of today consisted in escaping from enemies by foot, horse, or paddle, in living in close proximity to domestic animals, in pursuit of game with bow or gun, in subsisting on fish caught singly by hand, in personal combat with fist or sword, in throwing missiles, striking with a club or pursuing an enemy, in seeking safety in trees or caves, in living in tents or tree houses, and in sleeping and cooking by a campfire, then we might venture to explain the play life of the child as "an instinctive activity existing for purposes of practice or exercise and without serious intent." But these are not the pursuits of adult men, except in their hours of sport. Most of the plays of children find their significance, not in their likeness, but in their unlikeness to man's laborious duties. In fact, the plays of children bear a striking resemblance to the sports of men, and the latter would not be sports if they did not stand in direct contrast to work.

As regards the imitative plays of children, their resemblance to the serious activities of adult life is, of course, closer, and to them the Groos theory of play would seem to be less strained in its application. But the imitative plays themselves are not instinctive for the reason that they are imitative. If it is meant merely that imitation itself is an impulse which has been perpetuated by natural selection owing to its usefulness in preparing children for mature life, this view might be maintained, of course, if one still wished to put so much emphasis upon natural selection.

Other objections to the Groos theory may be passed with a mere reference. Perhaps the most serious of them is the failure of this theory to explain adult sports and to correlate them with the plays of children. Again, one is troubled by the frequent use of the word "serious" as applied to the activities of the adult, while the plays of children are spoken of as "sham," "make-believe," or "selfillusory." This distinction can no longer be made.

Child life and its plays are quite as serious and quite as real as the life of the man. If we are to speak of "ends," it would be difficult indeed to show that the life of the grownup is any more final or purposeful than the life of the child. Would it not be just as appropriate to say that the man's toil and sweat are a preparation for the radiant childhood of the son and daughter whom he may beget, as that the plays of childhood are a preparation for the prosaic work-life of the father? And as for seriousness, to the boy hastily swallowing his dinner or rushing through some uninteresting task to join his fellows in a game of ball or a trip to the river, it is the latter and not the former that are serious and real. It is a notable fact that most children take but a passing or trifling interest in what they eat, and scarcely remember their food of yesterday. It is a peculiarity of the adult masculine mind to be very intent on the bread-winning aspect of life and on the preservation of the species.

Perhaps nature exploits man for these particular aspects of life, which in themselves are but partial views. They might even be looked upon as necessary evils, subordinate in "purpose" to childhood, play, sport, art, and sympathy, which are more real and final.

In reference to the Groos theory of play, some critics have been misled by the fact that certain games, like baseball, seem to provide valuable training in such qualities as obedience, cooperation, quickness of decision, for attitude in defeat, and endurance. That the game cultivates these virtues to some extent is doubtless true. One can hardly suppose, however, that natural selection has operated to form an instinct for baseball because of its especial usefulness in providing such training. Other explanations for the fascination of this game are much simpler, as we shall see. Women, also, have need of these virtues, but they do not care to play baseball.

Professor Groos has more recently supplemented his work by a catharsis theory of play, already anticipated by American writers. According to this particular form of the catharsis theory, play is a kind of safety-valve for the expression of pent-up emotion, as for instance in the fighting plays of children, where the pent-up emotion is anger. According to this view, one would understand the emotions to be some kind of internal forces which would do damage if they could find no escape. It is not, however, probable that Professor Groos or any one holds this naive view of the emotions, and the whole relation may be more simply expressed if we suppose that the fighting plays are among the natural or spontaneous activities of children and as long as they are freely indulged in, the child is free from hurtful emotions. If these activities are repressed, then no doubt would occur certain internal disturbances of a less healthful character. Where spontaneous responses are inhibited, readjustments are necessary and emotions are present. When the spontaneous response is resumed, the emotion subsides. In this way children's plays might seem to have a catharsis effect. In spontaneous unrestricted play, however, there would seem to be no such element present or necessary.

In the sports of men, indeed, a decided Catharsis effect is present. They are essentially purifying. But, as we shall learn in these studies, the catharsis effect is primarily due to a restoring of disturbed balance in the psychophysical organism. It is thus more nearly described as rest than as purification. Play brings relief from that peculiar form of fatigue which follows from our modern strenuous life. It rests those parts of the nervous system which our daily work most stresses.

But adult play has probably a catharsis effect of another kind. It has been shown by the researches of Walter B. Cannon and his associates [1] that under the influence of strong emotion, say of fear or anger, a whole series of internal changes takes place in the organism, which are adaptive in their character and prepare the muscular system for the strenuous responses which the threatening situation demands. Of these the increased blood-sugar and the increased adrenin in the blood are typical. In the life history of our race these internal preparations for great muscular activity have been followed normally by the activity itself, say flight or combat. The circle is thus completed as nature meant it to be. But in our modern life of constant inhibition, where the emotions themselves are present often enough and the internal preparation for great muscular exertion takes place, the muscular responses themselves, owing to social restrictions and other causes, are necessarily greatly limited, if not altogether repressed. Hence arises a feeling of irritability, having its source perhaps in the poisoning of the blood by the presence of these unused activating substances. All kinds of active sports, therefore, involving muscular activity serve as substitutes for the original responses phylogenetically determined. Thus it would appear that sports have an actual catharsis effect in the case of adults, and that in children, while this effect is theoretically absent, it is, of course, actually present in increasing degree as the child becomes a man. This catharsis effect of play, laughter, and profanity should not, however, be interpreted in such a way that these forms of relaxation are considered to be mere drainage channels for shunting off accumulated energy. 1 All forms of play and sport, as well as laughter and profanity, have themselves been phylogenetically determined. They are indeed the older and more original responses, and their principal catharsis effect is not due to their draining off accumulated energy and using up the various energizing substances in the blood, but rather to the complete rest which they afford to parts of the brain over-stressed in our modern life of work.

The third theory of play has been called the Recapitulation theory. This takes full cognizance of the phylogenetic significance of play, and indeed is based upon it. As regards the latter, all future theories of play must take carefully into account the numerous and striking similarities between the plays of children and the pursuits and customs of primitive and prehistoric man as they have been pointed out by President G. Stanley Hall and his associates.

But the question arises as to the reason for this resemblance, and if the correct reason is not found, the whole significance of play may be lost. The theory in question does not explain this resemblance except by referring it to a so-called law, the law of recapitulation, according to which each individual passes through a series of stages in his development corresponding to the stages of racial development. Even in the sphere of embryology the validity of this law has been much questioned, and it is looked upon with increasing distrust when applied to the period of postnatal or psychological development. It should be said, however, that this theory of play is the only one that has successfully attacked the specific problem of accounting for the form taken by children's play. Perhaps the most serious difficulty with this theory is its failure to explain the plays of adults and to correlate them properly with those of children. Our main purpose in the present chapter is to examine more carefully the grounds of the resemblance between children's plays and the pursuits of primitive man and, more particularly, to explain if possible the similarity which exists between both of these and the sports of the mature man of the present time. To this end the following introductory definitions and propositions may be offered, which, if found useful and valid, will considerably simplify the psychology of play. The term "play" may be applied to all those human activities which are free and spontaneous and which are pursued for their own sake alone. The interest in them is self-developing and they are not continued under any internal or external compulsion. Play will thus include practically all the activities of children and the larger share of those of adults, such, for instance, as baseball, football, tennis, golf, polo, billiards, and countless other games and sports; diversions such as travelling, hunting, fishing, yachting, motoring, flying, dancing; vacation outings, games, races, spectacles, fairs, tournaments, and expositions; the theatre, opera, moving pictures, lectures, and entertainments; the enjoyment of music, painting, poetry, and other arts; the daily paper, the magazine, the short story, and the novel. The term "work," on the other hand, will include all those activities in which by means of sustained voluntary attention one holds one's self down to a given task for the sake of some end to be attained other than the activity itself. Such activities involve mental stress, strain, effort, tension, concentration, and inhibition.

The plays of children and the sports of adults are to be closely coordinated and explained by reference to the same general principles. There is a striking similarity between the plays of children and the sports of men on the one hand and the pursuits of primitive man on the other. This similarity is due to the fact that those mental powers upon which advancing civilization depends, especially voluntary and sustained attention, concentration, analysis, and abstraction, are undeveloped in the child and subject to rapid fatigue in the adult.

The question may be asked how, according to the above definitions of work and play, we shall classify that form of work which becomes so interesting as to be self-developing and requires no effort of attention to pursue it. A man may become so interested in his garden or in his inventions or in his professional pursuits that his work may take on some of the characteristics of play. Nevertheless, this kind of work demands the exercise of mental powers of a high degree of complexity, and is far more fatiguing than play or sport as above defined, though far less so than that kind of work which has been called toil, or drudgery, where interest fails and the strain of attention is at its maximum. Hence the chilcts activities and the play activities of the adult tend always to take the form of old racial pursuits.

If we look at the matter physiologically, it is very evident, in the case of the adult, that there are some brain centres, or some brain tracts, or some forms of cerebral functioning, that are put under severe strain in our modern strenuous life and that there must be some kind of activity which will relieve these centres, or these tracts, during a considerable portion of each waking day and involve other centres not so subject to exhaustion. Such activity we call play or sport. Perhaps the word "relaxation" would be a more exact description of it. For our present purpose it does not matter in the least what these centres are or what manner of cerebral functioning this is.

It is only necessary to note the evident fact that there is some kind of cerebral activity associated with those peculiar mental powers the development of which has made possible human progress. Nor, again, is it necessary for our present purpose to make any exact enumeration of these so-called higher mental processes which distinguish the modern civilized man. Generally speaking, however, they include a constantly increasing power of sustained attention of the voluntary kind, controlled association, concentration, and analysis, together with a constantly increasing power of inhibition. The individual becomes increasingly able to hold steadily in view the image of a desired end, to inhibit the old and habitual responses which are no longer appropriate to that end, to analyse a given situation in thought, so that the response may be to certain elements in the situation rather than to the situation as a whole, and thus to meet a given situation with a new response. Only the fully developed adult mind is capable of much thinking of this kind, and at best it is highly fatiguing and cannot be continued through many hours of the waking day, so that all, or almost all, the hours of the child's day and the larger number of hours of the adult's day must be filled with responses of the simpler, more elemental, and racially older kind. Consequently children's play and adult sport tend to take the forms of old racial activities, involving brain tracts that are old, well worn, and pervious.

It is well known that the present tendency in both historical and anthropological study is to place less emphasis on the differences in the mental constitution of different races of men. 1 All existing races and all historical ones, so far as we can see, are much alike in their mental powers. But from our present point of view these races are all modern.

It is clearly evident that in comparing modern civilized man with the highest of the lower animals or with his prehistoric, if not even with his primitive, ancestors, there has been an unmeasured advance in the powers above mentioned. Even this assumption, however, is not necessary so far as our present theory is concerned. It is merely necessary to notice that in seeking relief from the fatigue involved in that sustained and voluntary attention, controlled association, analysis, and abstraction which are essential to our or to any advancing civilization, we fall back upon a set of activities which no longer involve these processes, but which through ages of use have become familiar and easy.

All the evidence that we have points to the validity of the law that those peculiar forms of mental activity which have developed late in the evolution of man are most affected by fatigue a law fully sustained by the study of psychasthenics and their incapacity for higher mental operations, as well as by the observation of people normally fatigued, while it is known that the disintegration of the nervous system in disease follows the reverse order of its development.

Hence we understand why children's play and adult sport take the form of hunting, fishing, camping, outing, swimming, climbing, and so on through the long list. The more elemental these activities have been in the history of racial development, the greater release they afford, when indulged in as relaxation, from the tension of our modern life.

Those forms of mental response which are developed late in the history of the race, and late in the life of the child, that tense and strenuous activity upon which modern progress depends, the power to hold ourselves by sustained attention and sustained effort down to hard and uninteresting tasks for the sake of some ultimate end, the consecration of the mental forces upon probed Science, philosophy and invention Kie inhibition of old and undesirable responses, all these bring quick and extreme fatigue, and demand rest for the corresponding parts of the brain. In sleep these higher mental processes enjoy almost complete suspension. But the exercise of these powers during the long hours of our waking day would result in speedy collapse. It is clear therefore that our daily activity must be made up quite largely of responses of the simpler type, which shall give exercise to our muscles and sense organs and invoke older and more elemental forms of mentality, and at the same time allow the higher ones to rest. Such is relaxation in all its forms, and of such consists almost wholly the life of the child. For the brain tracts associated with the above-mentioned forms of mental activity are undeveloped in the child, as they are in early man, so that we may say with considerable truth not that the child ought not to work, but that he cannot work.

In the following pages we shall review some of the instances of the striking resemblance between the habits of our human ancestors and the plays of children and men, beginning with the simpler illustrations drawn from the plays of children and proceeding to the more instructive ones connected with the sports of adults.

Haddon and Tylor have studied the history of the kite and the top and of marbles, and have shown their very ancient character and their connection with early religious and divinatory rites. The same may be said of casting lots, throwing dice, games of forfeits and games with common playing cards. The mental habits of our ancestors, as we know, survive in the counting-out rhymes, in the charms and talismans and superstitions of children. One recalls the magic formula used by Tom Sawyer for driving away warts: You got to go by yourself in the middle of the woods where you know there is a spunkwater stump, and just as it's midnight you back up against the stump and jam your hand in and say: and then walk away quick eleven steps with your eyes shut, and then turn around three times and walk home without speaking to any one, because if you speak, the charm's busted.

The mental habits of the child seem like echoes from the remote past, recalling the life of the cave, the forest, and the stream. The instinct exhibited in infancy, as well as in boyhood, to climb stairs, ladders, trees, lampposts, anything, reminds us of forest life; the hide-and-seek games which appeal so powerfully even to the youngest children recall the cave life of our ancestors, or at least some mode of existence in which concealment from enemies, whether human or animal, was the condition of survival; while the instinct of infants to gravitate toward the nearest pond or puddle, the wading, swimming, fishing, boating proclivities of every youngster, seem like a reminiscence of some time when our fathers lived near and by means of the water.

During a long period in the evolution of life among the higher animals and in the early history of man, the one all-important factor was speedy for upon it depended safety in flight from enemies and capture in pursuit. This ancient trait has persisted and survives today in a deep instinctive joy in speed, whether exhibited in running or coasting or skating or in the speed mania which lends such delight to motoring, flying, fast sailing, and fast riding.

Again, the ancient life of pursuit and capture persists upon every playground in the familiar games of tag, blackman, pull-away, and a hundred others. Indeed, for the exhibition of this instinct, no organized game is necessary. Sudden playful pursuit and flight are seen wherever children are assembled. The ancient life of personal combat is mirrored in the plays of children in mimic fighting and wrestling. The passion of every boy for the bow and arrow, sling, sling-shot, gun, or anything that will shoot, reveals the persistence of deep-rooted race habits, formed during ages of subsistence by these means.

There was a time when man lived in close relation with and dependence upon wild and domestic animals. This period is reflected in many forms in the child's life, in his animal books, his animal toys, his Teddy bears, in his numerous animal plays. The former dependence of man upon the horse is shown in the instinct of the child of today to play horse, to ride a rocking-horse, or a stick, or anything. The child's first musical instruments, the rattle, the drum, and the horn, were the first musical instruments of primitive man.

These illustrations could be multiplied indefinitely. They show the limitations of the Groos theory of play, for none of the plays of this class have much to do in preparing the child for the life of today, or in giving him special practice for his future work. We ourselves are so much slaves of the past in our habits of thought that we do not easily realize how far from the actual life of the present day is this play-life of the child. The real world of today is that of the laboratory, the school, the library, the bank, the office, the shop, the street, the factory, the farm and the railroad. Notwithstanding the child's imitative bent, his world, as shown in his tales, his dreams, and the plays he loves best, is that of the forest, the stream, the camp, the cave, the hunting-ground, and the battlefield.

Those things which have such a vital and absorbing interest for the boy have had at one time in our racial history an actual life and death interest for mankind. Take, for instance, the jackknife. How many knives has your boy had and lost, and what rich joy there is in every new one! We see how the practice and preparation theory of play fails here. The knife has no significance in society now. It has degenerated to mere fingernail purposes. But at one time it meant life in defence and food in offence. Your boy's supreme interest in the knife is a latent memory of those ancient days. Those who could use the knife and use it well survived and transmitted this trait to their offspring. The same could be said of the sling, the bow and arrow, and of sports like boxing, fencing, and fishing.

Consider the fascination of fishing: This is not a practice and preparation for the real life of today, but a reverberation of phyletic experience. In a summer resort where the writer was a visitor the past summer, day after day the whole male population of the hotel resorted to the fishing grounds. They paid two dollars and a half a day for a guide, seven dollars a day for a motorboat, and a cent and a half each for worms. Surely a stranger uninitiated into our habits would have been amazed to see these returning fishermen at night indifferently handing over their catch to the guide. It was the fishing they desired, not the fish, and yet great was their woe when one large fish was lost in the act of landing. It is estimated by the New York "Times" that on Sundays and holidays when the weather is fine, twenty-five thousand people in New York City go fishing at a minimum cost of one dollar each, and of these no doubt more than ninety-five per cent go for fun and not for the fish. At some stage in the history of human development fishing was without doubt a general means of subsistence. Those who could catch fish survived and handed down this instinct. Likewise the fascination of gathering wild nuts and berries is out of all proportion to the value of them when gathered. But nuts and berries were once of vital concern to our fathers.

It is in baseball and football, however, that we best see the phylogenetic significance of play. The daily paper is a good index of popular interest. Here we shall often find perhaps seven, perhaps twenty columns devoted to baseball, while no other single subject whether in politics, art, literature, or science, aspires to two columns. How shall we explain the absorbing interest in baseball and football as well as in horse-racing and prizefighting? Here again, phylogenetic experience becomes the key to the problem of modern sports.

In baseball we have a game combining three of the most deep-seated racial instincts, the instinct to throw, to run, and to strike. During untold periods of the life history of our race, survival has come to him who could throw the straightest, run the swiftest, and strike the hardest. To throw something at something is almost as natural for a boy as to breathe. Throwing, batting, running are no longer of any service in this age of mind, but they were the conditions of survival in the distant past. Baseball reinstates those ancient attitudes and brings a thrill of cherished memories. Any one who has ever held a bat in hand and assumed the expectant attitude of the batter knows the peculiar thrill which is explained only by recalling that his distant ancestors in just that attitude beat down with a real club many an opposing foe, whether man or beast, and those who held clubs in this position and struck hard and quickly survived and transmitted this instinct. Dr. Gulick says:

Baseball is a complex of elements all of which date back certainly to our prehuman ancestors. The ability to throw a stone with accuracy and speed was at one time a basal factor in the struggle for survival. The early man who could seize a bough of a tree and strike with accuracy and great power was better fitted to survive in the brutal struggles of those early days than the man not so endowed. He could defend his family better, he was better fitted for killing game, he was better fitted for overcoming his enemies. The ability to run and dodge with speed and endurance was also a basal factor.

The instinct to throw, as the same author shows, belongs to boys only, scarcely appearing in the case of girls. The awkward throw of girls, like the left arm throw of boys, is well known. The plays of girls reveal their own set of instincts recalling the habits of primitive woman. "We are the descendants of those men who could throw and those women who loved children."

Football excites still greater enthusiasm than baseball because it reinstates still more primitive forms of behaviour. The fascination of football, like that of other sports which have a deep appeal to the human mind, is explained only by the facts of mental evolution. We have to go back in human history to those ancient scenes and those ancient pursuits which have left an indelible imprint on the human brain, and we have to remember that in our hours of relaxation we demand a complete release from those newer forms of mental activity which condition progress and civilization, and a temporary return to the older and easier ones.

The one great elemental fact in human history is the fact of war. Mankind has come up through a history of warfare. It has been man against man, group against group, tribe against tribe, nation against nation, from the beginning. Man is at home on the battlefield.

There he has received his training and gained his strength. His soul is full of latent memories of strife and conflict. The football field is a mimic representation of this age-old field of battle. Here again is found the face-to-face opposition of two hostile forces, the rude physical shock of the heavy opposing teams, the scrimmage-like, melee character of the collisions, the tackling, dodging, and kicking, and the lively chases for goal as for cover.

Football is more fun than baseball and attracts larger crowds, because it is more dramatic, more like a fight. It awakens in us deep-seated slumbering instincts, permits us to revel for a time in those long-restrained impulses, relieves completely the strain of the will, and so serves all the conditions of relaxation.

By inner imitation the spectators themselves participate in the game and at the same time give unrestrained expression to their emotions. If at a great football game any one will watch the spectators instead of the players, he will see at once that the people before him are not his associates of the school, the library, the office, the shop, the street, or the factory. The inhibition of emotional expression is the characteristic of modern civilized man. The child and the savage give free expression in voice, face, arms, and body to every feeling. The spectators at an exciting football game no longer attempt to restrain emotional expression. They shout and yell, blow horns and dance, swing their arms about and stamp, throw their hats in air and snatch off their neighbours' hats, howl and gesticulate, little realizing how foreign this is to their wonted behaviour or how odd it would look at their places of business. So also the defeated players cry like babies, as did the heroes of ancient Troy.

The excitement of the spectators cannot be explained by the importance of the scenes before them, for, as in the case of the horse-race, they have little or no relation to the serious life of the present; but the scenes are those which were once matters of life and death.

The prevalence of gambling in connection with football, as well as in horse-racing, prizefighting, and other popular sports, illustrates the reversion to primitive morals accompanying the return to early pursuits.

This prevalence of gambling and of other obvious evils 2 connected with intercollegiate athletics has suggested to some the desirability of abolishing these sports. A very different conclusion, however, seems to be forced upon us by the study of the laws of relaxation in its broader aspects. Not until we understand the psychology of alcohol and of war and of the foolish amusement crazes shall we recognize the full significance and the full value of athletic contests and intercollegiate rivalries. The evils mentioned are real enough and most deplorable, but it does not follow that they would not be present in other or worse forms in different connections if there were no intercollegiate athletics.

The intense interest aroused in intercollegiate sports is no doubt to some extent an echo of the old ancestral rivalries between social groups. They appeal, therefore, to deepseated human instincts and fulfil to a marked degree all the requirements of relaxation and recreation.

It should, of course, be remembered that the social value of these sports relates rather to the spectators than to the players. For the latter, indeed, they may become a form of work. But the participants as spectators are numbered by the thousands, and for all of these the games serve as valuable forms of relaxation. The substitution of intramural football and baseball for the intercollegiate games would result in the loss to a large extent of the valuable holiday and festival aspects of the latter sports.

Furthermore, the intense interest in intercollegiate football and baseball has resulted in a very wide actual participation in these games by the students in colleges, universities, and in public and private schools throughout the country.

The law that the more elemental the character of our responses, the greater their value as relaxation and release from the tension of the strenuous life, is well illustrated in the circus and amphitheater of the Romans. When we recall the sports of ancient Rome, we see again that in sport we have a psychological factor of the greatest importance and a profound psychological problem. Juvenal's phrase "bread and games" has become familiar. The popularity of any emperor was nearly proportional to his liberality in the matter of games and spectacles. Emile Thomas says: "After the sack of Rome by Alaric, the miserable remnant of the original inhabitants, and the peasants who flocked in from the environs to the number of ten thousand, loudly demanded games in the Circus, which had to be celebrated among the smoking ruins."

The Colosseum, whose magnificence receives a new meaning from our point of view, accommodated eighty-seven thousand people. The Circus Maximus was one of the most imposing of Roman structures. It is said that four hundred and eighty-five thousand spectators were in actual attendance at once upon its spectacles. 1 The shouting could be heard in the suburbs of Rome. The upper wooden seats collapsed at one time, killing eleven hundred people. Rome had theatres, too, but the largest of these, that of Pompey, had seats for only forty thousand spectators, and despite the political interest which attached to many of the theatrical exhibitions, we must believe that the interest in the theatre was insignificant when compared with that of the amphitheater and circus. Trajan gave a single entertainment lasting one hundred and twenty-three days.

Now, what was the character of these amusements which so fascinated the Roman populace? They were horse-races, gladiatorial combats, and the exhibition and contests of wild animals. Man's racial history has been one long battle with the lower animals, defensive for life and safety, offensive for food and sustenance. So far as the workaday world of the Romans is concerned, it was much the same as ours, taxing the same higher mental powers and demanding relaxation in the form of older and simpler pursuits.

In the gladiatorial combats we see the hand-to-hand encounters of early man, almost as far removed from the actual daily life of the Romans as it is from ours. In the display of wild animals and in their deadly combats with each other and with man, we see mirrored in Roman sports the old life of the forest and plain. The mood of the spectator at the Colosseum changes also to suit the character of the spectacle, and for the time he is no longer the civilized Roman of the second century, but boisterous, cruel, intoxicated with the sight of blood. So strong was the craving for the old feral scenes that professional hunters were kept in the remotest parts of Asia and Africa to capture alive every species of beast to be exhibited and killed for the amusement of Rome. Eleven thousand animals were produced by Trajan at a certain spectacle. Much has been said about the brutalizing effect of these games upon the Romans; but if we have correctly outlined the psychology of sport, we see in such games as these not a brutalizing agency, but an afterglow of brutality left behind. The modern circus, menagerie, and zoological gardens offer similar entertainment on a smaller scale, and appeal to the same instincts.

The human race has reached a stage of evolution in which such sports as gladiatorial shows, prize-fights, and 'bullfights hark too far back and are no longer endured, but before we condemn them too harshly it would be well to compare the number of men and animals killed in these ancient exhibitions with the number of men and horses killed in a modern war.

Success today does not depend upon swiftness of foot or swiftness of horse, yet our sports take the form of foot-races and horseraces. There was a time when swiftness of foot and swiftness of horse were vital. So in our sports these old scenes are reenacted. Stage managers, story-writers, and moving-picture shows seek always 'for a new thrill. It is sometimes thought that the new and unexpected is thrilling. The reverse is true. The thrilling is the old and elemental. When love and warfare fail, the story-writer can always fall back on the horse-race for thrills. The horse has little significance for the life of today and it is fast becoming less, but he has had an intimate relation with the life history of the race. It is difficult to read any well-told story of a horse-race or chariot-race, or any account of human rescue by means of equine or canine intelligence, without an emotional disturbance out of all proportion to the importance of the events. In fact they have no significance now. They belong to the past.

In this connection it is interesting to recall that some years ago an English magazine published the results of a census which it had made of the order of popularity of Browning's shorter poems. The list contained about fifty of these poems, including such matchless gems as "Evelyn Hope," "Abt Vogler," "My Last Duchess," "Rabbi Ben Ezra," etc. But the first place of all the fifty was given to the poem entitled, "How they brought the Good News from Ghent to Aix," a poem without significance of thought or sentiment, but depending for its interest upon the incident of a desperate horseback ride from Ghent to Aix. The compelling force of this poem will be felt by the reader, if we quote some of the first and last lines:

* I sprang to the stirrup, and Joris, and he;
* I galloped, Dirck galloped, we galloped all three;
* "Good speed!" cried the watch as the gate-bolts undrew;
* "Speed!" echoed the wall to us galloping through; Behind shut the postern, the lights sank to rest, And into the midnight we galloped abreast;
* And there was my Roland to bear the whole weight Of the news which alone could save Aix from her fate;
* With his nostrils like pits full of blood to the brim, And with circles of red for his eye-sockets' rim.

Then I cast loose my buffcoat, each holster let fall, Shook off both my jack-boots, let go belt and all, Stood up in the stirrup, leaned, patted his ear, Called my Roland his pet-name, my horse without peer; Clapped my hands, laughed and sang, any noise, bad or good, Till at length into Aix Roland galloped and stood.

* And all I remember is friends flocking round;
* As I sat with his head 'twixt my knees on the ground;
* And no voice but was praising this Roland of mine, As I poured down his throat our last measure of wine.

Which (the burgesses voted by common consent) Was no more than his due who brought good news from Ghent.

From the phylogenetic standpoint which we have thus gained, both children's play and adult sport come into clearer light. Thus we understand why adult sport resembles the activities of early man. The older, the more basal, the more primitive, so to speak, the brain patterns used in our hours of relaxation, the more complete our rest and enjoyment. Just in proportion as the sport is primitive, so much greater is the sweet peace which it seems to bring to the troubled soul, simply because it involves more primitive brain tracts and affords greater release from the strenuous life.

So while we find one hundred and fifty spectators at an intercollegiate debate, we find a thousand at an automobile race, five thousand at a horse-race, thirty thousand at a great baseball game, seventy thousand at a great football game, and three hundred thousand at a gladiatorial show. The nervous tracts which function in such activities as hunting and fishing and swimming and boating and camping, in football and baseball and golf and polo, and in horse-racing and bullfighting, are deep worn, pervious, and easy. During countless generations the nerve currents have flowed through these channels. Witnessing these rude contests, pictures of former ages, or taking part in these deep-seated, instinctive actions brings sweet rest and refreshment. 'The racially old is seized by the individual with ease and joy." The soothing restfulness of the open grate fire is thus probably due to latent or subconscious memories of the campfire, which so long brought rest and comfort to the early man.

From this point of view, the dancing craze is less difficult to understand. In explaining such phenomena it will not do to rely too much on the behaviour of the crowd, as some writers have done. To call it a craze, a fashion, an epidemic, and to refer it to the laws of imitation which govern a crowd, is not to explain it. Imitation alone is a very feeble social force. It becomes a powerful force only when the imitated action satisfies some need. The desire to dance, whether it be conscious or unconscious, may be very strong, but, as long as it is under the ban of social disapproval, the desire may be largely repressed. When these social restrictions are removed, then the practice may become general, and if the desire is strong enough, it may spread like an epidemic. This is about as far as the law of imitation helps us in explaining a dancing craze.

Dancing is a pastime as old as the human race. The muscles involved are the larger muscles of the trunk and legs, fundamental, as they have been called. The brain patterns concerned are, therefore, the oldest and earliest in racial development. Progress has been, first, in the direction of the finer and more differentiated movements of the arms, hands, eyes, and vocal organs, and then, in our own times, more and more toward purely intellectual activity. Rest and relaxation, therefore, always tend to take the form of exercise of the fundamental muscles. As compared with other forms of relaxation which we have been studying, such as hunting, fishing, horse-racing, ball-playing, etc., dancing is ultra-primitive, both in respect to the fundamental character of the muscles involved, and also in respect to the simple rhythmical form of the movements. It affords, therefore, a complete rest of the higher brain and provides a very perfect means of relaxation.

If we consider the manner of life of civilized man of the twentieth century and compare it with that of one hundred years ago, we shall understand the peculiar fascination of the dance at the present day. From the beginning of his racial history, there has been one set of muscles which man has continuously used, however intermittent the use of the others has been, and these are the muscles of the legs. Until recent years he has been on his feet most of the time when not asleep standing, walking, running, climbing. Now he sits in a chair, working his brain or his eyes or his hands, or else he rides in a carriage, automobile, street-car, or train. It is doubtful whether this sudden and radical change can take place without disastrous consequences. At any rate, we can understand why dancing as a mode of recreation should in these circumstances appeal to us so powerfully as to take the form of an epidemic when once fashion has given its sanction.

When we speak of dancing as a very perfect means of relaxation, we refer, of course, to healthful forms of the dance as exhibited in the folk-dances and in the dances of children. The modern social dance as it exists in America, in which the sex element has become too prominent, associated also as it is with night hours, electric lights, dust, and bad air, has slight recreational value as compared with the earlier and healthier forms of folk-dancing. To understand the truth of this, it is only necessary to ask ourselves whether the dancers of today are likely to be the fathers and mothers of the future citizens of America. Sociologists are already well aware that we must look in quite another direction for these. The game of golf, again, has a peculiar restorative power surpassing all medical or other therapeutic arts. We may be physically and mentally weary from a morning's work. Despite the strenuous physical exertion of an afternoon at golf, our fatigue is lessened, not increased. Fresh air does not explain it. It is a return to the primitive outdoor life. We stride over hill and through ravine; we stumble into ditches; we carry a club and strike viciously at the ball; we follow the ball with the eye and search for it in the grass as our forefathers searched for their arrows and missiles; we use our legs and our arms; we let the nerve currents course through the more ancient channels; we revel unconsciously in latent memories and old race habits and come back to our work rested, renewed, and refreshed.

But you may say golf and bowling and baseball and prizefighting require skill and close attention and tax mind as well as muscle. But this is not the point. Our remote ancestors had skill. To see quickly and correlate nicely eye and hand, or eye and foot, was an early acquisition. It is not this that fatigues us in modern life. It is the everlasting, high-pressure grind. It is holding ourselves down to hard working and hard thinking and long-sustained tasks. It is analysis, concentration, effort, dead lift of mind, the kind of mental work that digs Panama canals, perfects automobiles and airships, discovers new laws of mind and matter in the laboratory, thinks out new fields for the investment of capital, scrutinizes countless court records for precedents in law which may clear our clients, holds the ship's captain on the bridge in times of peril, keeps the soldier at his post and the clerk at his desk through the long hours and the weary days. As the strenuous life increases in city and country, there is an increased demand for relaxation, whether in the form of baseball or football, horse-racing or gambling, or in the form of the automobile craze, or the auction-bridge craze, or the dancing craze, or the moving-picture craze. These are all methods of escape from the clutch of the modern strenuous life, exhibited in all countries, but most noticeably in America, for whatever it is that is driving the human race forward in the path of progress so rapidly and relentlessly seems to have gripped the Anglo-Saxon people particularly hard.

Even these many forms of relaxation are not sufficient to relieve the overwrought brain, and so in ever-increasing amounts we have recourse to artificial means of relaxation through narcotics, such as alcohol, tobacco, and other drugs. Alcohol, by its slight paralysis of the higher and later developed brain tracts, accomplishes artificially what is effected naturally by play and sport, that is, it liberates the older, freer life of the emotions and the more primitive impulses.

Thus, from our new point of view, the difficulties in regard to children's play disappear. The reason why children play and why their plays take reversionary forms is now evident. The higher brain tracts, those making work possible, are not developed. If a child does anything, he must play, i.e., his activity must take the form prescribed by the brain patterns already developed, and these are the old racial ones. He is equipped with a nervous mechanism adequate for old racial activities and for the most part with these only. The little girl hugging and nursing her doll is not the victim of an instinct whose purpose is to prepare her for later maternal duties. She is simply doing what her mother and her grandmothers have done since the beginning. If they had not done so, she would never have been born.

The child does not play because of surplus energy, for under normal conditions all his energy is expended in play; the child is a playing animal. Nor does he play because of an instinctive need of practice and preparation for life's serious duties, for the form of the latter is constantly changing while the plays of children remain much the same from year to year and century to century. Nor, finally, does he play because it is necessary for his complete growth that he should pass through the several stages of racial history. He plays because he is a child, and to the child's natural and active life we give the name "play" to distinguish it from the life of conscious self-direction, of strain and effort and inhibition which evolution has imposed upon the adult human being.

When we say that all of the activity of the young child takes the form of play, the statement should be regarded as a general one. As the term "play" is actually used, there are certain minor classes of responses which are not included. The child's instinctive shrinking from a large furry animal is as much a part of his original nature as his tendency to run and jump and climb and wade. His responses in the taking of food, likewise, and in protecting himself by crying are original inherited responses. But to crying and sucking and shrinking from objects of fear we do not give the name "play," because, being of the immediate life-serving kind, they bear a closer resemblance to those responses to which in later life we give the name "work," and we reserve the term "play" for that larger and characteristic class of activities which are distinguished from the conscious self-directive life of the man. The play reactions of children, therefore, belong to their original nature. Social heredity may account for the forms of organization of many of the plays of children as well as the sham character which they assume when compared with their originally serious form, but the elements of the great mass of the plays which are dearest to the hearts of children are truly instinctive. The educational; application of this theory of play presents difficulties than the older theories. It is not necessary that the child should live through and live out any series of savage stages. It is merely necessary that he should be kept active with the mental and physical equipment that he has, that work should not be too early imposed upon him, and that his plays should be so organized and supervised that, while retaining the elementary form of his instinctive responses, they may be physically, morally, and socially harmless.

For instance, a boy, if he is a boy, must throw. It is just a question of whether he shall throw stones at a cat, at a street-car, at little children, or whether he shall throw a curved ball to the catcher. The latter is harmless, the former dangerous. Again, a boy's instinct of 1 Compare James's Psychology, n, 429, n. rivalry is very strong. He must do something daring, get ahead of some one, as those of his ancestors who survived did before him. If a proper playground is provided, all these things may be done without injury to society. Again, in response to the dancing instinct, the children must be taught the graceful and healthful folk-dances.

In our modern cities supervised play has become necessary for social order for the reason that the old conditions of spontaneous, healthful play have been taken away.

Says Luther Burbank, quoted by George E. Johnson: Every child should have mud-pies, grasshoppers, water-bugs, tadpoles, frogs, mudturtles, elderberries, wild strawberries, acorns, chestnuts, trees to climb, brooks to wade in, water-lilies, woodchucks, bats, bees, butterflies, various animals to pet, hay fields, pine cones, rocks to roll, sand, snakes, huckleberries, and hornets; and any child who has been deprived of these has been deprived of the best part of his education.

As regards adults, the social applications of the theory are equally obvious. There must be large periods of relaxation from the high-tension life of today. If they are not provided in the form of healthful and harmless sports, there will be irritability, abnormal fatigue, and antisocial outbreaks. There will be auction-bridge crazes and dancing crazes and moving-picture crazes, and there will be ever-increasing resort to the temporary harmonizing effect of alcohol, tobacco, and coffee. Even in the life of the family the harmonizing influence of games is seen. The friction sometimes exhibited among its members, in some cases taking the extreme form of nagging, wrangling, and quarrelling, is no doubt due in large part to the fatigue of the higher brain. In such cases it will often be found that participation in some simple game, particularly an outdoor game, such as golf, tennis, or even quoits, will completely relieve the situation, bringing sympathy, harmony, and peace. In society, the larger family, the same effect must follow upon the larger participation in healthful sports. It is sometimes a matter of surprise to us in periods of national prosperity, when wages are good and work obtainable, that unrest increases, together with crime and insanity.

It may be because the high tension with its consequent fatigue is not relieved. What is needed is less work and worry and more healthful relaxation. Worry is a good example of the high-tension life that is a part of our civilization. Worry is only a perverted form of provision. It is well enough for preachers to tell us not to worry, but worry is one of the conditions upon which civilization depends, namely, solicitude and care for the future. As a nation we are just beginning to worry, for instance, about the depletion of our forests and soil, and it is well that we are doing so. But sometimes we become excessively solicitous about the future, whether it be about the rent or the winter's supply of coal or our future health or the health and morality of our children, and this is what is usually spoken of as worry. It is very wearing, for the reason that it brings constant strain upon delicate and recently developed brain tracts and makes relaxation imperative.

If we have correctly described the theory of play and the psychology of relaxation and their relations to the conditions of our modern life, it will be evident at once that the need will not be supplied merely by providing more playgrounds for children and more holidays and sports for grownups, vital as these are. The difficulty goes deeper and calls for emphasis of still other forms of relaxation than play and sport. There are many of these, such, for instance, as music, which is one of the best, and rhythmic dancing, when freed from objectional features. An ever-ready and convenient form of relaxation is the modern novel, in which the attention is sustained objectively as in the chase or the drama, but its value as relaxation is greatly less than that of the old and social storytelling. Society in all its forms is a healthful means of relaxation. All valuable games and sports are social and the mere mingling with our fellows lowers the mental stress and tension. Primitive man was wholly social and survived only in cooperative groups. The reversionary character of crowd behaviour has been made well known to us.

Religion may be mentioned finally as a mode of relaxation of the highest value. Religion is a letting go the stress and tension of the individual and resigning one's self to an outside power, whether that power be God or the Church. The function of religion in this aspect is that of a sustainer, and religion loses much of its usefulness if the individual, as is often the case, feels it his duty to sustain his religion. His religion must sustain him. Clubs, societies, fraternities of all kinds, exercise a similar function. The great charm of all fraternal societies is that they relieve the stress, the burden, the tension of the individual and shift the responsibility upon the society as a whole. The society is back of him, to some extent will do his thinking for him, decide moral questions for him, relieve him from fear.

Just as man has physically lifted himself from the earth, overcoming gravity, so mentally he has raised himself above the other animals by the fatiguing exertion of his higher mental powers. The first animals were marine animals. They floated in or upon the water without effort. Then came creeping land animals prone upon the ground but not so completely supported as in the water. Gradually the animal lifted himself upon four legs and at last, by infinite labour, erect upon two, and the tension is correspondingly great. The horse rests very comfortably upon his four legs if allowed to stand, and needs to lie down scarcely an hour in the twenty-four. Man sustains himself with constant effort in an erect position and must sit much of the time on a chair, and at night reverts to the original position of the worm, flat upon the bed. This illustrates the whole theory of relaxation. It is always some form of reversion to primitive attitudes, physical or mental, and it brings rest and peace and harmony.

The rhythm of moral and social progress probably follows the same law. Periods of rapid progress are followed by periods of rest and relaxation. From time to time we are shocked by waves of vice and epidemics of immorality. We hear suddenly of conditions of astonishing laxity of morals in the small towns of our Western States, which are supposed to be models of propriety, and we say that the world is going to the bad. But our judgment is too hasty. These things are really incidental to progress. What we witness is a kind of moral relaxation, a relapse to more primitive conditions, as a result probably of progress that is too rapid, of tension too great. Something like moral fatigue takes place and a reaction follows.

Just at present we are hearing it said that our country has gone "amusement-mad." Well, our manner of life has been very strenuous. The tension has been high. Something was bound to happen. Other forms of relaxation have failed us just when we needed them most particularly art and religion. We are told that the art of ancient Greece was the product of the Greek genius. Perhaps it was the cause of it. Both art and religion entered intimately into the daily life of the Greeks. They have departed from ours.

In fact the world has lately been getting too severely serious and laborious. Too much hard thinking is demanded to keep up the modern pace. Whether in journalism, in literature, in scientific research, in mechanical invention, in social and educational reform, in labour movements, or in the feverish struggle for wealth, the higher brain is taxed to a degree incommensurate with the possibility of physiological adjustment. Our physical constitution cannot so quickly adapt itself to this suddenly increased demand upon certain specific nervous functions comparatively new and unstable. Reactions of one kind or another are therefore inevitable. In America we have the amusement crazes, obsessions of dancing, motoring, baseball, football, moving pictures, etc., together with a healthy revival of athletic sports, playground and recreation movements, and interest in outdoor life. In Europe, where the temper of the people lends itself less readily to these forms of release, we have witnessed the reaction in its most repulsive form, in a debauch of bloodshed, and a return to the most brutal and the most elemental kind of behaviour, that of war, which rests the higher brain completely. It is really a physiological situation that the peace societies have to contend with. Mankind cannot so easily escape from its long past.

In conclusion, it should be said that it is doubtful whether the tendency shown in children's play and in adult sport to take the forms of old racial activities can be subsumed under such names as survival, reversion, or recapitulation. These biological terms are all too narrow, and they carry a certain reproach which does not pertain to the play and sport activities. It is a wholly unwarranted assumption that those peculiar forms of mental activity which in a special manner characterize the adult masculine mind are of any higher order than those which are exhibited in play in the broader sense in which we have used the term.

The latter represent more fundamental forms of human behaviour and perhaps more valuable. Just at the present time evolution seems to be tending toward the development of those high-tension masculine traits by which man adapts himself to his environment and which produce something which we call progress or civilization, a civilization, however, in no way remarkable except in the way of its frenzied reactions. It is the age of work, the age of stress and effort and tension, the expensive, centrifugal age, the age of outer conquest but not of inner harmony. At such a time, comforts, luxuries, and inventions abound, side by side with profound misery. Is it not possible to think of a higher civilization than ours a civilization faintly realized by the ancient Greeks where the play motive will be ascendant, where a greater degree of repose, of measure, and of harmony will be attained, and where humanism will be more prized than expansionism?

Sex Tourism

The term sex tourism is mostly associated to the prostitutes more particularly women in Asia. Although prostitution is illegal in most countries more particularly, for those minors, still, the said type of tourism is still in full bloom in many of the poor countries in the world. In fact according to the survey conducted in Germany and Switzerland, there are about 8% of the respondents who have answered that they had sex with someone whom they had only met during their holiday that could be a fellow traveller, a local and more particularly a prostitute (2003).

In fact according to statistics, in Costa Rica, the capital city of San Jose, there are about 2, 000 child prostitute alone, that are regularly sold to the foreigners as a part of their sex-tour packages (2007). One thing that have affect the fast growth of the said industry is when HIV/AIDS have arrived to Southeast Asia, the industries started to implement different health check up. Nowadays, the said type of tourism has also involved in the use of the Internet for their marketing strategy.

Educational Opportunity

Educational Tourism

During the past decades, the educational tourism have evolved and developed number of ways such as the student exchanges or the urge of the young people to travel to another country in order to study and learn as well as analyse the language and culture of other people; special holidays on the other hand, is the urge to travel to learn something new (1999). There is no doubt that educational industry has already become one of the most popular types of special interest tourism. According to and (1997), the world market for international education travel was estimated to increase from 4.8 million trips up to more or less 8 million trips in 1996, showing that it had increase 66% of its total trips.

Tourism industry has been one of the most important industries in the world during the past few decades that have helped many countries and nations to improve their economies by increasing sales, employment and the foreign currency earnings (1991). Tourism has been part of the normal daily life of many people in the world (2006).

That is why most of the countries and places in the world are doing their best in focusing on their tourism industry because of the fact that the said industry has obtained the leading position of becoming the most important source of income and foreign investments (2006). (2006) believes that the growth of the tourism industry will continue to expand in the near future and will maintain its growth to become the most important industry in the world.

Special Interest Tourism

Special interest tourism is a controversial and a hot label that often used incorrectly or interchangeably to define a form of tourism that refers to the mass tourism (2000). According to the World Tourism Industry or WTO, special interest tourism can be defined as the specialized tourism that involved individual or group tours by those people who wishes to develop their given interests or visit sites and places that has a relation or connection with their specific interest or subject (2003). According to, people are travelling because of their particular interest for a particular subject that are available or can be seen in a given country or place (2003).

On the other hand those people who are into the special interest tourism are called special interest tourist. They are motivated by their desire and urge to pursue their particular interest, hobby or activity than can be a sport like, scuba diving, golf or mountain climbing or bird watching; another thing that can motivated them is their love for heritage interest like folk music, educational pursuit and periodical architecture. They are choosing their destination based on the can offer them a better and unique way of enjoying their hobbies and interest (2000 century).

Conclusion

There is no doubt that tourism had been the most important industry of any country that is why most of them are doing their best in order to maintain and preserve all of their resources that can attract the attention of their target tourist. With accordance to the three chosen tourism, I must say that all of them are in great performance in the international tourism industry. Perhaps of all the special tourism that I had chosen, the education tourism is the most fast growing and the most in demand in the world. On the other hand, the sex tourism is the most controversial and most judged.

Shopping

One-day Shopping Tourism as a Situation Specific Experience

Motives for a Shopping Trip : The motivational basis for purchasing and shopping has been studied by consumer behaviour researchers for decades. The seminal attempt to classify buyers according to their orientation was made by Stone (1954). He identified four different shopper types: the economic consumer, the personalizing consumer, the ethical consumer and the apathetic consumer. Later, several studies have been conducted in order to increase understanding on shopping orientation. According to Tauber (1972) shopping behaviour is motivated by a variety psychosocial need beyond those relating to the products being acquired. In this way, Tauber identified both personal and social motives to be influential in shopping behaviour. Personal satisfaction gained from shopping according to Tauber are: 1) the opportunity to enact a culturally prescribed role; 2) diversion from daily routines; 3) provision of self-gratification; 4) learning about new trends, fashions and innovations; 5) obtaining physical exercise; and 6) receiving sensory stimulation from the retail environment. The satisfaction of a social nature arises from 1) social interaction outside the home; 2) communication with others having similar interests; 3) affiliating with reference group; 4) obtaining increases in social status; 5) achieving success in bargaining and negotiation. Later, Bellenger and Korgaonkar (1980) introduced their twofold shopper typology: economic shoppers, who dislike shopping or are neutral toward it and recreational shoppers, who enjoy shopping as a leisure-time activity.

Westbrook & Black (1985) introduced a motivation-based shopper typology based on Tauber's work. According to Westbrook & Black, there are seven major dimensions of shopping motivation: 1) anticipated utility; 2) role enactment; 3) negotiation; 4) choice optimization; 5) affiliation; 6) power and authority; and 7) stimulation.

These dimensions may vary across individuals and shopping situations due to personality, learning, products being shopped and the types of retail institutions. Dawson, Bloch & Ridgway (1990) used Westbrooks & Blacks results as starting point in their research of how shopping motives and emotional states influence retail outcomes.

They divided motives to product-oriented motives and experiential motives. Product-oriented motives include 1) find variety of new products; 2) find unique crafts or foods; 3) see new things; 4) find good prices; and 5) keep up with new crafts or foods when experiential motives are 1) watch other people; 2) enjoy the crowds; 3) see and hear entertainment; 4) meet new people; 5) experience interesting sights, sounds and smells; 6) get out of the house. Babin, Darden & Griffin (1994) use same kind of duality in their research of shopping value.

Babin et al. argue, that shopping includes both 1) utilitarian outcome resulting from some type of conscious pursuit of an intended consequence and 2) an outcome related more to spontaneous hedonic responses.

As the entertainment aspect of retailing came more recognized, also the hedonic shopping motivations came more apparent. Arnold & Reynolds (2003) focused only on hedonic shopping motivations and developed a scale, which consists of 1) adventure; 2) gratification; 3) role; 4) value; 5) social; and 6) idea shopping motivations.

One remarkable feature in the studies on shopping motivation is that both utilitarian and hedonistic motivations are apparent and important in explaining different aspect of purchasing behaviour. According to Arnold & Reynolds (2003) the importance of the recreational and hedonistic aspects is emphasized in modern markets. Shopping goes beyond mere purchasing and product acquisition in that it emphasizes recreation and gratification.

The growth of the size of shopping malls and the change of their style into more entertaining has led to increase in consumers' interest. It appears as, for example, long shopping trips and increase in time spent in shopping malls. Ikea is one of those shopping centres, which tempt customers from long distance to receive stimulation, buy products and spend leisure time. Travellers spend hours in a car, bus or train just to spend one day in Ikea. The aim of this paper is to understand the main motives of this kind of a shopping trip. The objective is to describe and analyse the motivation orientation of the people going on a one-day trip to Ikea by bus. This study represents a new approach of shopping orientation study in that it concerns the whole trip, not only the store.

Motivational Orientation for One-day Shopping Trip to Ikea

This one day shopping tourism trip to Ikea cannot be specified solely as tourism or shopping. For some consumers, the trip might be just travelling and for others it is mainly shopping. Shopping is experiential and satisfying in nature and not only instrumental in getting the products and services needed. In this way it can be seen to be something in between everyday and holiday. It contains tourism-like features when both movement and changing places are included. On the other hand, shopping is an important activity in tourism, shopping and dining have said to be the most popular activities among tourists. In its broadest sense, shopping is seen as a significant element of tourism. Sometimes shopping may be the foremost motivation for travelling. When the prime reason for the trip is to shop, tourist shopping has been defined as 'shopping tourism', while 'tourism shopping' is used when shopping is just one of many other activities undertaken during the trip.

The similarities between shopping and tourism are evident especially in outshopping, i.e. when the shopping trip is extended beyond the boundaries of one's local retailing area. What is evident is that consumers do not go to a shopping trip just for purchasing or goods. It can be presumed that on a shopping trip motives to travel and motives to purchase are both present. In this research the interest lies in the tension between the recreational motives and the purchasing oriented motives on a one-day bus trip to Ikea. On these shopping trips, travellers spend hours in a bus, shop hours in Ikea and spend hours on the way back home. The first challenge here is to analyse the ability of the motivational orientations to categorize differently motivated travellers.

In order to analyse the motivational orientation of Ikea travellers a Likert-scale consisting of 25 items based on previous research on shopping and travelling motives was developed. Altogether 104 persons were interviewed on bus on their way to Ikea. The motivational data was factor analysed in order to reveal the orientation dimensions. Thinking about the aim of this study, two factor model appeared to be the most clear to interpret. Only the most heavily (>.50) loaded statements.

The two factors explain 38 per cent of the total variance.

Items describing recreational reasons for participating a shopping trip, push from everyday life and pull of the experiential aspects of a shopping trip were loaded on the first factor. In order to capture both the pull and push motivations the factor is termed as "variety from everyday". Items loaded on the second factor conventionally included elements of purchasing behaviour, namely information gathering and product buying. This factor is named as "purchasing". The two factors resemble well the motivational orientations of recreational and task-orientation found by Kaltcheva & Weitz (2006).

In order to reveal different shopping traveller groups a cluster analysis was conducted by using the factors as variables. The five cluster solution presented, offers a grouping that can be justified with good reasons argued for.

The two factors of purchasing and variety from everyday life turned out to be able to discriminate between the clusters of consumers. However, because of the relative small sample size we are not able to make any far reaching interpretations of the clusters. The results suggest, however, that the recreational factor of variety from everyday life seems to be somewhat better discriminator than the task-related purchasing factor. Most of the travellers attended on the Ikea trip in order to buy something. Especially consumers in group A went to Ikea in order to purchase something. On the other hand group B consumers were not inspired by purchasing. They were presumably there just to escort or to elapse time. The C and D shoppers emphasized the recreational and experiential aspects of the shopping trip with the difference that for the C consumers purchasing was more important. On the other hand, the E consumers regarded the shopping trip more as an everyday activity that has to be attended to in order to get something needed.

Clusters are relatively close to origin. It can be assumed, that travellers' motives on this kind on shopping trip to Ikea are not strongly related to variety from everyday life or to purchasing, but various things combine in the motivation structures of the travellers. Falk and Campbell (1997) argue that while shopping, hedonistic and utilitarian motivations become so closely intertwined it is not reasonable to separate them. Consumers often justify their shopping with some rational reason, which might also increase the amount of utilitarian motives. Shopping trip is a sum of several elements, which is why it should be considered as different, partially overlapping processes.

Shopping Trip as an Experience

Since the hedonistic motives to shopping became apparent, the consumer has been seen as an individual emotionally involved in a shopping process, in which the multisensory, imaginary and emotive aspects are sought and appreciated. Shopping is not only buying, but also a socioeconomic means to socialize, enjoy oneself and the company of another person. In this way, shopping can be seen as an experience with an important emotional meaning, founded on the interaction with the products and services consumed. According to Schmitt (1999), an experience is a sum of different elements: sense, feel, think, act and relate.

In order to gain deeper understanding of a shopping trip as an experiential phenomenon, 104 Ikea travellers were interviewed on the way back home from Ikea. The travellers were asked to describe their trip and the best and worst things of it. These descriptions were analysed with content analysis using the elements of experience by Schmitt (1999) as a loose conceptual grid. All of these elements were present in Ikea traveller's descriptions. In addition, to own and to be privileged came up in the descriptions.

Owning has an important role on a shopping trip: buying things and the joy of possessing get travellers into a good mood. Thinking on a shopping trip is both creative and thoughtful. A shopping trip is imagination, gaining new insights and pondering of things. A shopping trip to Ikea is full of stimulation for senses: people try different tastes, see attention awaking new things, smell the scents of new goods, touch coverings of soft pillows and smooth leather couches and listen to the sounds of the department store. Sitting in a bus is a large part of physical action on a shopping trip to Ikea. However, the trip also includes a lot of other kind of action: eating, talking and laughing. To relate is an important element in a shopping trip. Good company might make the trip worth going and friends are needed for backup while making purchasing decisions.

Feelings on a shopping trip can be everything from wonderful and lovely to awful and horrible.

Travellers' descriptions of their trip express a large spectrum of experiences. Every consumption experience is unique and includes thinking, action, relating, feeling and sensing in varying degree. We can assume that this consumption experience itself is somehow valuable, although the desired products are not always found, the prices are too high or the time runs out too fast. Also Westwood (2006) argues that for shopping tourists, already sense of being somewhere different was a defining feature of their experience. Ikea travellers have an experience that makes them somehow privileged compared to those, who have not visited Ikea.

Wonderful Shopping or Endless Torture?

It is amazing, how many different elements are attached to one shopping trip to Ikea. Pleasantness or unpleasantness of the trip is a consequence of many different elements. Sometimes one element affects a lot and sometimes small things create large entities. The pleasantness of the trip might derive from good company, meeting an old friend or spending time with family. Good plans, new ideas, reasonable purchases and money saving make the trip nice. People can relax and enjoy buying and travelling on the Ikea trip. Seeing new products and the large store is exciting and shopping in good company cheers up. The store's selection is nice to watch; scents from cafeteria arouse hunger and food tastes amazingly good after wandering.

For some of the travellers, motivational orientations defines the pleasantness or unpleasantness. One of the travellers, who was strongly oriented for variety from everyday life found, that the best thing about the trip was "*The trip itself (possibility to get away from home once in a while)*", when the worst thing was, that Ikea was only "*An ordinary store*". One of the purchasing-oriented travellers described the best thing about the trip "*I got all the things I needed*".

But for many of the travellers on Ikea-trip, situational factors seem to define the pleas ant and unpleasant elements of the experience. One traveller, who was not purchasing oriented at all, thinks that the best thing about the trip was "*many good purchases*", when the worst thing was that "*all of the plans did not come true, I could not find suitable things*".

Sometimes one good or bad occurrence is the one that is remembered about the trip. For some travellers, the fact that restaurant closed earlier than they assumed, was definitely the worst thing about the trip, despite of their motivational orientation. In one trip, there were some problems with the seats on the bus on the way back and everybody could not sit next to their friend. This was worst thing about the trip to many travellers, although they were purchasing-oriented.

This might be due to the experiential and intensive nature of the one-day shopping trip. This trip is not solely purchasing or leisure, it combines rationality and emotionality. This trip includes many different aspects, and the comprehensive experience is a combination of all of these.

According to Buttle (1992) shopping trips are basically made in terms of logical force, but motives for shopping are also linked to particular shopping context. Our findings support Buttles conclusions: most of the Ikea travellers are purchasing oriented, and attend the trip to buy desired products. Tourism, on the other hand, is considered to be hedonic activity, which determines the shopping context. On the shopping trip to Ikea, travel context brings in the hedonic motives for the trip.

Travellers' motivational orientation differs in the way they wish to gain also immaterial consequences on the trip. Most of the travellers are oriented to buy something, but they are not all interested in the recreational aspects of the trip. According to Westwood (2006) leisure-like aspects are more important than purchasing while shopping. This might be true with shopping-oriented travellers, but our results indicate that there are also purely purchasing oriented travellers on a trip to Ikea. The fact, that some consumers try to justify their shopping with rational reasons, might affect to this.

Because of the small differences in Ikea-travellers' motivational orientation, we suggest that a shopping trip should be seen as different processes, which might also be overlapping. We examined these processes as experiential aspects of a shopping trip. Ikea travellers' experience includes the elements suggested by Schmitt (1999) and in addition the elements named to own and to be privileged arouse from travellers descriptions.

These elements can be assumed to occur from the special characteristics of the shopping trip. Pleasantness and unpleasantness on this kind of intensive one-day shopping trip seems to arise from situational factors. For some travellers, motivational orientation defines the best and worst things about the trip. But it is not unusual, that same elements affect the pleasantness or unpleasantness, despite the motivational orientation of the travellers.

This might be due to the experiential nature of the trip. One-day shopping trip to Ikea is not purely a shopping trip; it is an intensive experience, which includes many different elements.

Offering experiences is a great opportunity for retailers to succeed. Experiential retailing aims to offer customers satisfactory total consumption experiences by chancing the store atmospherics.

Types of Tourist

Tourism is a travel for predominantly recreational or leisure purposes. Tourism also refers to the provision of services in support of this act. Tourism is defined as the study of man (the tourist) away from his usual habitat, of the touristic apparatus and networks responding to his various needs, and of the ordinary (where the tourist is coming from) and nonordinary (where the tourist goes to) worlds and their dialectic relationships. Such conceptualisations extend the frame beyond the earlier trade-oriented notions or definitions mostly devised to collect data and calculate tourist arrivals, departures, or expenditures. Significantly, it is this holistic view which accommodates a systemic study of tourism: all its parts, its interconnected structures and functions, as well as ways it is influenced by and is influencing other forms and forces relating to it.

Tourism Behaviour

The concept of behaviour in tourism considers customers and their behaviour specifically as it relates to tourist activities. Some distinctive behaviour topics include cross-cultural interaction, authenticity, tourist-guide interaction and post travel attitudes. This subsumes both the observable behaviour of tourists and their mental and psychological processes involving decision-making, motivations and cognition. The study of tourist satisfaction provides a link to business and management research. Knowledge of the behaviour of tourists in space and time is valuable to assist planners and managers of attractions and environments. Tourist behaviour and experience is assessed by survey studies as well as observational and field research.

Decision Process

Many models have been proposed to simulate the decision-making process for tourism-related products. However, this is a very complicated procedure, and it increases in complexity as more people become involved. The concepts of image, utility maximisation, knowledge acquisition and others are all involved. In addition, various socioeconomic characteristics affect decision making in different ways. Tourism has become one of the world's most powerful components of economic development. Many countries have established tourism development as a high priority concern.

However, increases in discretionary time and money, as well as the variety of vacation choices, have given the potential traveller more flexibility of choice. As a result, the factors influencing travel decisions are becoming more complex. If a travel or tourism organisation wants to influence a travel decision, it needs to understand who is making the decision and how that decision is made.

The 'decision process' has been described as a simple association between a stimulus and a response. It has also been described as a very complex interaction among many behaviour determinants (, 1966). An effective travel decision-making model must incorporate important factors affecting the decision (such as sociodemographic, sociological and psychographic characteristics) and provide an understanding of the relationships between these variables. Travel decisions may also be affected by factors such as travel characteristics, destination attributes and past travel patterns. One of the key steps in tourism planning and marketing is to develop travel behaviour choice models by analyzing these travel factors.

Consumer Behaviour

Consumer behaviour can be viewed as the study of how, why and how often individuals make decisions to spend their available resources (such as money, time or energy) on consumption-related items (and, 1990). Many factors affect the consumer decision process. Factors can come from marketing (including such things as perceived product quality, price and distinctiveness), social sources (which includes family and reference groups), individual differences (such as sociodemographics, lifestyle and personality types), or psychological processes (like motivation, or destination perceptions).

Sociodemographics, travel characteristics and psychographic variables have all been recognized as important factors influencing travel decisions. One of the strategic approaches in tourism planning and decision-making is to develop travel choice models by analyzing these travel factors. Models can be defined as 'systems of hypotheses relating one or more dependent variables to several independent variables' (1989).

In studying travel and tourism, dependent variables could be the choice of a tourist destination, hotel or accommodation, the likelihood of taking a future trip, the length of stay or the total number of visits. On the other hand, independent variables could include factors such as sociodemographics, psychographics, travel characteristics, destination attributes or economic variables.

Tourism Motivations: Factors affecting the Decision Making Process: According to the sociologist Max Weber, motivation lies at the core of human behaviour. Consequently, the study of motivation is central to any social scientific undertaking since it provides understanding, explanation and prediction. It goes beyond the how questions of description to the why questions of interpretation and causality. As one domain of interpersonal activity, tourism is no exception to this general observation. Indeed, 'why do people travel?' is probably the most fundamental issue in tourism research today (2000). (1994), points out that there are several concrete social influences conditioning the decision to travel. He identifies the family, reference groups, social class, the surrounding culture and the work place as the most important of these. The latter is particularly significant since it is conductive to compensatory and spill over effects in various types of travel.

1. Social interaction is commonly identified as a tourism motivation. Early research on the latter incorporated the underlying hypothesis that an individual has a need for love and affection and the desire to communicate with others. Further explorations revealed enhancement of kinship and friendship relationships and the facilitation of varied and increased social interaction as motives which directed vacation choice and behaviour.
2. Cultural motivators are strong push factors for the development of tourism. Cultural motivators lead the tourist into learning about and experiencing the culture of societies other than their own.

Senior Tourism

An exponential increase in the number of senior citizens throughout the world has made this group an attractive niche market for tourism with its own particular needs. Tourism marketers in countries like Australia, Canada and the United States are beginning to sharpen their focus on older people. Seniors roughly constitutes up to a third of the adult population in each of these countries. Many of these seniors have the desire and means to travel for pleasure, discovery and learning. The main purpose of travel is Holiday. Seniors stay more in lower cost accommodation. They tend to stay more with friends, relatives or their own property.

Trip Characteristics

1. Senior Tourists travel longer.
2. Senior Tourists travel to more destinations.
3. Senior Tourists have less ties to employment.

Senior Tourists are people of later age (after 55) who travel for leisure and whose earning and family obligations decrees and finally disappear. A-first-distinction can be made in young-old (aged 55-64), old (aged 65-74) and very old (aged 75 and over).

Economic Aspects

The WTO forecasts that earnings from international tourism will grow an average of 6-7% annually – double the growth rate for the world economy as a whole. In the coming decades tourism activity will become one of the main economic sectors of the world. Senior Tourists are attractive as consumers because:

1. They have the financial means.
2. They have time.
3. They have a better education than in the past.
4. They belong to a generation, which has travelled.
5. They are relatively healthy and know that activities like tourism and recreation contribute to a healthy lifestyle.

Senior Tourists differ in age (chronological-biological), health, economic status, tourism experience and cultural background.

People do not change their travel behaviour because they turn 60 or retire. Travel experience and patterns will have an important influence on travel behaviour.

Youth Tourism

Youth Tourism has taken many forms over time, most of which seem to have been a simple expression of youthful energy and curiosity about the world beyond their bounded society. Their travels were usually a form of alternatives to prevailing tourism. Historically, these involved travels to medieval universities and such institutions as the "Grand Tour", with its year abroad for young scholars and their tutors.

Youth travel itself is not a new phenomenon. For centuries, young people have been travelling around the world with their families, in groups, or on their own. The World Tourism Organization (WTO) defines the 'young' tourism market as travellers 16-25 years old, who take a trip of at least one night's stay. The Canadian youth market is defined as young people 30 years of age and under, who are travelling outside the family unit, not for business, and not primarily to visit friends or relatives, and whose travel includes at least one overnight stay.

Youth Travel Market

Different groups within the youth travel market have unique characteristics and motivations for travel, and require different products to suit their needs. The youth travel market is divided into two broad categories: independent you travel and youth travel group.

Youth Group Travel

This group is consisting of six or more unrelated young people travelling together. Youth travel group is divided into two groups: student travel or school-based youth group travel and non-school based youth group travel. Youth travel is specifically sanctioned by the sponsoring school, board or school district. School based youth group travel may be driven by curriculum-related activities an/or semi-curricular or extracurricular activities like music performances and sports competition.

Travel and activities are generally undertaken as a group, accompanied by teachers, school personnel and/or adult chaperones. Non-school-based youth group travel is often referred as youth travel grope. This travel is organized by a group such as a sports team, church group, cultural/musical performance troupe or Scouts/Guides. Travel is often undertaken as a group, but may also occur in smaller groups, led by parents or other adult chaperones. Youth group travellers are price sensitive, in the sense that they are more strongly influenced by price related issues that the average business or convention traveller.

Independent Youth Travel

Sometimes referred to as 'free independent youth travellers', or foreign independent youth travellers', independent youth travellers travel alone, or in small informal groups. Today's independent youth travellers tend to be well educated, well informed, and Internet savvy. Students between the ages of 18 and 26 mostly comprise this group, although some are young professionals who are either unemployed or taking time off between school and settling down.

Most independent youth travellers head for destinations farther from home stay longer and spend less daily but more in total than the average adult tourist spends. They appear to be price sensitive for travel, housing and food, but less for entertainment, shopping and attractions. Domestic independent youth travellers tend to plan shorter trips, to one or two specific destinations. Foreign independent travellers tend to have longer stays, and are experience-driven.

Independent Youth Traveller Characteristics

1. Between 15 and 30 years old.
2. Well-educated – most often students or previous students.
3. Travel independently, or with 1-2 friends.
4. Risk-friendly, experience oriented.
5. Responsive to destination/experience based marketing initiatives.
6. Detailed pre-trip planning.
7. Lower incomes, but willing to save/combine travel with work in order to finance travel.
8. Lower daily spending, but longer stays resulting in higher overall spending per trip.

Organised Mass Tourists

The organized mass tourist was the least adventurous and was confined to his environmental bubble, while the drifter was most adventurous and felt at ease with strangeness. The organized mass tourist preferred guided tours, air-conditioned bus with fixed itinerary because of the need of maximum familiarity and minimum novelty.

The degree to which strangeness and familiarity prevailed in the tourist role determined the nature of the tourists' experience as well as the effect on the host society. Cohen (1979) further distinguished five modes of tourist experience by analyzing the different meanings which interest in and appreciation of the culture, social life. The typology further confirmed the different behaviour of travellers in relation to their motivation

Individual Mass Tourist

The individual mass tourist was similar to the organized mass one but he allowed more flexibility in his time and itinerary and so his tour was not well preplanned. He would make the major arrangements through a travel agent, as familiarity was dominant in his total trip experience, but he still accepted somehow the experience of novelty.

The explorer tried to leave the environmental bubble by associating himself with the local people visited and the language they spoke. However, the explorer was still cautious to avoid too rough a visiting experience, and therefore he normally needed comfortable accommodation and reliable transportation.

The Explorer

The explorer tourists are thole one, who travel to or into (unfamiliar or unknown regions), esp for organized scientific purposes. Archeologists, Environmental schientist etc. are the examples of this group.

Exploration is the act of searching or travelling a terrain for the purpose of discovery, e.g. of unknown people, including space (space exploration), for oil, gas, coal, ores, caves, water, (Mineral exploration, botanical exploration, or prospecting), or information.

Although exploration has existed as long as human beings, its peak is seen as being during the Age of Discovery for Europe's contact with the rest of the world, and Major explorations after the Age of Discovery for scientific exploration in the modern era.

The Drifter

A Drifter is an itinerant person. Such people may be called drifters, tramps, rogues, or hobos. A vagabond is characterised by almost continuous travelling, lacking a fixed home, temporary abode, or permanent residence. Vagabonds are not bums, as bums are not known for travelling, preferring to stay in one location.

Historically, "vagabond" was a British legal term similar to vagrant, deriving from the Latin for 'purposeless wandering'. Following the Peasants' Revolt, British constables were authorised under a 1383 statute to collar vagabonds and force them to show their means of support; if they could not, they were jailed. Under a 1495 statute, vagabonds could be sentenced to the stocks for three days and nights; in 1530, whipping was added. The assumption was that vagabonds were unlicensed beggars.

By the 19th century the vagabond was associated more closely with Bohemianism. The critic Arthur Compton-Rickett compiled a review of the type, in which he defined it as men "with a vagrant strain in the blood, a natural inquisitiveness about the world beyond their doors." Examples included Henry David Thoreau, Michael John Arthur Bujold, Walt Whitman, Leo Tolstoy, William Hazlitt, and Thomas de Quincey. A notable 20th century vagabond was the Hungarian mathematician Paul Erdos.

Allocentric vs. Psychocentric

Allocentric tourist – enjoys varied activities and gets a thrill from the unexpected

Psychocentric tourist – nonadventurous and self-inhibited

Allocentric tourists are constantly searching for the new destination, as package tours start spreading into past midcentric and even allocentric destinations. Examples of this include the Caribbean becoming increasingly more midcentric (people between the extremes) as travel becomes less expensive.

- o In 1974, Stanley Plog developed a theory which allowed the US population to be classified into a series of interrelated psychographic types. These types range from two extremes:
- o The 'psychocentric' type is derived from & apos; psyche & apos; or ' self-centred & apos; where an individual centres thoughts or concerns on the small problem areas of life. These individuals tend to be conservative in their travel patterns, preferring 'safe' destinations and often taking many return trips. For this latter reason, market research in the tour-operating sector labels this group as ' repeaters & apos;.
- o The 'allocentric' type derives from the root 'allo' meaning 'varied in form'. These individuals are adventurous and motivated to travel/discover new destinations. They rarely return to the same place twice, hence their market research label ' wanderers & apos.

The Expectation-Evaluation Paradigm

Tourists and vacationers go through a complex decision-making process in determining their level of post-purchase satisfaction. Most tourist satisfaction models follow a positivists approach, in which tourists are viewed as rational beings who evaluate their level of satisfaction or dissatisfaction through a disconfirmation paradigm. That is, tourists purchase a trip with certain expectations (i.e., destination, amenities, and activities), and subsequently evaluate satisfaction based on whether than absolute truth, and that such research produces findings "with a focus on meaning and understanding the situation or phenomenon under examination".

He recommends building multiple methods approaches that involve the researcher with those being researched and focus on in-depth study of a small sample.

Stewart and Floyd (2004) capture the rationale for including post-positivistic philosophies within recreation and leisure studies with their observations: "The anxiety amongst leisure researchers is a reflection of a broader crisis within the social sciences about any account that claims to have directly or completely captured someone's lived experiences and social reality". They cite an increasing interest in post-positivistic philosophy as a means for addressing this inability to fully represent people's lived experiences.

Employing a post-positivistic philosophy, this study focuses on understanding and interpreting the process and factors of satisfaction evaluation, rather than on prediction and control. Utilizing mixed qualitative methods, this study examines the complexity involved in tourists' satisfaction with their travel experiences, moving beyond the rational decision-making principles found in positivistic approaches such as Moutinho's, towards an interpretivistic approach.

"Travellers want more than merely observing things and listening to lecture, they want to get actively involved". Tourists may have expectations about the level of active involvement they will experience during a trip that would lead tô a disconfirmation paradigm, however active involvement seems to be a more complex variable in the evaluation of satisfaction than what can be captured and measured using Moutinho's model.

For this reason, it has been chosen as a variable to be further explored. Geva & Goldman (1999) define group dynamics as "...the relations and interactions among group members, the cohesion and morale of the tour group, manner in which free time was spent...". Bettenhausen (1991) suggests that belonging to a group had a great impact on an individual's sense of self, in shaping behaviour and attitudes, in creating a shared culture, and in creating the "rites, rituals, and social roles that provide continuity and order". Arsenault and Gale (2004) report findings from their study of Travel Suppliers and Tour Operators, which indicate a relationship between small group interaction, bonding, friendship formation, and satisfaction via the dimension of positive memory creation

The Tourist Experience

Tourism is a quest for experiences that are in contrast to, and sometimes an extension or intensification of, daily experience. In this sense, tourism is a pioneering example of the emerging "experience economy". The quality of experiences constitutes the key to the success of tourism development. However, despite the importance of the "tourist experience," this is still an ambiguous term. Although various constituents of the tourist experience, such as motivations (curiosity, novelty, change, authenticity meaning, identity, self), satisfactions, feelings, and emotions, have been well researched in psychology, anthropology, sociology, and other disciplines, the literature on the tourist experience as a *gestalt* phenomenon has still been understudied. This is not to deny that there exists a small literature on the tourist experience per se. But many questions still remain unanswered. For example, how is the formulation of the tourist experience related to itineraries?

Itinerary is a frequently used term in the tourism industry, especially in tonnst brochures, but it is rarely seen as an academic term. The reason for this situation could be simple. The itinerary is seen as too self-obvious, too simple, and too trivial to deserve serious academic treatment. At best, it is treated as a component of tourism linking to tour operation. Such a common-sense view of the itinerary should be challenged! however. Rather than being trivial, itineraries act as important media through which the tourism industry interacts with the tourist in the production and consumption of the tourist experience. Itineraries shape the formulation and organization of the tourist experience and become an arena in which the tourist experience is socially produced. As *temporal-spatial carriers* of tourist experience, itineraries are significant in the ways that tourism is consumed and in the ways that tourists' experiences are shaped.

Surely, the tourist experience cannot completely be equated with, or reduced to, itineraries, but it is equally true that the tourist experience is shaped by itineraries. There are at least two reasons that the itinerary deserves study in its own right. First, a number of paradoxes involved in tourism have their roots in itineraries. These paradoxes involve dualisms including authenticity and inauthenticity, autonomy and passivity, freedom and determinations, agency and structure. For example, while tourism is regarded as a quest for authenticity, what is experienced often ends up as "staged authenticity" of the front zone, partly because of the temporary and transient nature of itineraries that constrain tourists from penetrating the back zone of toured reality. While tourism is hailed as freedom, it often ends up as the loss of freedom, partly because of the rigidity of itineraries. While tourism is thought to restore the autonomy and agency that have decreased in daily routines, it creates its own constraints over autonomy and agency because of the constraining, pre-determining, and disciplining nature of itineraries. As Minea and Oakes put it in this volume's introduction, tourism is a performance through which various binaries, such as subject and object, are constantly re-enacted. Relatedly, itineraries are performances in which the paradoxes of modernity are enacted and embodied. The itinerary is thus one of the best dimensions of tourism from which the paradoxes and ambivalence of modernity can be revealed.

Second, as spatial-temporal carriers of tourism commodities, itineraries constitute the media that bridge experiences and goods, services and products, hospitality and attractions, movement and rest, time and space, the quantitative side and the qualitative side of tourism, the ordinary supportive consumption and extraordinary peak consumption, tourist consumers and tourism suppliers. Thus, the itinerary is one of the best domains of tourism from which the mechanisms of social, economical, and cultural production of tourism can be better understood.

This chapter deals with the issue of how the production and consumption of itineraries bring about and reinforce a series of paradoxes in tourism, and how the formation of itineraries are related to wider social, economical, and cultural processes. Just as tourism reveals the ambivalence of modernity and globalization, the same is true of the itinerary. The itinerary provides an alternative perspective from which the paradoxes of tourism can, perhaps more clearly, be revealed.

The following pages consist of three parts. The first concentrates on the issue of how itineraries constitute the *commodity form* of the tourist experience and how the commoditization of itineraries leads to a number of paradoxes. The second examines how itineraries become a way of circulation of tourism products and the associated paradoxes. The third focuses on the role that itineraries play in shaping the consumption of tourism, and the consequential "consuming paradoxes".

Finally, in the conclusion, the paradoxes of tourism are discussed in relation to the rationalization of the tourist experience within the context of postmodernity.

Itineraries as the Commodity form of Tourism

In contemporary societies, the tourist experience is sold as a commodity, which is a result of the commoditization of travel and associated pleasant experiences under the condition of modernity. However, what is the commodity *form* of tourism? This is still an unanswered question. For a commodity to come into being, it must have a form.

For example, for a commodity to become the object of desire, it must be designed in order to take a particular appearance of colours, shape, size, and so on. This type of appearance can be called the *material form* of a commodity. However, in addition to the material form of commodities, there also arise *dematerialized forms* of commodities. In postindustrial economies, the commoditization of information and services leads to the *dematerialization* of commodity forms. The increasingly dominant part that the economy of services plays in postindustria] economies makes the nonmaterial form of commodities increasingly significant. As an integral element of the service industry, tourism also assumes a nonmaterial form, which is exemplified by itineraries.

The itinerary is a system of links between the temporal and spatial arrangements of tourist activities on the tourist journey. From the perspective of the tourism industry, an itinerary is a salable product that links, bridges, and puts together the various components that are necessary to the consumption of tourism. These components include accommodation, transportation, restaurants, attractions, entertainment, and tourist sites. Obviously, for tour operators and travel agencies, itineraries are the commodity form of mass tourism products.

But they are the nonmaterial form, despite the fact that tourism contains such material elements as food, means of transport, and hotels. The itinerary is nonmaterial because it is "virtual", existing in both tourists' and suppliers' imaginations; illustrated in tourist brochures, guidebooks, or TV programs; and only instantiated or materialized in the stage of consumption. Although itineraries are the non-material form, this does not mean that itineraries have nothing in common with the material form. The material commodity form consists of the arrangements of material elements. By contrast, the nonmaterial commodity form is constituted by the temporal and spatial arrangement of procedure, process, and activities. Thus, itineraries, as the nonmaterial commodity form of tourism, are temporal-spatial connections.

They constitute the temporal-spatially organizing processes in which discrete tourist "raw materials" are integrated and sold as a packaged commodity. At the same time, they themselves become the boundaries organized and constrained by the larger economic, social, political, and cultural contexts. Why does tourism take the commodity form of itineraries? The answer should be found from the process of the commoditization of travel experiences.

First, the commoditization of travel experiences is confronted with the problem of *intangible* experiences. In order to turn intangible experiences into "tangible" products in managerial terms, a certain organizing form must be imposed upon the journey.

Thus, itineraries are a way in which travel experiences are objectified, operationalized, and temporally and spatially "materialized." In a literal sense, we cannot sell experiences or pleasures per se, but we can sell the itineraries that are the "containers," carriers, or confines of experiences and pleasures. In short, itineraries are the "tangible" temporal-spatial carrier of intangible travel experiences, which can be produced, circulated (in the form of tourist brochures), and sold in the tourist market. Second, the essence of the commoditization of travel experiences is to make profit through creating an exchange value of tourism commodity. In so doing, travel experiences, as a qualitative subjective state, must be turned into precisely quantifiable and priceable products. Itineraries thus become the quantifiable, profitable, and saleable products of travel experiences.

Third, the commoditization of travel experiences reduces risk and uncertainty arising out of journeys. In order to transform the "raw materials" of risky and uncertain travel into tourism commodities, itineraries become a necessary form through which risks, chances, and uncertainties linking to journeys are eliminated or diminished. For examples, flight seats, hotel rooms, and restaurant tables are secured; safety and hygiene are ensured; access to attractions is guaranteed with tickets booked in advance. With itineraries, the risk-related and uncertain journeys are turned into clearly arranged, certain, standardized, and predictable commodities of tourist experiences.

Itineraries thus embody the rationalism in capitalist commoditization, and hence act as a rational way in which the tourism industry controls and manages mobile experiences. Itineraries are particularly attractive to *mass tourists* who want to create order out of chaos, risks, and uncertainties on their journeys to unfamiliar environments, even though they might also want to defy that order at the same time.

Itineraries are thus an indispensable commodity form of modern tourism and act as an integral dimension of the commoditization of the tourist experience. However, while tourism is successfully commoditized with the help of itineraries, it also faces a paradox derived from itineraries. Part of the essence of the tourist experience is to get out of daily routines, order, schedules, and constraints. As mentioned above, in order to turn the tourist experience into a commodity, it is necessary to make tourism assume a commodity form, namely, itineraries. The latter, however, imposes an emergent routine, order, schedule, and constraint upon the tourist experience.

Thus, tourism, the very act of escape from daily constraints, ends up as an alternative constraint. In relation to the *elimination of chance, risk, and uncertainty* and the increase of security and certainty, tourism is wheeled to the position of diminishing the real charms and appeals of travel, namely, a suitable extent of risk-taking, challenge, improvisation, independence, flexibility, freedom, creativity, and authenticity. Thus, while tourism is put on with the commodity form of itineraries, it paves a way to the demise of the authenticity of travel. As a response to such a strong commoditization of tourism, an increasing number of tourists tend to abandon overscheduled and itinerized mass tourism and adopt more individualist, independent, and flexible forms of travel.

These individual tourists take responsibility for then-own itineraries and leave enough room for adapting and changing primary schedules. The increasingly popular "backpacking" form of travel is such an example. This process can be called the *decommoditization* of itineraries. What Edensor (1998,105-14) describes about tourist behaviours at the Taj is a typical example of differentiation of decommoditized itinerary from commoditized itinerary.

For package tourists, visits to the Taj are highly regulated, predetermined, restrained, and disciplined in time and space. As a result of commoditization of itineraries, package tourists are usually allowed to stay for a quite limited time and to walk around within a limited range when they visit the Taj. By contrast, backpackers have much wider room for improvisation and for changing their itineraries as much as they wish.

For ex ample, they usually spend much more time and cover a wider spatial range at the Taj. Decommoditization of itineraries is thus a tourist action that seeks to transcend the rigidity, constraints, and disciplines of the itinerary of package tourism and that seeks more individual freedom, autonomy, and creativity. However, after getting rid of the itineraries of package tourism, independent travellers find themselves involved in an alternative form of commoditization.

For example, independent travellers often have to buy guidebooks in order to plan an itinerary. Here, guidebooks, such as Lonely Planet and Rough Guides, are themselves a specific way of commoditization of itineraries, or more precisely, the commoditization of the *knowledge* of potential itineraries. In guidebooks, itineraries become the content, rather than the commodity form, of guidebooks. The consumption of this content accompanies independent travellers' journeys. The itineraries described in guidebooks are thus the *hidden* itineraries of the tourism system that shape and organize independent travellers' concrete itineraries.

These *hidden itineraries,* such as the network of schedules, traffic lines and prices, and booking systems of transportation and hospitality, constitute alternative constraints on travel. While the itineraries of package tours are the first level of touristic constraints, the itineraries of the tourism system as a whole are the second level of touristic constraints. Thus, while independent travellers can get rid of the first level of itineraries (overt itineraries) that are sold by travel agencies as packaged tours, they cannot get rid of the second level of itineraries (covert itineraries), itineraries that are hidden in the tourism system and are described by guidebooks and other travel materials.

Itineraries as the Way of Circulation of Tourism Products

Itineraries are not only scheduled journeys, but also mark a spatialization of those journeys. To put it another way, itineraries are about "what" will happen "when" and "where." While the issue of the scheduled journeys has been touched on above, we now turn to the issue of the spatialization of tourism, namely, the issue of "where" tourist activities will take place.

Itineraries are not only the commodity form of tourism, but also the form of access to tourist attractions. Itineraries are the way to circulate tourism products in tourist markets. In the market of goods, it is commodities that are circulated and delivered to consumers for consumption. In the market of temporal spatial experiences of tourism, however, it is tourist consumers that are "circulated" and "delivered." They are taken to tourism products, that are not deliverable in a literal sense. Thus, when tourists travel to destinations, are in a sense "delivered" to tourists. Itineraries can thus be regarded as a way of the circulation of tourism products, despite the fact that itineraries are themselves an integral part of those products.

As a result, once tourist sites are visited by tourists, the "experiences" of these sites are in reality "delivered" and "circulated" to the tourist simultaneously. Therefore, the directions of tourist flows or itineraries are of significance to tourist destinations.

Itineraries are thus not only the way in which people move, but also the way in which landscapes, cultures, and heritage are "circulated". The integration of places into the networks of tourist itineraries turns the places into "experiential commodities" circulated among tourists. Thus, it is no small wonder that tourist destinations compete for access to the network of tourists' itineraries. The simultaneity and synchronization of *circulation* and *consumption* of the tourism products makes the directions and coverage of tourists' itineraries vital to the success of tourism development.

Paradoxes may occur when tourist destinations vie for inclusion into the network of tourists' itineraries. In reality, to compete for this inclusion is to develop a favourable image that is in congruence with targeted potential tourists' tastes and demands.

In this sense, to promote the circulation of a product of "tourist destination" is an issue of developing and establishing a desired image about the destination. In general, a favourable tourist image of a destination tends to allow tourists to include this destination into his or her itineraries, whereas a negative image, on the other hand, tends to deter potential tourists from visiting the destination. However, a favourable image of a destination may involve a paradox.

For example, in sightseeing tourism, the inclusion of a destination into his or her itineraries this time simultaneously implies the exclusion of this place next time, for sightseers always want to seek variety and novelty. Therefore, while a favourable image increases a destination's attractiveness, it may at the same time pave a way to the demise of that attractiveness. That is why a destination has its own life cycle. In postmodernity, with the help of mass media and the Internet, images increasingly become cultural fashions, whereas cultural fashions are always transient and temporary. Moreover, with the bombardment of images, images seem to become an autonomous world, a world that is "virtual reality." Thus, while image-making on the part of a destination is originally aimed at directing potential tourists' journeys and competing for the inclusion of the destination into their itineraries, it may often end up as distracting those tourists because they may get lost in the bombardment of tourist images. In this situation, word of mouth regains its significance in a world with too much information and too many images.

Itineraries as Menus for Tourism Consumption

Tourism is essentially an activity of consumption. What is consumed in tourism consists of two types of "materials." The first is the "material" serving of such daily consumption needs as eating, drinking, and sleeping. This does not mean that the material of this kind needs to be same with that of everyday life. Rather, a certain variety is necessary. Moreover, the consumption of this material takes place in a nondaily context, that is, the context of a journey, mobility, and an itinerary. New meanings of the consumption of the daily material can be derived from such a nondaily context. The second is the "material" of attractions at destinations and the journey itself. This type of material is beyond the reach of daily consumption. The consumption of the first type can be called "consumption *on* the journey," and the consumption of the second type can be called "consumption o/the journey." The consumption *on* the journey is the primary tourism consumption, and the consumption o/the journey is the secondary tourism consumption. The former is the extension of daily consumption to the journey; it is the base and support of the secondary consumption. By contrast, the latter is a transcendence of daily consumption; it is an extraordinary consumption. Both kinds of consumptions constitute *mobile* consumerism, or mass consumption *on the move.*

In both the primary and the secondary consumption, itineraries function as the temporal-spatial carriers of the two. In the primary tourism consumption, itineraries act as the nondaily *context* where daily functions of consumption are performed. In the secondary tourism consumption, itineraries become not only an *object* for consumption (journeys, services, and experiences), but also a *means* of "consumption *elsewhere*" consumption that takes place in other places and that transcends daily consumption. The secondary tourism consumption can thus be called *"peak consumption"*.

The rise and the spread of mobile or touristic consumerism relates to the rise of tourist citizenship in contemporary societies. Tourist citizenship means a specific type of consumer citizenship, a democratized right to consume extraordinary experiences that transcend one's daily reach and that are accessible only through travel. In relation to this, itineraries act as the *carrier* of extraordinary experiences. However, problems arise with the question of "what is the extraordinary experience?" The extraordinary is always relative. What is extraordinary for children could not be so for adults. What is extraordinary for the first-time travellers could not be so for experienced travellers. For island residents, the sea is not the source of extraordinary experience. However, the sea is so for inhabitants from desert areas. Therefore, the extraordinary is relative to different potential tourists with different experiential backgrounds and characteristics. Relatedly, in tourism marketing, tourism is segmented into different typologies and packaged as various types of products in order to serve the varying needs of potential tourists with different tastes.

As a result, the functions of itineraries as illustrated in tourist brochures are similar to the functions of menus in restaurants. Just as menus help customers in selecting courses of foods that best fit their tastes and preferences, so itineraries presented in tourist brochures serve clients in choosing types of tourist experiences that best satisfy them. In short, itineraries function as menus for tourism consumption.

According to Levi-Strauss (1983), for foods to be edible, they must be cooked. In this sense, cooking is a cultural practice. The same is true of potential tourist resources. For these resources to be consume-able by potential tourist consumers, they must also be culturally "cooked." Itineraries are thus one of the cultural ways of "cooking" these resources. Just as menus represent certain cuisines by means of which foods are cooked, itineraries embody touristic "cuisines" by means of which potential tourist resources are "cooked" and "packaged." As itineraries are often displayed and illustrated in tourist brochures, it is more precise to regard itineraries *as presented in tourist brochures* that are the "menus" of tourist experiences.

Just like a certain type of cuisine produces some consistency in foods, itineraries also embody a certain theme or consistency in tourist experiences. A "touristic cuisine" that produces this consistency is "thematized." As a result of thematization, each itinerary is often centred around certain common themes, such as the itineraries of "Beautiful China," "Classic China," "China Adventure," and "the Silk Road." All these itineraries select some of the components from the "raw materials" of China and combine them as a thematic itinerary. Itineraries are thus the cultural combination of tourist experiences, in which the criteria for inclusion and exclusion of the components of tourist resources are culturally, as well as economically, determined.

In short, it is culture that determines what type of packaged tourist experiences suit what kind of potential tourists. Via such criteria of selection, discrete tourist spots are integrated as a whole and objectified as an itinerary. Itineraries thus reflect people's views, evaluations, and imagery of the world.

They are the categorization of peoples, cultures, places, and heritage in the world. In this sense, itineraries form *institutional circuits* in which contemporary people are "circulated" to examine and renegotiate the meanings of their relationships with the world. Itineraries are not only culturally structured as thematic experiences, but also dramatized as progressive stories. Itineraries are *scripts* in which the tourist journeys—like courses for a meal—can be organized as the beginning, the middle, the climax, and the end. Accordingly, tourists are performers who make their own stories with the itinerary unfolding across time and space. Just as dramatization creates meaning, the intensified dramatization of human experiences in itineraries indeed helps foster and reproduce meanings in human Use. Therefore, the consumption of itineraries is in reality a way of *consumption of meanings,* that are created beyond the confines of daily life and that make human life more colourful and meaningful.

However, with the mass production and consumption of itineraries or tourism, there arises a paradox of objectification of meanings, a paradox inherent in what Simmel (1990) calls "the objectification of culture" in western modernity. Itineraries are the temporal-spatial carriers of tourist experiences and their associated meanings. Under the condition of the commoditization of tourism, itineraries are often supplied in massive, homogenized, and standardized ways. The new marketing strategy of the segmentation of tourism does not forsake these standardizations but merely divides them into several domains. As a result, the meanings related to itineraries are objectified, standardized, and thematized.

In pre-modern ages, every single journey was linked to unique, subjective, and personal meanings. Under the condition of modernity, by contrast, such subjective and personal meanings of travel are increasingly diminished. Instead, tourism is packaged as various types of itineraries with thematic, categorized, homogenized, and objectified meanings In tourism advertisements, there are a number of "musts."

Once these "musts" are seen, this means "you have been there." If you go to Paris, you "must" find the scene of a romantic couple kissing each other. If you go to London, you "must" enjoy beers in a typical English pub. If you go to Beijing, you "must" see the torrent of bicycles on streets, Tiananmen Square, the Forbidden City, and the Great Wall at Badaling. All these "musts" signify the typical, objectified, standardized, and commonly acceptable meanings derived from the journeys to these places. Itineraries are thus organized in terms of socially, culturally, and objectively sanctioned and defined "worthiness" of visits. This site is included in our itineraries, just because everybody says it must be seen. That activity is also an item of our itinerary, just because everybody thinks such a kind of activity is a "must" in such a place. To miss such a "must" is not only a pity, but also a loss of value we pay for the journey Thus, in a hidden way, itineraries lead to a cultural and social conformism to objectified and stereotyped meanings that are already circulated within society, mass media, and the tourism industry.

However, for individual tourists, the problem could be, "why 'must' we see this site or participate in that activity at such a place?" "Could we look at the place from our own perspectives and find something meaningful with our own eyes?" Yes, you could. However, even independent travellers are in pursuit of the experiences that are informed by guidebooks, brochures, maps, and holiday programs on TV that are seen at home.

Thus, it becomes obvious that tourism is a kind of cultural practice in which each tourist participates to reproduce the code of meanings regarding the status quo, what is "sacred," and what is "heritage." The meanings derived from itineraries are thus unavoidably objectified and stereotyped. Accordingly, the consumption of these meanings serves to reproduce consumerist values of a society. Thus, tourists begin with a search for personal meanings but end up with the disappearance of *personal* meanings. Tourists want to keep a distance from reality but end up with a stronger conformity to the objectified semiotic order that a society needs.

Such a paradox is one of exemplifications of what Miles (1998,5) calls the "consuming paradox." In this, the consumers' pursuit of freedom through economic means ends up maintaining "a dominant order that potentially constrains personal liberty". He describes the consuming paradox as the idea that, on the one hand, consumerism appears to offer us individuals all sorts of opportunities and experiences, on the other hand, as consumers we appear to be directed down certain predetermined routes of consumption which ensure that consumerism is ultimately as constraining as it is enabling. (Miles 1998,147) Itineraries embody the same consuming paradox.

As the form of circulation and consumption of tourism products, itineraries are the bearer of touristic consumerism. On the one hand, itineraries offer tourists "menus" for free choices and ease and order on the journey. On the other hand, itineraries direct tourists to the "predetermined routes of consumption" (Miles 1998,147), which may trigger complaints about the very ease and order linking the itineraries because of their constraints on freedom and spontaneity. Itineraries initially offer tourists menus for free choice, but they finally deprive tourists of freedom of choice on the journey. Itineraries are thus constraining as well as enabling. While tourism becomes a reaction to the ambivalence of modernity (Wang 2000), it itself brings about its own ambivalence.

Conclusion

The quest for the tourist experience is essentially a reaction to the Logos-modernity which is about the realm of institutions characterized by reason and rationality (Wang 1996, 2000). However, in so doing, the tourist experience is itself rationally organized. The tourist experience appears to be an escape from the overwhelmingly rationalizing institutions, but finally ends up as the rationalization of that experience, with the tourism industry being its rational agent. Itineraries, then, become a way in which the tourist experience is rationally organized. In this sense, the paradoxes of tourism derived from itineraries represent the paradoxes of the Logos-modernity that is characterized by overarching rationalization in contemporary societies.

In effect, the rationalization of experiences often turns the tourist experience into its opposite, namely, the non-flexible and rigid schedules and itineraries.

The Tourist as Outsider or Guest

Everyone who has ever travelled to another country knows that feeling. The feeling of being the outsider, the one who doesn't blend it, that everyone knows is totally outta place. And most of us know that when some tourist shows up in your home town, you feel the exact same way about them. Some try their best to blend in, others don't care that you laugh at them.

The Tourist Resort Zone

The Descriptive Approach

Tourist destinations are in a state of continuous change. This development is more intense in the case of island destinations due to their geographic limitations

Transport is a fundamental component of tourism, providing the vital link between the tourist generating areas and destinations. Hence there are very close links between the transport and tourism industries where a two-way relationship exists. On the one hand good accessibility, which is determined by the transport services provided, is essential for the development of any tourist destination. Conversely for the transport industry, there can be substantial benefits from tourism because of the additional demand which this type of travel can produce.

Aviation is an increasingly important mode of transport for tourism markets. Whilst geography has meant that, in modern times, air travel has always been the dominant mode for long distance travel and much international tourism, moves towards deregulation, and in particular the emergence of the low cost carrier sector, have also increased aviation's significance for short and medium haul tourism trips. Thus, developments in aviation are having very major implications for many leisure and business tourism markets. However, the characteristics and needs of leisure travellers are generally so very different from business travellers that this necessitates a separate consideration of these markets if a detailed understanding of the relationship with aviation is to be gained.

In spite of the obvious closeness between the aviation and the leisure tourism industries, there are very few specialist texts on this subject. Most tourism focused books consider aviation as just one component of the tourism industry which needs to be discussed, whereas aviation specialist texts rarely concentrate on just leisure travel. In addition there is very little literature that gives a detailed appreciation of the complexities and potential conflicts associated with the development of coherent and effective aviation and tourism policies. Therefore it is the aim of this book to fill this important gap which exists with a comprehensive, in-depth study of the relationship between aviation and leisure travel.

7

The Role of Destination Image

Introduction

The unprecedented growth in the tourism industry during the last fifty years has created major challenges in tourism marketing. As more and more areas of the world are developed for tourism, the destination choices available to consumers continue to expand. Furthermore, today's consumers, facilitated by increased leisure time, rising levels of disposable income and more efficient transportation networks, have the means to choose from among this much larger variety of destinations. As a result, tourism marketers are now faced with influencing consumer decision making in an increasingly complex and competitive global marketplace.

One of the most significant marketing challenges arising from this situation is the need for an effective destination positioning strategy. In order to be successfully promoted in the targeted markets, a destination must be favourably differentiated from its competition, or positively positioned, in the minds of the consumers. A key component of this positioning process is the creation and management of a distinctive and appealing perception, or image, of the destination.

Tourism has been long accepted as an economic activity of attracting tourists and catering to their needs, which has rapidly grown into the world's largest industry and surpassing other important sectors such as automobiles, steel, agriculture and so forth. As demand for tourism increased, more and more areas developed for tourism and the choices of destination available to tourists continue to expand. As a result, destinations compete, and this phenomenon would lead to a fierce competition between tourism destinations. In this case, to be successfully promoted in targeted market, a destination must be favourably differentiated from its competition and has strong image to be positioned in the mind of the tourists. Thus, destination image play an important role in making the tourism destination viable for long-term tourism business Tourists today have to be enticed since the tourism destination is an intensely competitive and many destinations competing with one and another to attract the same potential tourists.

Therefore, a better understanding of destination image is vital in order to develop appropriate marketing strategies that based on tourists' perception and behaviour so that more competitive destinations' products are delivered to current and potential tourists.

The research of destination image can be traced back to the early of 1970s. In this era, images signify a pretesting of the destination which, can be referred as transpose representation of the destination into potential tourist's mind. Natural environment or beautiful beaches are the images held that likely to detract or contribute to the important role in tourism development and this become the concerns of Hunt study. His influential work has been expanding and later, several studies also highlighted the aspect of image and travel behaviour such as Mayo (1973), Gunn (1972), which since then and after 30 years, destination image become the most researched topics in the field of tourism.

Factors that Influencing the Destination Image Formation

The understanding of image formation is a one way to develop a competitive image or good impression of tourist destinations to the market. A positive image of tourist destination is considered as pulling factors among the flood of total impression that attract visitors to the destination. However, there are several types of factors that vital in the destination image formation which is pushing the tourists to the destination.

Previous section has explained the importance of variety and types of information sources in image formation. Thus, this section attempts to highlight personal factors which refer to individual's personal characteristics, as well as psychological characteristics which influence destination image formation. On top of that, the differences in tourists' cultural values and past travel experiences are also important factor to be included.

Past Travel Experience

Previous studies have shown a significant effect on what tourist has perceived and acted based on previous experiences. According to Perdue (1985), past travel experience explain the reason why repeat visitors only visit several or specific destination. It is because of specific intention or certain level of knowledge that pulled them to the destination again. On the other hand, first time visitors travelled to more destination and visited more attractions than repeat visitors (Oppermann, 1997).

This was supported by Fakeye and Crompton (1999) study that shows repeat visitors rated attraction-based images significantly higher than first-timer or even the potential tourists. Potential tourists have limited knowledge about the attributes of a particular destination and they have no previous experience, while previous visits affect familiarity with the destination.

For instance, Millman and Pizam (1995) found that individuals with past experience at a destination had a more positive image of the destination, and is more likely to revisit compared with individuals who were aware of, but had never experienced in the destination. They also found that individuals with no awareness of a destination were similar in their intention to visit compared with individuals with some level of destination awareness. This has enlightened that past experience reduces the risk of unfamiliarity of the environment and unsatisfactory experience which in turn result in accepting or rejecting a destination in a choice set.

Destination awareness is about knowledge or how much the tourist knows about the destination product. This term of awareness was used in purchasing and consumption behaviour which reveals whether the consumer has experienced or familiar with the product, and followed by repeat purchase.

In this case, for repeat visitation to be occurred there must lead to a first trial or first visit. Nevertheless, the awareness may not always lead to purchasing behaviour. In other words, information collected by tourists is not necessarily influence their travel behaviour perhaps there are many situational factors that may affect tourists travel behaviour. If satisfaction occurs as the result from the first visit, repeat visitation will follow.

Personal background characteristic, psychological factors and cultural values Every individual is different in nature. Personal characteristic, psychological factors and cultural values do affect the formation of image. The amount of external stimuli which is being exposed to the tourist determines the level of beliefs toward the attributes of the destination. Nevertheless, the internal factors such as sociodemographic characteristics perhaps lead to the various developments of mental picture about the destination, which produces their own version of images prior to individual's needs, motivation, knowledge, preferences and other personal characteristics.

A tourist destination can be described as a combination of services, resources and experiences. The destination image is basically measured through the cognitive-affective dimension which tells what images should be promoted based on what tourist has perceived or preferred. On the other hand, the amount of external stimuli which is being exposed to the tourist as well as, the motivational aspects that took place will initiate the action based on the image preferred.

The development of mental images will be later modified during the actual contact of the destination. As a result, the outcome of the experience affects the overall perception of the destination. This influences the post-decision for the future selection of holiday or visitation whether revisited or rejected.

The proposed theoretical framework identified the process as discussed in the literature. The question remains on how this process being examined as a complete cycle of image preference. This involve before the tourist making visit, during and after visitation as well as, the next process in intention to revisit. Therefore, this paper proposed a theoretical framework that need for further inquiries based on the given phenomenon.

Measures of Physical Attractiveness

Definition

To define a Tourist Attraction is not simple. Here are two definitions:

1. A physical or cultural feature of a particular place that individual travellers or tourists perceive as capable of meeting one or more of their specific leisure-related needs. Such features may be ambient in nature (e.g. climate, culture, vegetation or scenery),

or they may be specific to a location, such as a theatre performance, a museum or a waterfall.

2. Positive or favourable attributes of an area for a given activity or set of activities as desired by a given customer or market, including climate, scenery, activities, culture.
   (a) Man made attractions are physical structures (Sydney Harbour Bridge) or events (Olympics).
   (b) Natural attractions are physical phenomena deemed unusual and /or beautiful (Bungle Bungles).
   (c) Secondary attractions have tourist appeal, but are not the primary reason for visiting a location.
   (d) A negative attraction is an attribute of an area that tends to make some customer or market choose not to visit as for example pollution or crime.

Types of Attractions

There are basically two types of attractions:

- Built Attractions.
- Natural Attractions.

In attempting to embrace the core values of these definitions, Tourism Western Australia has developed the following set of essential and desirable recognition criteria for assessing a Tourist Attraction. The use of these criteria will ensure that uniform standards provide a fair and equitable assessment of all Tourist Attractions.

A Tourist Attraction will need to meet all of the essential recognition criteria before a recommendation is made to Main Roads Western Australia or a local government for the erection of appropriate road signs.

Built Attractions – Recognition Criteria

Essential Criteria

Most importantly:

- Tourism must clearly be an important part of the business In addition, the attraction must:
  - * Provide a substantive tourist experience in addition to, or part of, the commercial establishment's normal activities.

  * Have all relevant State and Local Government licenses and approvals to operate as a commercial tourist attraction including health, planning, parking and disabled access facilities.
  * Be a member of a recognised local tourism organisation.
  * Be open on weekends and three other days of the week including public holidays.
- Clearly display opening times (if not open 7 days):
  * At the entrance to the property or establishment.
  * In brochures and all promotional mediums (advertisements, web sites, etc.).
- Be open at least between 10am and 4pm.
- Produce a leaflet or brochure describing the attraction.
- Be distinctly signed at the property line so that the attraction can be easily identified.
- Be clean and well presented at all times.
- Have clean and conveniently located toilet facilities.

Desirable Criteria

It would be desirable for the attraction to also:

- be open every day.
- be Quality Assured by Tourism Council Western Australia.
- provide a parking area for coaches and caravans.
- keep a record of visitor numbers (e.g. by way of a visitors book).

Other Considerations

Arts & crafts outlets, nurseries, garden centres and the like are generally not considered to be tourist attractions unless the premises are significantly large and they provide some kind of value added experience such as having a well known or established artist in residence, or they conduct interpretative tours of their premises.

Wineries must provide wine tastings and cellar door sales. Wineries, which are only 'open by appointment', are not considered to be a tourist attraction for road signage purposes. Historic sites, buildings, etc. must be classified by the Heritage Council of WA.

Natural Attractions-recognition Criteria

Natural attractions comprise geographic or other natural features of tourist interest:

- National Parks and Reserves.
- Waterfalls, lakes, dams and other water catchment areas.
- Beaches.
- Caves, rock formations.
- Scenic lookouts, viewing areas, vistas and areas of impressive natural beauty.

Essential Criteria

The natural attraction must:

- be managed by a recognised agency or body.
- be recognised by Tourism Western Australia as a significant feature of tourist interest.
- be accessible to the public at least 9 months of the year.
- clearly display when the attraction is closed (if not open year round).
    - at the turn-off to the attraction.
    - in brochures and all promotional mediums (advertisements, websites, etc.).
- have adequate designated parking areas at the site.
- be distinctly signed at the entrance point so that the natural attraction can be easily identified.
- have clean and well presented visitor facilities.
- have access roads, walking tracks and viewing platforms maintained in a safe and satisfactory condition all year-round by the management body responsible.

Desirable Criteria

It would be desirable for the natural attraction to also:

- have clean and conveniently located toilet facilities.
- provide a parking area for coaches.
- be interpreted.

The Economic Impacts of Tourism

Businesses and public organizations are increasingly interested in the economic impacts of tourism at additional, state, and local levels. One regularly hears claims that tourism supports X jobs in an area or that a festival or special event generated Y million dollars in sales or income in a community. "Multiplier effects" are often cited to capture secondary effects of tourism spending and show the wide range of sectors in a community that may benefit from tourism.

Tourism's economic benefits are touted by the industry for a variety of reasons. Claims of tourism's economic significance give the industry greater respect among the business community, public officials, and the public in general. This often translates into decisions or public policies that are favourable to tourism. Community support is important for tourism, as it is an activity that affects the entire community. Tourism businesses depend extensively on each other as well as on other businesses, government and residents of the local community.

Economic benefits and costs of tourism reach virtually everyone in the region in one way or another. Economic impact analyses provide tangible estimates of these economic interdependency and a better understanding of the role and importance of tourism in a region's economy.

Tourism activity also involves economic costs, including the direct costs incurred by tourism businesses, government costs for infrastructure to better serve tourists, as well as congestion and related costs borne by individuals in the community. Community decisions over tourism often involve debates between industry proponents touting tourism's economic impacts (benefits) and detractors emphasizing tourism's costs. Sound decisions rest on a balanced and objective assessment of both benefits and costs and an understanding of who benefits from tourism and who pays for it.

Tourism's economic impacts are therefore an important consideration in state, regional and community planning and economic development. Economic impacts are also important factors in marketing and management decisions. Communities therefore need to understand the relative importance of tourism to their region, including tourism's contribution to economic activity in the area.

A variety of methods, ranging from pure guesswork to complex mathematical models, are used to estimate tourism's economic impacts. Studies vary extensively in quality and accuracy, as well as which aspects of tourism are included. Technical reports often are filled with economic terms and methods that non-economists do not understand. On the other hand, media coverage of these studies tend to oversimplify and frequently misinterpret the results, leaving decision makers and the general public with a sometimes distorted and incomplete understanding of tourism's economic effects.

How can the average person understand these studies sufficiently to separate good studies from bad ones and make informed choices? The purpose of this bulletin is to present a systematic introduction to economic impact concepts and methods. The presentation is written for tourism industry analysts and public officials, who would like to better understand, evaluate, or possibly conduct an economic impact assessment. The bulletin is organized around ten basic questions that either are asked or should be asked about the economic impacts of tourism.

What is an Economic Impact Analysis?

A variety of economic analyses are carried out to support tourism decisions. As these different kinds of economic analysis are frequently confused, let's begin by positioning economic impact studies within the broader set of economic problems and techniques relevant to tourism. These same techniques may be applied to any policy or action, but we will define them here in the context of tourism. Each type of analysis is identified by the basic question(s) it answers and the types of methods and models that are appropriate.

Types of Economic Analysis

Economic impact analysis — What is the contribution of tourism activity to the economy of the region? An economic impact analysis traces the flows of spending associated with tourism activity in a region to identify changes in sales, tax revenues, income, and jobs due to tourism activity.

The principal methods here are visitor spending surveys, analysis of secondary data from government economic statistics, economic base models, input-output models and multipliers. (Frechtling 1994a) Fiscal impact analysis – Will government revenues from tourism activity from taxes, direct fees, and other sources cover the added costs for infrastructure and government services? Fiscal impact analysis identifies changes in demands for government utilities and services resulting from some action and estimates the revenues and costs to local government to provide these services.

Financial analysis – Can we make a profit from this activity? A financial analysis determines whether a business will generate sufficient revenues to cover its costs and make a reasonable profit. It generally includes a short-term analysis of the availability and costs of start-up capital as well as a longer-range analysis of debt service, operating costs and revenues. A financial analysis for a private business is analogous to a fiscal impact analysis for a local government unit.

Demand analysis – How will the number or types of tourists to the area change due to changes in prices, promotion, competition, quality and quantity of facilities, or other demand shifters? A demand analysis estimates or predicts the number and/or types of visitors to an area via a use estimation, forecasting or demand model. The number of visitors or sales is generally predicted based on judgement (Delphi method), historic trends (time series methods), or using a model that captures how visits or spending varies with key demand determinants (structural models) such as population size, distance to markets, income levels, and measures of quality & competition.

Benefit Cost analysis (B/C) – Which alternative policy will generate the highest net benefit to society over time? A B/C analysis estimates the relative economic efficiency of alternative policies by comparing benefits and costs over time. B/C analysis identifies the most efficient policies from the perspective of societal welfare, generally including both monetary and nonmonetary values. B/C analysis makes use of a wide range of methods for estimating values of non-market goods and services, such as the travel cost method and contingent valuation method.

Feasibility study – Can/should this project or policy be undertaken? A feasibility study determines the feasibility of undertaking a given action to include political, physical, social, and economic feasibility. The economic aspects of a feasibility study typically involve a financial analysis to determine financial feasibility and a market demand analysis to determine market feasibility. A feasibility study is the private sector analogue of benefit cost analysis. The feasibility study focuses largely on the benefits and costs to the individual business or organization, while B/C analysis looks at benefits and costs to society more generally.

Environmental Impact assessment – What are the impacts of an action on the surrounding environment? An environmental assessment determines the impacts of a proposed action on the environment, generally including changes in social, cultural, economic, biological, physical, and ecological systems. Economic impact assessment methods are often used along with corresponding measures and models for assessing social, cultural and environmental impacts. Methods range from simple checklists to elaborate simulation models.

Benefit cost analysis and economic impact analysis are frequently confused as both discuss economic "benefits". There are two clear distinctions between the two techniques. B/C analysis addresses the benefits from economic efficiency while economic impact analysis focuses on the regional distribution of economic activity. The income received from tourism by a destination region is largely offset by corresponding losses in the origin regions, yielding only modest contributions to net social welfare and efficiency. B/C analysis includes both market and non-market values (consumer surplus), while economic impact analysis is restricted to actual flows of money from market transactions.

While each type of economic analysis is somewhat distinct, a given problem often calls for several different kinds of economic analysis. An economic impact study will frequently involve a demand analysis to project levels of tourism activity. In other cases demand is treated as exogenous and the analysis simply estimates impacts if a given number of visitors are attracted to the area. A comprehensive impact assessment will also examine fiscal impacts, as well as social and environmental impacts. Be aware that an economic impact analysis, by itself, provides a rather narrow and often one-sided perspective on the impacts of tourism. Studies of the economic impacts of tourism tend to emphasize the positive benefits of tourism.

On the other hand environmental, social, cultural and fiscal impact studies tend to focus more on negative impacts of tourism. This is in spite of the fact that there are negative economic impacts of tourism (e.g., seasonality and lower wage jobs) and in many cases positive environmental and social impacts (e.g., protection of natural & cultural resources in the area and education of both tourists and local residents). An economic impact assessment (EIA) traces changes in economic activity resulting from some action.

An EIA will identify which economic sectors benefit from tourism and estimate resulting changes in income and employment in the region. Economic impact assessment procedures do not assess economic efficiency and also do not generally produce estimates of the fiscal costs of an action. For many problems economic impact analysis will be part of a broader analysis. Environmental, social, and fiscal impacts are often equally important concerns in a balanced assessment of impacts.

What Economic Impacts does Tourism have?

Tourism has a variety of economic impacts. Tourists contribute to sales, profits, jobs, tax revenues, and income in an area. The most direct effects occur within the primary tourism sectors —lodging, restaurants, transportation, amusements, and retail trade. Through secondary effects, tourism affects most sectors of the economy. An economic impact analysis of tourism activity normally focuses on changes in sales, income, and employment in a region resulting from tourism activity.

A simple tourism impact scenario illustrates. Let's say a region attracts an additional 100 tourists, each spending $100 per day. That's $10,000 in new spending per day in the area. If sustained over a 100 day season, the region would accumulate a million dollars in new sales.

The million dollars in spending would be distributed to lodging, restaurant, amusement and retail trade sectors in proportion to how the visitor spends the $100. Perhaps 30% of the million dollars would leak out of the region immediately to cover the costs of goods purchased by tourists that are not made in the local area (only the retail margins for such items should normally be included as direct sales effects). The remaining $700,000 in direct sales might yield $350,000 in income within tourism industries and support 20 direct tourism jobs. Tourism industries are labour and income intensive, translating a high proportion of sales into income and corresponding jobs.

The tourism industry, in turn, buys goods and services from other businesses in the area, and pays out most of the $350,000 in income as wages and salaries to its employees. This creates secondary economic effects in the region. The study might use a sales multiplier of 2.0 to indicate that each dollar of direct sales generates another dollar in secondary sales in this region.

Through multiplier effects, the $700,000 in direct sales produces $1.4 million in total sales. These secondary sales create additional income and employment, resulting in a total impact on the region of $1.4 million in sales, $650,000 in income and 35 jobs.

While hypothetical, the numbers used here are fairly typical of what one might find in a tourism economic impact study. A more complete study might identify which sectors receive the direct and secondary effects and possibly identify differences in spending and impacts of distinct subgroups of tourists (market segments). One can also estimate the tax effects of this spending by applying local tax rates to the appropriate changes in sales or income. Instead of focusing on visitor spending, one could also estimate impacts of construction or government activity associated with tourism.

There are several other categories of economic impacts that are not typically covered in economic impact assessments, at least not directly. For example:

- *Changes in prices* — tourism can sometimes inflate the cost of housing and retail prices in the area, frequently on a seasonal basis.
- *Changes in the quality and quantity of goods and services* – tourism may lead to a wider array of goods and services available in an area (of either higher or lower quality than without tourism).
- *Changes in property and other taxes* – taxes to cover the cost of local services may be higher or lower in the presence of tourism activity. In some cases, taxes collected directly or indirectly from tourists may yield reduced local taxes for schools, roads, etc. In other cases, locals may be taxed more heavily to cover the added infrastructure and service costs. The impacts of tourism on local government costs and revenues are addressed more fully in a fiscal impact analysis.
- *Economic dimensions of "social" and "environmental" impacts*-There are also economic consequences of most social and environmental impacts that are not usually addressed in an

economic impact analysis. These can be positive or negative. For example, traffic congestion will increase costs of moving around for both households and businesses. Improved amenities that attract tourists may also encourage retires or other kinds of businesses to locate in the area.

Direct, Indirect and Induced Effects

A standard economic impact analysis traces flows of money from tourism spending, first to businesses and government agencies where tourists spend their money and then to:

- *Other businesses* — supplying goods and services to tourist businesses,
- *Households* – earning income by working in tourism or supporting industries, and
- *Government* — through various taxes and charges on tourists, businesses and households Formally, regional economists distinguish direct, indirect, and induced economic effects.

Indirect and induced effects are sometimes collectively called secondary effects. The total economic impact of tourism is the sum of direct, indirect, and induced effects within a region. Any of these impacts may be measured as gross output or sales, income, employment, or value added.

Direct effects are production changes associated with the immediate effects of changes in tourism expenditures. For example, an increase in the number of tourists staying overnight in hotels would directly yield increased sales in the hotel sector. The additional hotel sales and associated changes in hotel payments for wages and salaries, taxes, and supplies and services are direct effects of the tourist spending.

Indirect effects are the production changes resulting from various rounds of re-spending of the hotel industry's receipts in other backward-linked industries (i.e., industries supplying products and services to hotels).

Changes in sales, jobs, and income in the linen supply industry, for example, represent indirect effects of changes in hotel sales. Businesses supplying products and services to the linen supply industry represent another round of indirect effects, eventually linking hotels to varying degrees to many other economic sectors in the region.

Induced effects are the changes in economic activity resulting from household spending of income earned directly or indirectly as a result of tourism spending. For example, hotel and linen supply employees, supported directly or indirectly by tourism, spend their income in the local region for housing, food, transportation, and the usual array of household product and service needs.

The sales, income, and jobs that result from household spending of added wage, salary, or proprietor's income are induced effects. By means of indirect and induced effects, changes in tourist spending can impact virtually every sector of the economy in one way or another.

The magnitude of secondary effects depends on the propensity of businesses and households in the region to purchase goods and services from local suppliers. Induced effects are particularly noticed when a large employer in a region closes a plant. Not only are supporting industries (indirect effects) hurt, but the entire local economy suffers due to the reduction in household income within the region. Retail stores close and leakages of money from the region increase as consumers go outside the region for more and more goods and services. Similar effects in the opposite direction are observed when there is a significant increase in jobs and household income.

Final demand is the term used by economists for sales to the final consumers of goods and services. In almost all cases, the final consumers of tourism goods and services are households. Government spending is also considered as final demand. The same methods for estimating impacts of visitor spending can be applied to estimate the economic impacts of government spending, for example, to operate and maintain a park or visitor centre.

Regional Economic Models

An input-output model (I-O model) is a mathematical model that describes the flows of money between sectors within a region's economy. Flows are predicted by knowing what each industry must buy from every other industry to produce a dollar's worth of output.

Using each industry's production function, I-O models also determine the proportions of sales that go to wage and salary income, proprietor's income, and taxes. Multipliers can be estimated from input-output models based on the estimated re-circulation of spending within the region. Exports and imports are determined based upon estimates of the propensity of households and firms within the region to purchase goods and services from local sources (often called RPC's or regional purchase coefficients). The more a region is self-sufficient and purchases goods and services from within the region, the higher the multipliers for the region.

Input-output models make a number of assumptions. The basic ones are that:

- All firms in a given industry employ the same production technology (usually assumed to be the national average for that industry), and produce identical products.
- There are no economies or diseconomies of scale in production or factor substitution. I-O models are essentially linear–double the level of tourism activity/production and you double all of the inputs, the number of jobs, etc.
- The model doesn't explicitly keep track of time, but analysts generally report the impact estimates as if they represent activity within a single year.
- One must assume that the various model parameters are accurate and represent the current year. I-O models are firmly grounded in the national system of accounts, which relies on a standard industrial classification system (SIC codes) and various federal government economic censuses, in which individual firms report sales, wage and salary payments and employment. I-O models will generally be at least a few years out-of-date, although this isn't usually a major problem unless the region's economy has changed significantly. An I-O model represents the region's economy at a particular point in time. Tourist spending estimates are generally price adjusted to the year of the model.
- Multiplier computations for induced effects generally assume that jobs created by additional spending are new jobs, involving new households in the area. Induced effects are computed assuming linear changes in household spending with changes in income. Estimates of induced effects may be inflated due to the violation of these assumptions. Induced effects tend to account for the vast majority of the secondary effects of tourism, and therefore should be used with caution.

What are Multipliers and Multiplier Effects of Tourism?

Multipliers capture the secondary economic effects (indirect and induced) of tourism activity. Multipliers have been frequently misused and misinterpreted in tourism studies and are a considerable source of confusion among non-economists. Multipliers represent the economic interdependency between sectors within a particular region's economy.

They vary considerably from region to region and sector to sector. There are many different kinds of multipliers reflecting which secondary effects are included and which measure of economic activity is used (sales, income, or employment).

For example,

* The Type I sales multiplier = direct sales + indirect sales direct sales.
* The Type II or III sales multiplier 1 = direct sales + indirect sales + induced sales direct sales.

Multiplying a Type I sales multiplier times the direct sales gives direct plus indirect sales. Multiplying a Type II or III sales multiplier times the direct sales gives total sales impacts including direct, indirect and induced effects. The multipliers defined above are called ratio type multipliers as they measure the ratio of a total impact measure to the corresponding direct impact. Comparable income and employment ratio type multipliers may be defined by replacing sales with measures of income or employment in the above equations. Ratio multipliers should be used with caution.

A common error is to multiply a sales multiplier times tourist spending to get total sales effects. This will generate an inflated estimate of tourism impacts. The problem is that tourism spending or sales is not exactly the same as the "direct effects", appearing in the multiplier formula.

Tourist purchases of goods (vs. services) are the primary source of the problem. To properly apply tourist purchases of goods to an input-output model (or corresponding multipliers), various margins (retail, wholesale and transportation) must be deducted from the "purchaser price" of the good to separate out the "producer price". In an I-O model, retail margins accrue to the retail trade sector, wholesale margins to wholesale trade, transportation margins to transportation sectors and the producer prices of goods are assigned to the sector that produces the good.

In most cases the factory that produces the good bought by a tourist lies outside of the local region, creating an immediate "leakage" in the first round of spending and therefore no local impact from production of the good.

Before applying a multiplier to tourist spending, one must first deduct the producer prices of all imported goods that tourists buy (i.e. only include the local retail margins and possibly wholesale and transportation margins if these firms lie within the region). Generally, only 60 to 70% of tourist spending appears as final demand in a local region. While all tourist purchases of services will accrue to the local region as final demand, only the margins on goods purchased at retail stores should be counted as local final demand. The ratio of local final demand to tourist spending is called the capture rate.

Capture Rate = Local Final Demand / Tourism Spending in Local Area

The distinction between Type II and Type III multipliers involves a technical difference in how the induced effects are computed. Type II approaches include households as a sector of the economy and invert the technical coefficient matrix including the household sector, while Type III approaches treat households as exogenous.

Capture rates, like multipliers, will vary with the size and nature of the region as well as the kind of tourist spending included. One must therefore be cautious in taking a multiplier or capture rate cited in one study and using it in another.

Another way of calculating a multiplier (generally the preferred approach among economists) is as a ratio of income or employment to sales. This kind of multiplier is sometimes called a Keynesian multiplier or response coefficient.

Type III Income multiplier = Total direct, indirect, and induced income direct sales.

Type III Employment multiplier = Total direct, indirect, and induced employment direct sales.

This income (employment) multiplier produces total income (employment) impacts when multiplied by the direct sales. One must still be careful in distinguishing between tourism spending/sales and direct sales effects. Some studies may embed the capture rate in the multiplier, expressing the ratio in terms of tourism spending rather than direct sales.

How are Tourism's Economic Impacts Measured?

The economic impacts of tourism are typically estimated by some variation of the following simple formula:

Economic Impact of Tourism = Number of Tourists.

* Average Spending per Visitor

* Multiplier.

The formula suggests three distinct steps and corresponding measurements or models: Estimate the change in the number and types of tourists to the region due to the proposed policy or action.

Estimates or projections of tourist activity generally come from a demand model or some system for measuring levels of tourism activity in an area. Economic impact estimates will rest heavily on good estimates of the numbers and types of visitors. These must come from carefully designed measurements of tourist activity, a good demand model, or good judgement. This step is usually the weakest link in most tourism impact studies, as few regions have accurate counts of tourists, let alone good models for predicting changes in tourism activity or separating local visitors from visitors from outside the region.

Estimate average levels of spending (often within specific market segments) of tourists in the local area.

Spending averages come from sample surveys or are sometimes borrowed or adapted from other studies. Spending estimates must be based on a representative sample of the population of tourists taking into account variations across seasons, types of tourists, and locations within the study area. As spending can vary widely across different kinds of tourists, we recommend estimating average spending for a set of key tourist segments based on samples of at least 50-100 visitors within each tourism segment.

Segments should be defined to capture differences in spending between local residents vs. tourists, day users vs. overnight visitors, type of accommodation (motel, campground, seasonal home, with friends and relatives), and type of transportation (car, RV, air, rail, etc.).

In broadly based tourism impact studies, it is useful to identify unique spending patterns of important activity segments such as downhill skiers, boaters, convention & business travellers. Multiplying the number of tourists by the average spending per visitor (be careful the units are consistent) gives an estimate of total tourist spending in the area.

Estimates of tourist spending will generally be more accurate if distinct spending profiles and use estimates are made for key tourism segments. The use and spending estimates are the two most important parts of an economic impact assessment. When combined, they capture the amount of money brought into the region by tourists. Multipliers are needed only if one is interested in the secondary effects of tourism spending.

Apply the change in spending to a regional economic model or set of multipliers to determine secondary effects. Secondary effects of tourism are estimated using multipliers or a model of the region's economy. Multipliers generally come from an economic base or input-output model of the region's economy. In many cases multipliers are borrowed (often improperly) or adjusted from published multipliers or other studies. One should not take a multiplier estimated for one region and apply it in a region with a quite different economic structure.

Generally, multipliers are higher for larger regions with more diversified economies and lower for smaller regions with more limited economic development. A common error is to apply a statewide multiplier (since these are more widely published) to a local region.

This will yield inflated estimates of local multiplier effects. Multipliers can also be used to convert estimates of spending or sales to income and employment. Simple ratios can be used to capture how much income or jobs are generated per dollar of sales.

These ratios will vary from region to region and across individual economic sectors due to the relative importance of labour inputs in each industry and different wage and salary rates in different regions of the country. Be aware that job estimates are generally not full time equivalents, making them difficult to compare across industries with different proportions of seasonal and part time jobs. Income or value added are generally the preferred measures of the contribution of tourism to a region's economy.

What are the Typical Approaches for an Economic Impact Assessment?

At the simple, "quick and dirty" end of the spectrum are highly aggregate approaches that rely mostly on judgement to determine tourism activity, spending and multipliers. Such estimates can be completed in a couple hours at little cost and rest largely on the expertise and judgement of the analyst. At the other extreme are studies that gather primary data from visitor spending studies and apply the spending estimates to formal regional economic models for the area in question. In between are a wide range of options that employ varying degrees of judgement, secondary data, primary data, and formal models.

Different levels of detail and corresponding expense (time and money) and accuracy are possible for each of the three steps — estimating tourist volume, spending, and multiplier effects. Four typical approaches illustrate the levels of detail that are possible and the associated methods.

1. Subjective estimates that rely mostly on expert opinion.
2. Secondary data in aggregate form, adapting existing estimates to suit the problem.
3. Secondary data in disaggregate form, permitting finer adjustment of data to fit the situation.
4. Primary data and/or formal models, usually involving visitor surveys and regional economic models.

The National Park Service's "Money Generation Model " is a simple fill-in-form for generating economic impacts. While an extremely simple approach, it captures the essential elements, of an economic impact analysis. The number of visits, average spending per visitor and an aggregate sales multiplier are entered on a simple work sheet to generate estimates of the direct and total sales effects of visitor spending. Sales effects are converted to income and jobs using simple ratios of income to sales and jobs to sales.

Tax effects of visitor spending can also be estimated by applying local tax rates In an engineering approach, one estimates the costs of producing a "trip" by itemizing typical costs for each input-e.g., a typical overnight visitor party of 4 staying two nights will incur $50 per night for motel room, $20 per person per day for meals, $10 for half tank of gas, and $50 for souvenirs = total of $320 per party per trip to sales estimates. With sound judgement in choosing the parameters, the MGM model can yield reasonable ballpark estimates of economic impacts at minimal cost.

This approach, however, provides little detail on spending categories or which sectors of the economy benefit from either direct or secondary effects. The aggregate nature of the approach also makes it difficult to adjust recommended spending rates or multipliers to different applications (USDI, National Park Service 1990.).

8

Tourism Impacts on the Environment

The quality of the environment, both natural and man-made, is essential to tourism. However, tourism's relationship with the environment is complex. It involves many activities that can have adverse environmental effects. Many of these impacts are linked with the construction of general infrastructure such as roads and airports, and of tourism facilities, including resorts, hotels, restaurants, shops, golf courses and marinas. The negative impacts of tourism development can gradually destroy the environmental resources on which it depends.

On the other hand, tourism has the potential to create beneficial effects on the environment by contributing to environmental protection and conservation. It is a way to raise awareness of environmental values and it can serve as a tool to finance protection of natural areas and increase their economic importance.

Tourism's Three Main Impact Areas

Negative impacts from tourism occur when the level of visitor use is greater than the environment's ability to cope with this use within the acceptable limits of change. Uncontrolled conventional tourism poses potential threats to many natural areas around the world. It can put enormous pressure on an area and lead to impacts such as soil erosion, increased pollution, discharges into the sea, natural habitat loss, increased pressure on endangered species and heightened vulnerability to forest fires. It often puts a strain on water resources, and it can force local populations to compete for the use of critical resources.

Depletion of Natural Resources

Tourism development can put pressure on natural resources when it increases consumption in areas where resources are already scarce.

Water Resources

Water, and especially fresh water, is one of the most critical natural resources. The tourism industry generally overuses water resources for hotels, swimming pools, golf courses and personal use of water by tourists. This can result in water shortages and degradation of water supplies, as well as generating a greater volume of waste water. In dryer regions like the Mediterranean, the issue of water scarcity is of particular concern. Because of the hot climate and the tendency of tourists to consume more water when on holiday than they do at home, the amount used can run up to 440 litres a day. This is almost double what the inhabitants of an average Spanish city use.

Golf course maintenance can also deplete fresh water resources. In recent years golf tourism has increased in popularity and the number of golf courses has grown rapidly. Golf courses require an enormous amount of water every day and, as with other causes of excessive extraction of water, this can result in water scarcity. If the water comes from wells, over pumping can cause saline intrusion into ground-water. Golf resorts are more and more often situated in or near protected areas or areas where resources are limited, exacerbating their impacts.

Local Resources

Tourism can create great pressure on local resources like energy, food, and other raw materials that may already be in short supply. Greater extraction and transport of these resources exacerbates the physical impacts associated with their exploitation. Because of the seasonal character of the industry, many destinations have ten times more inhabitants in the high season as in the low season. A high demand is placed upon these resources to meet the high expectations tourists often have.

Land Degradation

Important land resources include minerals, fossil fuels, fertile soil, forests, wetland and wildlife. Increased construction of tourism and recreational facilities has increased the pressure on these resources and on scenic landscapes. Direct impact on natural resources, both renewable and nonrenewable, in the provision of tourist facilities can be caused by the use of land for accommodation and other infrastructure provision, and the use of building materials. Forests often suffer negative impacts of tourism in the form of deforestation caused by fuel wood collection and land clearing. For example, one trekking tourist in Nepal-and area already suffering the effects of deforestation-can use four to five kilograms of wood a day.

Pollution

Tourism can cause the same forms of pollution as any other industry: air emissions, noise, solid waste and littering, releases of sewage, oil and chemicals, even architectural/visual pollution.

Air Pollution and Noise

Transport by air, road, and rail is continuously increasing in response to the rising number reported that the number of international air passengers worldwide rose from 88 million in 1972 to 344 million in 1994. One consequence of this increase in air transport is that tourism now accounts for more than 60% of air travel and is therefore responsible for an important share of air emissions. One study estimated that a single transatlantic return flight emits almost half the CO_2 emissions produced by all other sources consumed by an average person yearly.

Transport emissions and emissions from energy production and use are linked to acid rain, global warming and photochemical pollution. Air pollution from tourist transportation has impacts on the global level, especially from carbon dioxide (CO_2) emissions related to transportation energy use.

And it can contribute to severe local air pollution. Some of these impacts are quite specific to tourist activities. For example, especially in very hot or cold countries, tour buses often leave their motors running for hours while the tourists go out for an excursion because they want to return to a comfortably air-conditioned bus.

Noise pollution from airplanes, cars, and buses, as well as recreational vehicles such as snowmobiles and jet skis, is an ever-growing problem of modern life. In addition to causing annoyance, stress, and even hearing loss for it humans, it causes distress to wildlife, especially in sensitive areas. For instance, noise generated by snowmobiles can cause animals to alter their natural activity patterns.

Solid Waste and Littering

In areas with high concentrations of tourist activities and appealing natural attractions, waste disposal is a serious problem and improper disposal can be a major despoiler of the natural environment-rivers, scenic areas, and roadsides. For example, cruise ships in the Caribbean are estimated to produce more than 70,000 tons of waste each year. Today some cruise lines are actively working to reduce waste-related impacts. Solid waste and littering can degrade the physical appearance of the water and shoreline and cause the death of marine animals.

In mountain areas, trekking tourists generate a great deal of waste. Tourists on expedition leave behind their garbage, oxygen cylinders and even camping equipment. Such practices degrade the environment with all the detritus typical of the developed world, in remote areas that have few garbage collection or disposal facilities. Some trails in the Peruvian Andes and in Nepal frequently visited by tourists have been nicknamed "Coca-Cola trail" and "Toilet paper trail".

Sewage

Construction of hotels, recreation and other facilities often leads to increased sewage pollution. Wastewater has polluted seas and lakes surrounding tourist attractions, damaging the flora and fauna. Sewage runoff causes serious damage to coral reefs because it stimulates the growth of algae, which cover the filter-feeding corals, hindering their ability to survive. Changes in salinity and salutation can have wide-ranging impacts on coastal environments. And sewage pollution can threaten the health of humans and animals.

Aesthetic Pollution

Often tourism fails to integrate its structures with the natural features and indigenous architectural of the destination. Large, dominating resorts of disparate design can look out of place in any natural environment and may clash with the indigenous structural design.

A lack of land-use planning and building regulations in many destinations has facilitated sprawling developments along coastlines, valleys and scenic routes. The sprawl includes tourism facilities themselves and supporting infrastructure such as roads, employee housing, parking, service areas, and waste disposal.

Physical Impacts

Attractive landscape sites, such as sandy beaches, lakes, riversides, and mountain tops and slopes, are often transitional zones, characterized by species-rich ecosystems. Typical physical impacts include the degradation of such ecosystems.

An ecosystem is a geographic area including all the living organisms (people, plants, animals, and microorganisms), their physical surroundings (such as soil, water, and air), and the natural cycles that sustain them. The ecosystems most threatened with degradation are ecologically fragile areas such as alpine regions, rain forests, wetlands, mangroves, coral reefs and sea grass beds. The threats to and pressures on these ecosystems are often severe because such places are very attractive to both tourists and developers. Physical impacts are caused not only by tourism-related land clearing and construction, but by continuing tourist activities and long-term changes in local economies and ecologies.

Physical Impacts of Tourism Development

Construction activities and infrastructure development: The development of tourism facilities such as accommodation, water supplies, restaurants and recreation facilities can involve sand mining, beach and sand dune erosion, soil erosion and extensive paving. In addition, road and airport construction can lead to land degradation and loss of wildlife habitats and deterioration of scenery.

In Yosemite National Park (US), for instance, the number of roads and facilities have been increased to keep pace with the growing visitor numbers and to supply amenities, infrastructure and parking lots for all these tourists. These actions have caused habitat loss in the park and are accompanied by various forms of pollution including air pollution from automobile emissions; the Sierra Club has reported "smog so thick that Yosemite Valley could not be seen from airplanes". This occasional smog is harmful to all species and vegetation inside the Park.

Deforestation and intensified or unsustainable use of land: Construction of ski resort accommodation and facilities frequently requires clearing forested land. Coastal wetlands are often drained and filled due to lack of more suitable sites for construction of tourism facilities and infrastructure. These activities can cause severe disturbance and erosion of the local ecosystem, even destruction in the long term.

Marina development of marinas and breakwaters can cause changes in currents and coastlines. Furthermore, extraction of building materials such as sand affects coral reefs, mangroves, and hinterland forests, leading to erosion and destruction of habitats. In the Philippines and the Maldives, dynamiting and mining of coral for resort building materials has damaged fragile coral reefs and depleted the fisheries that sustain local people and attract tourists.

Overbuilding and extensive paving of shorelines can result in destruction of habitats and disruption of land-sea connections (such as sea-turtle nesting spots). Coral reefs are especially fragile marine ecosystems and are suffering worldwide from reef-based tourism developments. Evidence suggests a variety of impacts to coral result from shoreline development, increased sediments in the water, trampling by tourists and divers, ship groundings, pollution from sewage, overfishing, and fishing with poisons and explosives that destroy coral habitat.

Physical Impacts from Tourist Activities

Trampling Tourists using the same trail over and over again trample the vegetation and soil, eventually causing damage that can lead to loss of biodiversity and other impacts. Such damage can be even more extensive when visitors frequently stray off established trails.

Trampling impacts on vegetation	Trampling impacts on soil
Breakage and bruising of stems	Loss of organic matter
Reduced plant vigour	Reduction in soil macro porosity
Reduced regeneration	Decrease in air and water permeability
Loss of ground cover	Increase in run off
Change in species composition	Accelerated erosion

Source: University of Idaho

Anchoring and other marine activities In marine areas (around coastal waters, reefs, beach and shoreline, offshore waters, uplands and lagoons) many tourist activities occur in or around fragile ecosystems. Anchoring, snorkelling, sport fishing and scuba diving, yachting, and cruising are some of the activities that can cause direct degradation of marine ecosystems such as coral reefs, and subsequent impacts on coastal protection and fisheries.

Alteration of ecosystems by tourist activities Habitat can be degraded by tourism leisure activities. For example, wildlife viewing can bring about stress for the animals and alter their natural behaviour when tourists come too close. Safaris and wildlife watching activities have a degrading effect on habitat as they often are accompanied by the noise and commotion created by tourists as they chase wild animals in their trucks and aircraft. This puts high pressure on animal habits and behaviours and tends to bring about behavioural changes. In some cases, as in Kenya, it has led to animals becoming so disturbed that at times they neglect their young or fail to mate.

Effects of other Industries on Tourism

Impacts from other industries often have a more dramatic effect on the environment and can seriously affect tourism.

* Oil spills, like the oil tanker disaster that occurred off the Galapagos Islands (Ecuador) in January 2001, can cause severe short-term damage to tourist attractions. In that case, a freight ship loaded with 160,000 gallons of diesel fuel and 80,000 gallons of other petroleum products ran aground on the coast of San Cristobal and spilled nearly all of its load. Unique local marine and land species and the tourism potential of the area were badly affected.
* Agricultural runoff or industrial discharges can cause water pollution and may cause algae blooms like those that occurred in the Adriatic Sea in the early 1990s. In spite of improved control of sewage from tourism developments, the Mediterranean sea floor is increasingly carpeted with these quick-growing invaders, many rising 30 inches or more above anchoring runners. They appear equally adept at colonizing rock, mud, and sand in a virtually continuous swath that can extend from the beach out to a depth of about 150 feet, smothering coral reefs, fish and other sea flora and fauna in the process.
* Destructive practices such as blast fishing, with poisonous chemicals like cyanide, and muro-aminetting (pounding reefs with weighted bags to scare fish out of crevices) directly destroy corals. They can also destroy a major draw for tourists.

Loss of Biological Diversity

Biological diversity is the term given to the variety of life on Earth and the natural patterns it forms. The effects of loss of biodiversity:

* It threatens our food supplies, opportunities for recreation and tourism, and sources of wood, medicines and energy.
* It interferes with essential ecological functions such as species balance, soil formation, and greenhouse gas absorption.
* It reduces the productivity of ecosystems, thereby shrinking nature's basket of goods and services, from which we constantly draw.
* It destabilizes ecosystems and weakens their ability to deal with natural disasters such as floods, droughts, and hurricanes, and with human-caused stresses, such as pollution and climate change.

Tourism, especially nature tourism, is closely linked to biodiversity and the attractions created by a rich and varied environment. It can also cause loss of biodiversity when land and resources are strained by excessive use, and when impacts on vegetation, wildlife, mountain, marine and coastal environments and water resources exceed the carrying capacity. This loss of biodiversity in fact means loss of tourism potential.

Introduction of Exotic Species

Tourists and suppliers-often unwittingly-can bring in species (insects, wild and cultivated plants and diseases) that are not native to the local environment and that can cause enormous disruption and even destruction of ecosystems.

Depletion of the Ozone Layer

The ozone layer, which is situated in the upper atmosphere (or stratosphere) at an altitude of 12-50 kilometres, protects life on earth by absorbing the harmful wavelengths of the sun's ultraviolet (UV) radiation, which in high doses is dangerous to humans and animals. For instance, one of the reasons scientists have put forward for the global decrease of amphibian populations is increased exposure to UV radiation. Ozone depleting substances (ODSs) such as CFCs (chlorofluorocarbon) and halons have contributed to the destruction of this layer. The tourism industry may be part of the problem; direct impacts start with the construction of new developments and continue during daily management and operations. Refrigerators, air conditioners and propellants in aerosol spray cans, amongst others, contain ODSs and are widely used in the hotel and tourism industry. Emissions from jet aircraft are also a significant source of ODSs. According to Tourism Concern, scientists predict that by 2015 half of the annual destruction of the ozone layer will be caused by air travel.

UNEP's OzonAction Programme works with governments and industries, including the tourism industry, to phase out ODSs and find safer alternatives. UNEP has developed extensive information and guidance on how many types of businesses can eliminate ODSs and contribute to preservation of the ozone layer. For further reading see the publication How the Hotel and Tourism Industry can Protect the Ozone Layer.

Climate Change

Climate scientists now generally agree that the Earth's surface temperatures have risen steadily in recent years because of an increase in the so-called greenhouse gases in the atmosphere, which trap heat from the sun. One of the most significant of these gases is carbon dioxide (CO_2), which is generated when fossil fuels, such as coal, oil and natural gas are burned (e.g. in industry, electricity generation, and automobiles) and when there are changes in land use, such as deforestation. In the long run, the accumulation of CO_2 and other greenhouse gases in the atmosphere can cause global climate change- a process that may already be occurring.

Global tourism is closely linked to climate change. Tourism involves the movement of people from their homes to other destinations and accounts for about 50% of traffic movements; rapidly expanding air traffic contributes about 2.5% of the production of CO_2. Tourism is thus a significant contributor to the increasing concentrations of greenhouse gases in the atmosphere.

Air travel itself is a major contributor to the greenhouse effect. Passenger jets are the fastest growing source of greenhouse gas emissions. The number of international travellers is expected to increase from 594 million in 1996 to 1.6 billion by 2020, adding greatly to the problem unless steps are taken to reduce emissions. For more information on the relationship between energy and the environment, see UNEP's Energy Programme, which provides information and publications on energy efficiency and alternative energy sources to reduce the environmental impacts of energy use and of transportation.

How Global Environmental Impacts Affect Tourism

Natural Disasters

Catastrophes like floods, earthquakes, wildfires, volcanoes, avalanches, drought and diseases can have a serious effect on inbound and domestic tourism and thus on local tourism industries. The outbreak of the foot and mouth disease epidemic in England earlier this year (2001), for instance, has severely affected Great Britain's inbound tourism market. A BHA/Barclays Hospitality Business Trends Survey found that 75% of hotels in England, 81% in Scotland and 85% in Wales continued to be affected by the foot and mouth outbreak, and over 60% forecast a decline in business in the June-September 2001 period.

Climate Change

Tourism not only contributes to climate change, but is affected by it as well. Climate change is likely to increase the severity and frequency of storms and severe weather events, which can have disastrous effects on tourism in the affected regions. Some of the other impacts that the world risks as a result of global warming are drought, diseases and heat waves.

These negative impacts can keep tourists away from the holiday destinations. Global warming may cause:

* Less snowfall at ski resorts, meaning a shorter skiing seasons in the Alpine region. In already hot areas like Asia and the Mediterranean, tourists will stay away because of immense heat, and out of fear of diseases and water shortages.
* Harm to vulnerable ecosystems such as rainforests and coral reefs because of rising temperatures and less rainfall. A major risk to coral reefs is bleaching, which occurs when coral is stressed by temperature increases, high or low levels of salinity, lower water quality, and an increase in suspended sediments. These conditions cause the zooxanthallae (the singlecelled algae which forms the colours within the coral) to leave the coral. Without the algae, the coral appears white, or "bleached"-and

rapidly dies. The Great Barrier Reef, which supports a US$ 640 million tourism industry, has been experiencing coral bleaching events for the last 20 years.

* Rising sea levels, the result of melting glaciers and polar ice. Higher sea levels will threaten coastal and marine areas with widespread floods in low-lying countries and island states, increasing the loss of coastal land. Beaches and islands that are major tourism attractions may be the first areas to be affected.
* Increased events of extremc weather, such as tornadoes, hurricanes and typhoons. These are already becoming more prevalent in tourist areas in the Caribbean and South East Asia. Hurricane Mitch in 1998, for instance, heavily affected tourism in the Caribbean. Wind damage, storm waves, heavy rains and flooding caused major losses in the local tourism sector.

How Tourism can Contribute to Environmental Conservation

The tourism industry can contribute to conservation through:

Financial Contributions

* ***Direct financial contributions:*** Tourism can contribute directly to the conservation of sensitive areas and habitat. Revenue from park-entrance fees and similar sources can be allocated specifically to pay for the protection and management of environmentally sensitive areas. Special fees for park operations or conservation activities can be collected from tourists or tour operators.
* ***Contributions to government revenues:*** Some governments collect money in more far-reaching and indirect ways that are not linked to specific parks or conservation areas. User fees, income taxes, on sales or rental of recreation equipment, and license fees for activities such as hunting and fishing can provide governments with the funds needed to manage natural resources. Such funds can be used for overall conservation programs and activities, such as park ranger salaries and park maintenance.

For Costa Rica, for example, tourism represents 72% of national monetary reserves, generates 140,000 jobs and produces 8.4% of the gross domestic product. The country has 25% of its territory classified under some category of conservation management. In 1999, protected areas welcomed 866,083 national and foreign tourists, who generated about US$ 2.5 million in admission fees and payment of services.

Improved Environmental Management and Planning

Sound environmental management of tourism facilities and especially hotels can increase the benefits to natural areas. But this requires careful planning for controlled development, based on analysis of the environmental resources of the area. Planning helps to make choices between conflicting uses, or to find ways to make them compatible. By planning early for tourism development, damaging and expensive mistakes can be prevented, avoiding the gradual deterioration of environmental assets significant to tourism.

Cleaner production techniques can be important tools for planning and operating tourism facilities in a way that minimizes their environmental impacts.

For example, green building (using energy-efficient and non-polluting construction materials, sewage systems and energy sources) is an increasingly important way for the tourism industry to decrease its impact on the environment. And because waste treatment and disposal are often major, long-term environmental problems in the tourism industry, pollution prevention and waste minimization techniques are especially important for the tourism industry. A guide to sources of information on cleaner production (free) is available here.

Environmental Awareness Raising

Tourism has the potential to increase public appreciation of the environment and to spread awareness of environmental problems when it brings people into closer contact with nature and the environment. This confrontation may heighten awareness of the value of nature and lead to environmentally conscious behaviour and activities to preserve the environment.

For instance, Honduran schoolchildren from the capital city of Tegucigalpa are routinely taken to visit La Tigra cloud forest visitor centre, funded in part by ecotourist dollars, to learn about the intricacies of the rainforest.

If it is to be sustainable in the long run, tourism must incorporate the principles and practices of sustainable consumption. Sustainable consumption includes building consumer demand for products that have been made using cleaner production techniques, and for services-including tourism services-that are provided in a way that minimizes environmental impacts.

The tourism industry can play a key role in providing environmental information and raising awareness among tourists of the environmental consequences of their actions. Tourists and tourism-related businesses consume an enormous quantity of goods and services; moving them toward using those that are produced and provided in an environmentally sustainable way, from cradle to grave, could have an enormous positive impact on the planet's environment.

Protection and Preservation

Tourism can significantly contribute to environmental protection, conservation and restoration of biological diversity and sustainable use of natural resources. Because of their attractiveness, pristine sites and natural areas are identified as valuable and the need to keep the attraction alive can lead to creation of national parks and wildlife parks. In Hawaii, new laws and regulations have been enacted to preserve the Hawaiian rainforest and to protect native species.

The coral reefs around the islands and the marine life that depend on them for survival are also protected. Hawaii now has become an international centre for research on ecological systems-and the promotion and preservation of the islands' tourism industry was the main motivation for these actions.

Grupo Punta Cana, a resort in the Dominican Republic, offers an example of how luxury tourism development and conservation can be combined. The high-end resort was established with the goal of catering to luxury-class tourists while respecting the natural habitat of Punta Cana.

The developers have set aside 10,000 hectares (24,700 acres) of land as a nature reserve and native fruit tree garden. The Punta Cana Nature Reserve includes 11 fresh water springs surrounded by a subtropical forest where many species of unusual Caribbean flora and fauna live in their natural state. Guests can explore a "nature path" leading from the beach through mangroves, lagoons of fresh water springs and dozens of species of Caribbean bird and plant life. The Punta Cana Ecological Foundation has begun reforesting some parts of the reserve that had been stripped of their native mahogany and other trees in the past.

Other environmentally protective policies have been put into effect at the resort, such as programs to protect the offshore barrier reefs and the recycling of wastewater for use in irrigating the grounds. The fairways of the resort's new golf course were planted with a hybrid grass that can be irrigated with sea water The grass also requires less than half the usual amounts of fertilizer and pesticides. The resort has also established a biodiversity laboratory run by Cornell University.

Tourism has had a positive effect on wildlife preservation and protection efforts, notably in Africa but also in South America, Asia, Australia, and the South Pacific. Numerous animal and plant species have already become extinct or may become extinct soon. Many countries have therefore established wildlife reserves and enacted strict laws protecting the animals that draw nature-loving tourists. As a result of these measures, several endangered species have begun to thrive again.

Alternative Employment

Tourism can provide an alternative to development scenarios that may have greater environmental impacts. The Eco-escuela de Espanol, a Spanish language school created in 1996 as part of a Conservation International project in the Guatemalan village of San Andres, is an example.

The community-owned school, located in the Maya Biosphere Reserve, combines individual language courses with home stay opportunities and community-led ecotours. It receives around 1,800 tourists yearly, mostly from the US and Europe, and employs almost 100 residents, of whom around 60% were previously engaged in mostly illegal timber extraction, hunting and *milpas*, or slash-and-burn agriculture.

Careful monitoring in 2000 has shown that, among the families benefiting from the business, the majority has significantly reduced hunting practices, and the number and extension of "slash-and-burn" agricultural plots. Furthermore, as most families in the village benefit directly or indirectly from the school, community-managed private reserves have been established, and social pressure against hunting has increased.

Regulatory Measures

Regulatory measures help offset negative impacts; for instance, controls on the number of tourist activities and movement of visitors within protected areas can limit impacts on the ecosystem and help maintain the integrity and vitality of the site. Such limits can also reduce the negative impacts on resources.

Limits should be established after an in-depth analysis of the maximum sustainable visitor capacity. This strategy is being used in the Galapagos Islands, where the number of ships allowed to cruise this remote archipelago is limited, and only designated islands can be visited, ensuring visitors have little impact on the sensitive environment and animal habitats.

The Social Impacts of Tourism

Today, tourism is one of the largest and dynamically developing sectors of external economic activities. Its high growth and development rates, considerable volumes of foreign currency inflows, infrastructure development, and introduction of new management and educational experience actively affect various sectors of economy, which positively contribute to the social and economic development of the country as a whole.

Most highly developed western countries, such as Switzerland, Austria, and France have accumulated a big deal of their social and economic welfare on profits from tourism. According to recent statistics, tourism provides about 10% of the world's income and employs almost one tenth of the world's work force.

All considered, tourism's actual and potential economic impact is astounding. Many people emphasize the positive aspects of tourism as a source of foreign exchange, a way to balance foreign trade, an "industry without chimney" — in short, manna from heaven. But there are also a number of other positive and negative sides of tourism's economic boom for local communities, which not always considered by advocates of tourism perspectives. Therefore in this paper I will consider the main social and environment impacts of tourism at the country level.

The Positive and Negative Social and Environmental Impacts of Tourism

Socially tourism has a great influence on the host societies. Tourism can be both a source of international amity, peace and understanding and a destroyer and corrupter of indigenous cultures, a source of ecological destruction, an assault of people's privacy, dignity, and authenticity. Here are possible positive effects of tourism:

- Developing positive attitudes towards each other.
- Learning about each other's culture and customs.
- Reducing negative perceptions and stereotypes.
- Developing friendships.
- Developing pride, appreciation, understanding, respect, and tolerance for each other's culture.
- Increasing self-esteem of hosts and tourists.
- Psychological satisfaction with interaction.

So, social contacts between tourists and local people may result in mutual appreciation, understanding, tolerance, awareness, learning, family bonding respect, and liking. Residents are educated about the outside world without leaving their homes, while their visitors significantly learn about a distinctive culture. Local communities are benefited through contribution by tourism to the improvement of the social infrastructure like schools, libraries, health care institutions, internet cafes, and so on. Besides, if local culture is the base for attracting tourists to the region, it helps to preserve the local traditions and handicrafts which maybe were on the link of the extinction.

For example in Uzbekistan, particularly in such famous regions as Samarqand, Buhara, and Horezm tourists contribute significantly to the preservation of traditional handcrafting wood carving, hammered copper work, handmade silk and carpets, and of course to preservation and maintenance of architectural and historical monuments. Since Uzbekistan proclaimed its independence in 1991 many museums and monuments were renovated or opened to promote the national culture and traditions.

Growing interest in this culture makes the local people proud of their way of life.

On the other side tourism can increase tension, hostility, and suspicion. Claims of tourism as a vital force for peace are exaggerated. Indeed there is little evidence that tourism is drawing the world together. In this context economic and social impacts on the local community depend on how much of the incomes generated by tourists go to the host communities.

In most all-inclusive package tours more than 80% of travellers' fees go to the airlines, hotels and other international companies, not to local businessmen and workers. On the other hand large hotel chain restaurants often import food to satisfy foreign visitors and rarely employ local staff for senior management positions, preventing local farmers and workers from reaping the benefit of their presence.

Tourism has the power to affect cultural change. Successful development of a resource can lead to numerous negative impacts. Among these are overdevelopment, assimilation, conflict, and artificial reconstruction.

While presenting a culture to tourists may help preserve the culture, it can also dilute or even destroy it. The point is to promote tourism in the region so that it would both give incomes and create respect for the local tradition and culture. There are also both negative and positive impacts of tourism on the local ecology. Tourism often grows into mass-tourism. It leads to the over consumption, pollution, and lack of resources.

However, from the ecological point of view tourism is often more acceptable and preferable than any other industrial production, as it is environmentally friendlier. The problem is that it is not easy to change the traditional way of life of the local communities. It often creates pseudo conflicts.

Undoubtedly in some regions or countries the alternative industries are even more harmful to the environment than tourism. Besides that in many countries of Asia and the Pacific, for example in Cook Islands, Samoa and others, tourism is the main source of income or the friendliest to the environment. It is at least better than chopping down the forests or destroying coral reefs.

Conclusion

Thus, the preceding paragraphs show that the impact of tourism on local communities can be both positive and negative, whether it comes to economic, social, or environmental effects. It depends to which extent tourism is developed in a particular region. Every region has its bearing capacity, that is to say the limit of the incoming influence that does not harm the host community.

If we overcome that limit negative impacts of tourism will follow. Here is a figure which shows the dynamics between people, resources, and tourism in successful tourism: each makes a positive contribution to the others.

All the three elements in this model are in co-interaction. Local communities use the natural resources but they also protect them. Tourists come to enjoy the nature and get knowledge about it, but they also can pollute and destroy it, or on the other side help to protect it by drawing attention to unique natural resources in the area. Local communities affect tourists by giving them knowledge of their culture and way of life.

Tourists' impact on the local populations can be first of all economic by generating income, developing resources, sharing knowledge and experience, etc. Whenever we develop a new tourist destination we should always bear in mind this co-interaction. In order to decrease the negative effects on local societies we can check the following points when arranging a tourism activity in a region or taking part in it (Fennell1999, lecture notes):

* Are local§ people involved in the tourism industry as employees?
* Does the§ organization cooperate with the local businesses?
* Does it have a§ respectful attitude to the local culture?
* Is there§ respect to nature and how is it protected?
* How much§ economic benefit will the local population get from tourism?
* Are tour§ operators concerned about ecological hotels, transport, and restaurants?

We can see it is a great challenge to make a profitable business running tourism in an area without some negative effect to the local communities. It is possible for the tourism industry to cooperate with other industries and bring benefits to both the tourism organizations and local businesses. The first step to achieve it is to understand the needs and desires of both the host community and the tourists.

Economic and Social Impacts

The economic and social impacts of tourism are a big subject that cannot be covered thoroughly here. They should be examined in detail for any large tourism development project. Economically, tourism can create jobs for local people and bring money into the country. However many tourists like their comforts from home, and it is often necessary to import a large part of their requirements, so that much of the money may leave the country again to pay for these imports. If the resorts and hotels have been financed by overseas investors, they will also want to export their profits.

The developers may want the government to improve the airport, roads and other infrastructure, and possibly to provide tax breaks and other financial advantages, which cost the country money. The remaining benefit to an island country from some kinds of tourism development may thus be small indeed. Other kinds of tourist facilities provided by villages or financed locally may be economically more interesting. The social impacts of tourism may also be important. Most jobs for local people in the tourist industry are as servants, house maids, waiters, gardeners and other menial work that may give people a sense of inferiority.

At the same time the tourists come from other societies with different values and lifestyles, and because they have come seeking pleasure, they may spend large amounts of money and behave in ways that even they would not accept at home. Local people seeing the tourist example may want to live and behave the same way. Tourists may also, out of ignorance or carelessness, fail to respect local customs and moral values. These and other social effects may be among the most important long-term impacts of tourism development.

Negative Social Aspects of Tourism

Tourism can undoubtedly bring benefits to an area protecting pristine habitats and conserving cultures and wildlife in some of the world's poorest countries and revitalising regions within developed nations where traditional industries have declined, but it often comes at a cost.

This effect is, of course, most keenly felt in the developing world where the stark juxtaposition of affluent consumerism with subsistence lifestyles jars most noticeably. As a holiday-maker it is impossible to avoid the simple truth that the loose change lying forgotten in your bag would feed many of the local people for the best part of a week.

If you notice their poverty, how can they fail to notice your wealth? The more well-attuned your social awareness, the more difficult it is to ignore that tourism is essentially rooted in this inequality. However, there are more problems than simply forcing people to come face to face with that particular reality.

Assimilating Values

It is not simply the disparity of economic influence which can affect tourist areas. Other factors such as the collapse of traditional lifestyles, values and moralities can also be influenced and eroded by contact with travellers from different lands. This issue is, however, a difficult one. As the age-old adage tells us "travel broadens the mind" and this is often taken to mean that by going to other countries and experiencing their ways, we become more open and accepting of doing things differently ourselves.

The problem is that this is, inevitably, a two-way street; if we are open to learn from the meetings we have with other cultures and societies on our travels, why should they be any the slower to assimilate some of our values? There will always be an element of the "grass always being greener" – but does that make a particular view any the more or less valid? In truth, the answer has to be "no" and in as much as from our perspective "they" remind "us" of what we have turned our backs on in the material west, then perhaps, at least for some, we may represent their aspirations.

In the west, social values are often more fluid and ill-defined, beyond the most broad of consensus; this model does not fit well alongside a more structured and traditional society and for those who do embrace the alien culture – however slightly – life can be difficult.

One outcome is mounting dissatisfaction and disaffection; the other is the gradual disintegration of a way of life which in many cases was the reason tourists came in the first place.

Practical Issues

Some of the negative effects of tourism are much less philosophical. In many areas, crime increases dramatically during the tourist season, falling back to more usual levels when the visitors have all gone home. Although much of this will be targeted at the supposed easy pickings of the tourists themselves, it is not without its repercussions on the local population and the police and consular authorities on the ground.

In some places, the price of many staple foods and other essential items can be hiked up considerably to maximise the catch of tourist dollars, but this artificial inflation can often catch local people too – who often can least afford it.

In addition, in countries which are rich in wildlife and natural beauty, although initiatives to bring in tourists often contribute to parts of the local economy, by no means everyone benefits. It is also one of eco-tourism's greatest ironies that attempts to safeguard the environment can also make life worse for indigenous people, particularly if vast swathes of their traditional lands become part of a protected reserve.

There is a well established principle in science that you often alter the thing you observe just by the act of observing it. In many ways, tourism is no different– it is impossible to visit "untouched" lands without leaving your touch upon them, somehow. With many of the world's most beautiful and fragile ecosystems inhabited by some of the poorest people, it is inevitable that tourism throws the often conflicting environmental, economic and social forces into sharp relief. Much of the damage is unintentional; even if we try to live up to the responsible traveller's mantra of taking nothing but photographs and leaving nothing but footprints, sometimes the footprints we leave will be deeper than we think.

Tourism: Yesterday, Today and Tomorrow

Tourism, the act of paying money to go from one place to another to see different and unique sights, has been a fact of civilized life since approximately the 12th century. Of course, back in those days it was basically the upper, classes that had the time, the money, and the interest in travelling from one spot to another.

The word "travel" by the way comes from the medieval English word "travail" which means suffering great hardship, and that is a very good description of travel in its earliest days. Much has been written about the journeys of Marco Polo, who until recently was considered the world's first tourist.

Celebrated in books, movies, musicals and television specials in several countries, Marco Polo is today a hero in Italy and in China:

> *Venice named its airport after a beloved native son. There's the Marco Polo bridge outside Beijing, and no tourist to the Chinese capital in the 1980s was ever allowed to miss the Marco Polo Carpet Shop at the Temple of Heaven. Across Asia, in tributaries of the storied Old Silk Road that linked West and East, Polo's name beckons modern travellers to restaurants, hotels and souvenir shops.*

Now the question of whether Marco Polo actually did his famous travels has come up for hot dispute after a British Librarian, Frances Wood, published a small book called Did Marco Polo go to China?

In that, she uses vast research to cast doubts freedom to explore on their own (all for the investment of a little time, patience and gasoline). The advent of air travel in the 1930's heralded the true beginnings of what is called "tourism" today. Today's Travel for the Masses Data from the American Society of Travel Agents (ASTA) suggests that at any given moment of any given day, more than 2 million people around the world are in the process of travelling from one place to another.

Indeed, depending on whose figures one believes, the "tourism" industry worldwide can be said to range from $80 billion to $200 billion per year. Of course, these figures on the low side represent direct travel expenses (airfare, car rentals, train and bus travel, cruise ships, and so on) while the higher figures represent the addition of hotels, restaurants, entertainment, and "attendant revenue flows" into the local economies. At a summit meeting of congressional representatives and tourism industry leaders, the importance of tourism to the American economy was emphasized. There it was stated that "for many years, the United States was second only to France as the world's top tourist destination.

Environmental Impacts of Tourism Facilities

Tourism development usually starts with the construction of hotels, resorts and other places for tourists to stay. In addition there may be restaurants, night clubs, and recreation facilities such as golf courses, tennis courts, swimming pools, and marinas. These facilities require a lot of space, and land is usually scarce on an island.

Land and resources used for tourism are not available for other uses; developers may even want to keep local people away from beaches, reefs and lagoon areas reserved for tourists only. Whenever possible, tourism developers prefer to build on the coast, where the hotel will front on a beach and perhaps a coral reef, yet the coast is the most fragile and vulnerable area on an island, with the greatest conflicts between uses.

The construction of these facilities can have the same kinds of impacts as any other construction projects, such as soil erosion, changes in water runoff, and damage to natural environments. If the resort is on the coast, the plans frequently call for changes in the coastline, such as the creation or improvement of a beach, the construction of an artificial island, or the dredging of a harbour or building of a dock for tour boats to use to pick up and leave off the tourists.

These changes may upset normal coastal processes and be very difficult to maintain. Coastal hotel sites themselves are often vulnerable to storm damage, erosion and other problems because of their exposed location.

Tourist developments also require resources that may be scarce on an island. Water may be in short supply, yet tourist use of water is usually much greater per person than among the local population. Tourists require large quantities of high quality food; if it cannot be produced locally, it will have to be imported.

The sewage from large hotels can be a source of pollution if it is not treated and disposed of carefully. Most hotel projects include waste water treatment plants, but these can be difficult to maintain in the islands and need to be monitored regularly. Tourist facilities also produce large amounts of solid waste which can add to the existing solid waste disposal problems on many islands.

Infrastructure Requirements

Any major tourist development requires a good airport where large jets can bring tourists from overseas countries. Visits by tour ships may require improved docking facilities. Roads may have to be built to resort sites, or improved for tour buses. Water and electricity supplies may have to be increased.

All these kinds of infrastructure require investments which must be added on to the direct cost of a tourism project. Building roads, airports and docks can have major environmental impacts which are beyond the scope of this unit. Their overall effects, however, may be positive as well as negative. Such facilities benefit local people as well as tourists, reducing the isolation of remote areas and increasing the convenience of travel within the country and overseas. Tourism development can thus support useful expenditures that could not be justified for the local people alone.

Damage from Tourist Use

Tourists are often unaware of how fragile some island environments are. They may trample vegetation and thus cause erosion, or disturb birds and wildlife. They may leave their rubbish behind, littering the environment. They are apt to break corals as the walk or swim over the reef. Even anchoring in a fragile reef area can result in significant damage to corals.

Tourists love to collect corals, shells and other pretty objects as souvenirs, but too much collecting can damage a reef or other site. Fishing is sport for a tourist, but it may take away resources needed as food in nearby villages. Where a few tourists may do little damage, thousands of them can be a disaster. Think of the difference between one tourist breaking off a piece of coral, and hundreds of tourists each taking a piece of coral; a reef could quickly be stripped of its corals and shells. Areas subject to heavy tourist pressure should be protected from damaging activities.

Laws may be needed to protect wildlife and to control collecting. The increasing demand for curios such as stuffed turtles, turtle shell jewellery, mounted butterflies, and traditional objects made with rare bird feathers or animal skins can threaten rare species with extinction. The manufacture and sale of such objects should be prohibited or strictly controlled. Coral, shells for handicrafts or collectors, and local trees used for carving can also be wiped out locally or reduced to low levels when too much is used to supply the tourist trade.

Planning Tourism Development

One major question to be answered in planning tourism development is what scale of tourism is appropriate for the local environment and culture. Every place has a carrying capacity that cannot be exceeded without bringing about serious changes or even the collapse of important resources or systems.

While some small-scale tourism can be fit in almost anywhere, large scale tourism can cause major problems if it is not planned very carefully. The number of tourists an area can absorb should be decided before tourism development goes to far, because there always will be pressures for bigger and bigger developments. The appropriate scale of tourism may be determined by the most limited resource, such as water or coastal land, or by the desire to prevent serious social or cultural impacts. How many people, for instance, can a community receive comfortably as visitors, or how would it feel to be outnumbered by the tourists on your own island?

Comprehensive Planning for Tourism

Unlike most development projects that only involve a specific site or area, tourism frequently depends to some extent on an entire country or island. It is therefore in the interest of the tourist industry to see that the overall planning of the country's development includes the requirements of tourism. As more governments begin environmental planning and make physical plans (including town plans, master plans and coastal zone plans), it is essential that these plans include the sites of particular scenic or recreational potential.

The coastlines, vistas, swimming beaches, waterfalls, mountains and lagoons that tourists visit and photograph are capital assets just like hotels, but they are generally not owned by the tourism interests that benefit from them. Only careful comprehensive planning, and often the understanding and support of the traditional owners, can protect these resources from degradation and destruction.

Planning helps in making choices between conflicting uses, or in finding ways to make them compatible. It should aim to locate unsightly or polluting activities, like industrial areas, fuel storage depots, rubbish dumps, etc., where they will not destroy the beauty of a town or coastline or conflict with tourist sites. In many island towns, there are already too many cases where urban pollution is making tourist beaches unsightly or unsafe. Planning early for tourism development can help to avoid damaging and expensive errors and also to prevent the gradual erosion of environmental values significant to tourism. Improvements that help tourism, like better transportation, tree planting, restoration of historic sites, urban beautification and cleanliness, also improve the environment for the local population. Tourism development can help to stimulate general community improvement.

Bibliography

Andrew, N; Flanagan, S & Ruddy, J: *Tourism Destination Planning*, Dublin, Dublin Institute of Technology, 2002.

Apostolopous, Y and Leivadi, S: *Sociology of Tourism, The: Theoretical And Empirical Investigations*, London, Retailed, 1996.

Ashworth, G J and Dietvorst, A G J: *Tourism and Spatial Transformations: Implications For Policy and Plan*, Wallingford, CAB International, 1995.

Ashworth, Greg and Larkham, P J: *Building a New Heritage: Tourism, Culture & Identity in the New Europe*, London, Routledge,1994.

Baum, Tom: *We're all Going on a Summer Holiday: Images of Tourism Past and Person*, Buckingham, University of Buckingham, 1995.

Beeho, A & Prentice, R: *Conceptualising The Experiences of Heritage Tourists*, 1997.

Beeton, Sue:: *Film-Induced Tourism*, Clevedon, Channel View, 2005.

Belie et al.: *Tourism and the Inner City: An Evaluation of /Impact of Grant Assist*, London, HMSO, 1990.

Benefice, Brian G, and Cooper, Chris: *Geography of Travel and Tourism*, The, London, Heinemann, 1987.

Bolshevism, Germy: *Coping with Tourists: European Reactions to Mass Tourism*, Oxford, Berghahn Books, 1995.

Boniface, Priscilla and Fowler, Peter: *Heritage and Tourism: In the Global Village*, London, Retailed, 1993.

Bosselman, Fred P: *In The Wake of the Tourist: Managing Special Places in Eight Countries*, Washington, DC, Conservation Foundation, The, 1978.

Briguglio, L and Vella, Leslie: *Competitiveness of the Maltese Islands in Mediterranean in Tourism*, Chichester, John Wiley, 1995.

Brown, Dona: *Inventing New England: Regional Tourism in the Nineteenth Century*, Washington DC, Smithsonian Institution, 1995.

Brunt, Paul: *Market Research in Travel and Tourism*, Oxford, Butterworth Heinemann, 1997.

Burkart, A and Medlik, S: *Management of Tourism*, The, London, Heinemann, 1975.

Chambers, Erve: *Native Tours: The Anthropology of Travel and Tourism*, Prospect Heights, Waveland Press, 2000.

Chandler, Harry and Carter, John: *Chandler's Travels: A Tour of the Life of Harry Chandler*, London, Quiller Press, 1985.

Clark, Colin: *Tourist Services and Guidance: Heritage and Information*, Strasbourg, Council of Europe Press, 1989.

Coccosis, Harry and Nijkamp, Peter: *Sustainable Tourism Development*, Aldershot, Avebury, 1995.

Cohen, Erik: *Towards a Sociology of International Tourism*, 1972.

Dann, Graham M S: *Language of Tourism*, The, Wallingford, CAB International, 1996.

Davidson, R and Maitland, R: *Tourism Destinations, London*, Hodder and Stoughton, 1997.

Davidson, Rob: *Travel and Tourism in Europe*, Harlow, Addison Wesley Longman, 1998.

Ecotec: *Calderdale: Tourism Impact Study*, Calderdale, ECOTEC/Calderdale Council, 1990.

Edensor, Tim: *Tourists at the Taj*, London, Retailed, 1998.

Edgell, David L: *International Tourism Policy, New York*, Van Nostrand and Reinhold, 1990.

Elliott, James: *Tourism: Politics and Public Sector Management*, London, Retailed, 1997.

Fairgrieve, James: *Geography in School*, London, University of London Press, 1926.

Foster, Douglas: *Travel and Tourism Management*, London, Macmillan Educational, 1985.

Frechtling, Douglas C: *Practical Tourism Forecasting*, Oxford, Butterworth Heinemann, 1996.

Gamble, P. R: *The Educational challenge for Hospitality and Tourism Studies*, Tourism Management, 13, 1992.

Ghimire, Krishna: *The Native Tourist*: Mass Tourism within Developing Regions, London, Earthscan, 2001.

Goeldner, C. R: *The Evaluation of Tourism as an Industry and a Discipline, Paper Presented to*, International Conference for Tourism Educators, Guildford, University of Surrey, 1988.

Gunn, Clare and Var, Turgut: *Tourism Planning*, London, Retailed, 2002.

Hall, C Michael *Tourism Planning: Policies, Processes and relationships*, Harlow, Prentice Hall, 2000.

Hall, Colin and Jenkins, John: *Tourism and Public Policy*, London, Retailed, 1995.

Hall, Colin Michael: *Tourism and Politics*: Policy, Power, & Place, Chichester, Wiley, 1994.

Harrison, Lyndon: *Tourism Means Jobs*, Chester, Lyndon Harrison, 1996.

Harron, S and Weiler, B: *Ethnic Tourism*, Belhaven/Wiley, 1992.

Inkpen, G: *Information Technology for Travel and Tourism*, Harlow, Addison Wesley Longman, 1998.

Inskeep, Edward *National and Regal Tourism Planing*: Methodologies & Case Studies, London, Routledge/WTO, 1994.

Irwin, William *The New Niagara*: *Tourism, Technology, And the Landscape of Niagara Fal*, University Park, PA, University of Pennsylvania, 1996.

Jack, G and Phipps, A: *Tourism and Intercultural Exchange*: *Why Tourism Matters*, Clevedon, Channel View, 2005.

Jakle, John: *Tourist, The: Travel in Twentieth Century North America*, University of North Nebraska, 1985.

Jennings, Gayle: *Tourism Research*, Chichester, Wiley, 2001.

Judd, D R: *Promoting Tourism* in US Cities, 1995.

Karski, A: *Urban Tourism* - A Key to Urban Regeneration?, 1990.

Kotler, Philip et al: *Marketing Places*: *Attracting Investment, Industry & Tourism etc*, New York, free press, 1993.

Labarge, Margaret Wade: *Medieval Travellers*: *The Rich and Restless*, London, Hamish Hamilton, 1982.

Laws, Eric: *Tourist Destination Management: Issues, Analysis & Policies*, London, Routledge, 1995.

Leed, Eric J: *Mind of the Traveller, The: From Gilgamesh to Global Tourism*, New York, 1991.

MacCannell, Dean: *Tourist, The: A New Theory of the Leisure Class*, London, Macmillan, 1976.

Machin, Alan: *Retracing the Steps: Tourism as Education, Janus*, Fin, ATLAS / FUNTS, 2001.

Opperman, Martin and Chon, Kye-Sung: *Tourism in Developing Countries, London*, International Thomson Business Press, 1997.

Patullo, Polly: *Last Resorts*: *The Cost of Tourism in the Caribbean*, London, Cassell, 1996.

Pearce, Douglas: *Tourism Today*: *A Geographical Analysis*, Harlow, Longman, 1995.

Pearce, P L: *Social Psychology Of Tourist Behaviour*, The, Oxford, Pergamon, 1982.

Peters, M: *International Tourism*, London, Hutchinson, 1969.

Ringer, Greg: *Destinations: Cultural Landscapes of Tourism*, London, Routledge, 1998.

Ritchie, Brent: *Managing Educational Tourism*, Clevedon, Channel View, 2003.

Robinson, H: *Geography of Tourism*, A, London, Macdonald and Evans, 1976.

Robinson, M, Evans, E & Chalazion, P: *Tourism and Cultural Change, Sunderland*, Business Education Publishers Ltd, 1996.

Rogers, H Anthea and Slinn, Judy A: *Tourism: Management of Facilities*, London, Pitman: M & E, 1993.

Schwaninger, M: *Trends in Leisure and Tourism for 2000 - 2010*, Prentice Hall, 1989.

Scottish Tourist Board: *Visitor Attractions: A Development Guide*, Edinburgh, Scottish Tourist Board, 1991.

Seaton, A V et al: *Tourism: The state of the Art*, Chichester, John Wiley, 1994.

Shaw, G and Williams, A: *Tourism and Tourism Spaces*, London, Sage, 2004.

Stevens, Terry: *Island Tourism*: Malta, , WTO, 1993.

Trench, R: *Travellers in Britain*, London, Aurum, 1990.

Tribe, John *Corporate Strategy for Tourism, London*, International Thomson Business Press, 1997.

Urry, John: *Tourist Gaze*, The, London, Sage, 1990.

Van den Berg et al: *Urban Tourism: Performance and Strategies in Eight European Cities*, Aldershot, Avebury, 1995.

Van Harssel, Jan: *Tourism: An Exploration*, New York, Prentice Hall, 1994.

Veal, A: *Leisure and Tourism*: Policy and Planning, Wallingford, CABI, 2001.

Wahab, S A: *Tourism Management*, Tourism International Press, 1975.

Walle, Alfred H: *Cultural Tourism*: A Strategic Focus, Boulder, Co, Westview Press, 1998.

Wilkinson, Paul: *Tourism Policy and Planning: As Studies from the Caribbean*, Elmsford New York, Cognizant Communications Corporation, 1997.

Yale, Pat: *From Tourist Attractions to Heritage Tourism*, Huntingdon, Elm, 1991.

Zarkia, Cornelia: *Philoxenia: Receiving Tourists*-but *not Guests-on a Greek Island*, Oxford, Berghahn Books, 1996.

Index

□□□